de Gruyter Studies in Organization 59

Strategic Alliances and Process Redesign

de Gruyter Studies in Organization

Innovation, Technology, and Organization

This international and interdisciplinary book series from de Gruyter presents comprehensive research on the inter-relationship between organization and innovations, both technical and social.
It covers applied topics such as the organization of:
— R & D
— new product and process innovations
— social innovations, such as the development of new forms of work organization and corporate governance structure

and addresses topics of more general interest such as:
— the impact of technical change and other innovations on forms of organization of micro and macro levels
— the development of technologies and other innovations under different organizational conditions at the levels both of the firm and the economy.

The series is designed to stimulate and encourage the exchange of ideas between academic researchers, practitioners, and policy makers, though not all volumes address policy- or practitioner-oriented issues.
The volumes present conceptual schema as well as empirical studies and are of interest to students of business policy and organizational behaviour, to economists and sociologists, and to managers and administrators at firm and national level.

Editor:
Arthur Francis, Glasgow University Business School, Glasgow, GB

Advisory Board:
Prof. Claudio Ciborra, University of Trento, Italy
Dr. Mark Dodgson, The Australian National University, Canberra, Australia
Dr. Peter Grootings, CEDEFOP, Berlin, Germany
Prof. Laurie Larwood, Dean, College of Business Administration, University of Nevada, Reno, Nevada

Alexander Gerybadze

Strategic Alliances and Process Redesign

Effective Management and Restructuring
of Cooperative Projects and Networks

Walter de Gruyter · Berlin · New York 1995

Prof. Dr. *Alexander Gerybadze*
Professor of Business Administration and Technology Management at St. Gallen University,
Switzerland. Former director at Arthur D. Little International, Inc.. Advisor to large corporations
and government institutions in the fields of Strategic Management of Technology, Cooperation
Project Redesign, and Industrial Policy.

⊗ Printed on acid-free paper which falls within the guidelines
of the ANSI to ensure permanence and durability.

Library of Congress Cataloging-in-Publication Data

Gerybadze, Alexander.
  Strategic alliances and process redesign : effectice management
  and restructuring of cooperative projects and networks / Alexander
  Gerybadze.
       (De Gruyter studies in organization : 59)
    Includes bibliographical references.
    ISBN 3-11-013989-8
  1. Strategic alliances (Business) 2. Joint ventures. 3. Venture
  capital. I. Title. II. Series.
  HD69.S8G473   19941
  658'.044--dc20   94-28393
                                                        CIP

Die Deutsche Bibliothek Cataloging-in-Publication Data

Gerybadze, Alexander:
Strategic alliances and process redesign : effective management
and restructuring of cooperative projects and networks / Alexander
Gerybadze. – Berlin ; New York : de Gruyter, 1995
   (De Gruyter studies in organization ; 59)
   ISBN 3-11-013989-8
NE: GT

Converted by: Frohberg GmbH, Freigericht. — Printing: Gerike GmbH, Berlin. — Binding:
Dieter Mikolai, Berlin. — Cover Design: Johannes Rother, Berlin.

Contents

Part IV: Policy Implications

8.   New Cooperative Solutions and Public-Private Partnership . . .   267

List of Figures

List of Tables

Part I: Introduction

Introduction
In Search of Useful Theories for Cooperation and Process Redesign

Cooperative projects, strategic alliances, and various new forms of network relationships have gained widespread attention in the business community as well as in academia. An increasing number of empirical studies reflects this changing trend in managerial behavior and in business relations[1]. Many scholars, research institutes and international committees have adressed the growing role of cooperation and strategic alliances, and have initiated studies on these pervasive phenomena, as well as on their causes and implications. The Organization for Economic Cooperation and Development (OECD) has adressed cooperation and networking as a core topic within its Technology and Economic Program (TEP).

Formal and informal cooperation relating to the production and the diffusion of scientific and technical knowledge and the creation of technology has become a widespread phenomenon in OECD economies. ... The growth of international and domestic inter-firm agreements ... represents a significant and novel development of the 1980's. ... New technologies are less and less the result of isolated efforts by the lone inventor or the individual firm. They are increasingly created, developed, brought to market and subsequently diffused through complex mechanisms built on inter-organizational relationships and linkages. These linkages possess a number of features which make the 'network mode' (Imai and Itami 1984) a distinct form of inter-firm organization that operates alongside and in combination with the two forms previously recognized by economic theory, namely markets and 'hierarchies' (OECD 1992, 67 f).

Based upon this assessment of recent changes in business practice and its reflection in economic theory, the TEP background report suggests that "the time is ripe for the development of a full-fledged economic theory of networks" (OECD 1992, 77). Economic theory, however, follows with a considerable time-lag. The large and rapidly increasing number of empirical studies on cooperation and network relationships between firms has so far not been appropriately reflected in the *theoretical* literature.

To overcome the widening gap between perceived empirical changes and their reflection in theory, we intend to develop some *building blocs for an economic theory of cooperation*. Advances in the theoretical explanation of new inter-firm relationships must adress the following three topics: it is *first* necessary to define

---

1 Chapter 1, particularly section 1.2, contains a detailed description of these perceived trends and a critical synopsis of the literature.

the term cooperation and the various new forms of relational contracting precisely, and to distinguish them from more "traditional" modes of governance and organization. *Second*, an appropriate new theory must explain why cooperative associations are formed and which economic incentives they offer to induce agents to participate. In addition to these inducement effects, economic theory must also explain, *third*, under which conditions cooperative associations can be regarded as stable modes of governance and organization, offering sustainable economic advantages to participating agents.

In order to develop such an economic explanation of sustainable comparative advantages for cooperative associations, we need to analyze institutional choices from an investment and finance point of view. Economic activities and investment projects can be organized and coordinated in a variety of institutional forms. We are only interested in those institutional arrangements which offer the *highest value* to investors. If cooperation turns out to be the mode for which the project value is maximized, it will be chosen as a sustainable solution. If it turns out to be inferior to some other solution, such as pure market contracting or complete integration within a firm, it will *not* be chosen, or it will just be applied temporarily.

This criterion of maximizing project values for all investors which participate in a cooperative association, involves both an efficiency and a distribution effect. The first *efficiency effect* relates to the value of the investment project as a whole; the second *distribution effect* influences distributive shares accruing to each participating agent. Cooperative modes of governance and organization are so "complicated" because both aspects have to be considered at the same time. Since agents remain legally and organizationally independent, problems of efficiency and distribution must be solved simultaneously and on a project-by-project basis. This typically involves considerable coordination costs, which may often offset potential economic advantages to cooperation.

In spite of non-negligible coordination costs, which explain why collaborative associations are most often only second-best alternatives to either market transactions or integration within a single firm (Gullander 1976), cooperation may offer sustainable comparative advantages under some very specific conditions. Complex investment projects which require coordination of a variety of capabilities and skills being distributed between several independent firms, lead to a resource allocation problem with the following *design attributes:* (1) critical assets are unevenly distributed and closely-held by individual agents; (2) a-priori information about the form of the optimal solution (how resources should be combined) is widely scattered among agents; (3) failing to achieve the right combination of resources and knowledge is "more costly than other kinds of errors, including slight misspecifications of the overall pattern, as long as the individual pieces fit" (Milgrom and Roberts 1992, 91).

For projects with such design attributes, neither hierarchy nor the price mechanism will solve the resource allocation problem, and we are forced to develop appropriate *cooperation designs*, i.e. intelligent problem-solving mechanisms or "a system in which the pieces must fit together in a predictable way, thus narrowing the search for efficient solutions" (Milgrom and Roberts, 1992, 91). Cooperation designs must be "custom-tailored" to each resource allocation problem to be solved, and they will assure that a project can be organized in time and at an appropriate quality level. Each participating agent can mobilize a-priori information and closely-held specific resources at more favorable cost than any other investor could; the value of the multilateral investment project will be increased, and each participating agent may receive an appropriate share of the added value[2].

Modern concepts in the theory of investment and finance, new approaches to business organization and corporate renewal, as well as new conceptualizations proposed by neo-institutional economists emphasize a *project orientation* as opposed to the entity orientation. While entity concepts view the *business firm as the unit of analysis*, more modern concepts focus on transactions or projects as basic units of analysis. To cope with complex investment processes, which demand new types of institutional arrangements, we will use the *investment project as the basic unit of analysis* in our following investigations.

This view offers the advantage of being "open" to a wide array of alternative organizational solutions and cooperation designs: some projects can most appropriately be maintained and coordinated through cooperative associations while for other projects, market exchange may be sufficient. Relatedly, while some investment projects may efficiently be governed and organized within an integrated firm, it may be advantageous for other types of projects to mobilize open, non-hierarchical network relationships with other firms or research institutes. Institutional structures should accordingly be "custom-designed" to project requirements. Appropriate institutions must be *created*, and not be taken for granted. If, in contrast to this "open", project-oriented perspective, we constrain ourselves to an analysis of allocation and distribution within an *existing* entity (such as a particular business firm XYZ), we cannot be sure of deriving a solution for which the value of a project will be maximized.

Similar ideas of *endogenous and flexible organization design* are a common theme within the more recent publications on organizational change and business restructuring. An increasing number of books and articles are published on "business process redesign and reengineering" (Davenport 1993, Hammer and Champy 1993), on "lean management", "simultaneous or concurrent engineering", "total quality management", "continuous improvement", "kaizen", and on the "virtual corporation" (Davidow and Malone 1992). All these new management concepts emphasize: (1) a stronger goal-orientation and greater customer-

---

2   Our theoretical arguments for the efficiency and sustainability of cooperation will be outlined in part II of our book.

focus, (2) an explicit process-orientation as opposed to more structural or static views; and they all promote (3) unconventional, "open" and flexible ways of matching resources to strategic objectives, process configurations and projects.

Most of these new management concepts are entity-driven: they focus on the business corporation as the unit of analysis, since large firms constitute the prime target-group for assignments of process reengineering. Business process redesign concepts have so far not explicitly dealt with strategic alliances and with new types of inter-firm arrangements. It is our intent to develop process redesign further to be applicable for studying cooperative projects and "open" network structures of business firms and research communities.

Alternative "frameworks of contractual relations" such as firms, cooperative associations or markets can be considered simultaneously and in an unbiased way. The overall objective will be to find a suitable *correspondence between strategic objectives and resources* (as illustrated in Fig. 1, in which the circle connecting strategic objectives and asset bases symbolizes the contractual arrangement being "custom-designed" to the underlying project requirements). As an example, the strategic objective pursued might involve the production and commercialization of a consumer good such as a new video recorder; specific resources (e. g. specialized inputs required for video recorder development and manufacturing) must be mobilized through a complex sequence of process steps, activities and transactions. Governance and coordination of this sequence of activities must be achieved through a particular nexus of contracts, which will often involve cooperative agreements, particularly if different firms have to jointly agree on a new video standard[3].

An economic theory of cooperation must go beyond descriptive and intuitive approaches promoted within the business community; it would have to convincingly show that a particular nexus of contracts *between markets and hierarchies* is most suitable for coordinating a particular sequence of activities in an efficient and sustainable way.

Existing theoretical treatments of cooperation and networking activities are still not precise enough in differentiating between "discrete structural alternatives" (Simon 1978). Is cooperation and networking *really a distinctive mode of coordination*? Or does it simply represent an amalgam or a mixture of institutional arrangements "somewhere in between markets and hierarchies", an "intermediary or hybrid mode of organization", or "ill-defined transactions in the middle-range" (Williamson 1985, 83)? The OECD study mentioned above argues in favor of a more decisive and rigorous treatment, which pronounces cooperation as a truely distinctive mode of coordination.

---

3   In chapters 2 and 5, we will introduce a new method for structuring complex and multilateral investment projects.

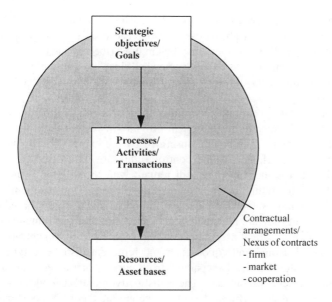

Fig. 1:   Cooperation Agreements as Relationships between Project
            Objectives and Resources/Asset Bases

But if cooperation and networking represent a truely distinctive mode of co-ordination, what exactly is it that constitutes this "third structural alternative"? A cooperation agreement can be defined as a nexus of contracts which requires that agents pool some activities while they still remain legally independent (see particularly our definition in section 1.1). Each agent will own some resources, which are *not* owned by the pooled organization. These resources which remain under the ownership of individual member agents will neither be provided as equity of the joint project organization, nor will they be provided on a rental basis.

This type of *distinctive contract mode* between rental agreements (market mode) and equity ownership (integrated mode) corresponds to the notions of "quoad usum" and "quoad sortem" in Roman contract law[4]. Both types of con-tracts, which we will call cooperative contract modes, were so far, according to our knowledge, not mentioned in the economic and organization literature. They must be seen as a *key for the understanding and explanation of cooperation.*

---

4   A definition and description of *"quoad usum" and "quoad sortem" contracts* can be found
    in Piltz (1991), Reimann (1991) and Reinhard (1991). We will analyze the application of
    this collaborative contract mode in sections 2.5, 3.3 and in chapter 7.

"Quoad usum" describes a relationship in which an individual agent grants a project organization the right to use a resource owned by him. Translated into English, this type of arrangement may be circumscribed by the term "made available for use". It can be considered "somewhat close" to the market mode, but it is nonetheless distinctly different, since resources are not exchanged on a sales or rental basis.

"Quoad sortem" constitutes a stronger form of a cooperation agreement: the owner of a highly-specific resource will provide this asset to a project organization. "Quoad sortem" may be circumscribed by the expression "implantation of values and control rights". Some control rights are transferred to the project organization, but ownership titles still remain with the original owner. He will acquire titles to the future income stream of the project. "Quoad sortem" contracts may be considered "somewhat close" to the hierarchical, equity based mode of coordination, but they are nonetheless distinctly different from integration, since property rights for critical assets are not held by the project organization.

Both "quoad usum" and "quoad sortem" represent distinctive types of contracts, that can thus be clearly separated from pure market agreements as well as from equity ownership contracts. These distinctive contract modes are a *constituent element of a cooperation design*. An economic theory of cooperation must show that it is advantageous in terms of project value and distributive shares to agree on this type of contract mode. Individual member agents must realize that it is to their advantage to pool resources without transfering ownership titles and without claiming rental income.

The efficiency and sustainability of cooperative contract modes must be explained by the *"difficult" or "critical" character of assets* to be involved in a project[5], and by a particular pattern of asset ownership distribution. If the resources required for a project are closely held by individual agents, if ownership titles are difficult to transfer, and if the value of resources is strongly dependent on closely-held knowledge, the advantages of cooperative contract modes outweigh their disadvantages.

These conditions for sustainable comparative advantage of cooperation are closely linked to an understanding of *capabilities and skills* of independent agents as *capital goods or assets*. It is our intent to emphasize the role of time needed to develop highly-specific capabilities and skills. Long periods needed to develop these capabilities (*entry times*) will explain why it is difficult to transfer ownership titles and why it may be economically advantageous to pool assets between independent agents. The durability of these assets (to be interpreted as *exit times*) will explain why agents are able to exploit quasi-rents, and also why they run the risk of being expropriated through a failure of the collaborative association. The

---

5   In chapters 3 and 5, we will define precisely under which conditions assets can be characterized as being "critical" or "difficult to coordinate".

specific combination of assets required for a multilateral investment project will explain the sustainable comparative advantages of certain modes of cooperation, but they may often also be used to assess project risks, and to explain why certain forms of cooperative associations will not be feasible.

While these considerations apply for all kinds of specific investments, a greater complication arises if the most critical assets are represented by knowledge. *Knowledge-based capital* is often characterized by very long entry times. The transmission of knowledge is complicated by the inherent characteristics of information (Arrow 1962). Knowledge is often "embodied" and inseparable from other specific resources. If knowledge-based capital represents a major share of the asset base required for an investment project, "complicated design features" outlined above will dominate choices, and resource allocation will primarily become a matter of choosing between alternative cooperation designs.

Specific knowledge-based capital is a focal point for the theoretical explanation of sustainable comparative advantages of cooperation. It will thus be the purpose of this book:

- to emphasize the role of *time* needed to build up, utilize and amortize the critical resources needed for sophisticated and complex investment projects;
- to *bridge recent advances in the economic theory of the firm* with ongoing developments in the management of corparate transformation and business *process redesign*;
- to develop a *theory of strategic investment processes* for which the selection and formation of appropriate institutional structures is endogenized;
- to develop a problem-solving approach, and a general framework for *structuring cooperative investment projects*; and
- to apply this framework to the *analysis of empirical case examples* which seem to require complex, collaborative solutions.

In *chapter 1* we will define the basic notions for cooperative investment projects and strategic alliances. A survey of the extensive literature will enable us to not only describe the growing importance of this subject, but also to summarize more recent empirical trends in cooperative investment behavior. "Traditional" economic explanations of cooperation will be critically assessed; we will argue that most existing economic explanations *cannot* explain sustainable comparative advantages of cooperation *unless* the important aspects of time, asset specificity, and knowledge formation and transmission are explicitly taken into consideration.

In *chapter 2* we will develop a new method of structuring complex investment projects for which appropriate institutional structures can be "designed" endogenously. Investors' strategic objectives represent the starting point for process evaluation and selection, for task analysis, and for the analysis of resource requirements. Appropriate institutional structures are interpreted as complex contractual arrangements, which can be "fine-tuned" to the underlying task requirements, and to the prevailing resource ownership pattern.

Chapter 3 introduces capital theoretical concepts for the analysis of cooperation. The formation of knowledge bases, and the establishment of contracts and institutional structures is interpreted as a process of capital accumulation. Knowledge formation, organizational learning, institutional change, strategic development and diversification, as well as business process redesign are analyzed in capital theoretical terms. The chapter concludes with a new interpretation of collaborative investment as an option.

Chapter 4 provides a survey on neo-institutional economics, and an economic explanation of "discrete institutional structures". The advantages and limits of vertical integration, of market transactions, and of alternative forms of cooperative arrangements will be discussed in detail. We will argue that the explanation of "hybrid", cooperative modes as superior and sustainable solution requires a more explicit understanding of time, and we will thus introduce the concepts of entry time and exit time.

In *chapter 5* we will outline a general framework for structuring complex investment projects, and for finding appropriate cooperation designs. The analysis of strategic objectives pursued within a group of agents leads to the joint specification of business processes, project tasks and resources, and to the analysis of distributed asset bases. The proposed model may serve as a generic framework for structuring institutional choices, and for the extension of process redesign concepts to strategic alliances and multi-agent networks. Chapter 5 also contains a delineation of the institutional boundaries of firms, who simultaneously participate in a number of cooperation projects and networks with other firms.

Chapters 6 and 7 contain empirical applications and analyses of particular investment and finance projects. In *chapter 6*, we will analyze multinational investment projects in the *telecommunication satellite industry*, for which international cooperation has been a pervasive mode of governance and organization. The comparison of three empirical projects shows that cooperation has *not* always been the superior mode of coordination, and that some projects have failed due to the inappropriate consideration of strategic objectives, task requirements and sustainable asset bases.

In *chapter 7* we will analyze cooperation agreements *within the venture capital business*. This segment of the capital market will be interpreted as a distributed knowledge pool, where financial funds are inextricably linked with highly-specific asset bases of financial investors. These asset bases take a long time to being built up, and it is very difficult to mobilize all the critical assets that are required for a start-up project without relying on cooperative agreements between investors. We will also show in chapter 7, that financial cooperation often involves *public agents* who control critical asset bases; finally we will analyze conditions under which the early participation of public institutions may be an essential element of collaboration agreements within the venture capital sector.

Based on our analysis of cooperation, strategic alliances and process redesign, we will propose a *"new agenda for public policy"* (see our final *chapter 8*).

Economic and industrial policy should be "designed endogenously" and in accordance with particular business process requirements. Areas of public involvement should be decomposed into projects with clear constituencies, relatively small groups of participants, and with a clear attribution of tasks and responsibilities. For each particular project, sustainable asset bases of participating private as well as public agents must be critically assessed. Our proposed framework of project structuring and business process redesign is applicable to many types of complex, large projects, and it is particularly suited for the design of public-private partnerships.

1 Cooperation and Strategic Alliances: Empirical Evidence and Theoretical Explanations

1.1 Basic Notions and Definitions for Cooperative Projects

Any sophisticated investment project requires a diversity of skills and the mobilization of different, often highly-specific assets. It involves very complex processes through which a certain configuration of skills and assets is achieved over time. The more specific and advanced the required skills and assets are, the more will a firm have to rely on a sophisticated division of labor and responsibilities. This again leads to greater requirements for coordination in order to secure the whole spectrum of specialized inputs at the desired quality level, in time, and at acceptable cost.

There are three different ways for a firm to coordinate its activities and to secure access to all specialized inputs required for its smooth and successful operation[1]. The *first* involves setting up links with independent market participants who will provide the appropriate skills and resources at the time needed. We will call this the *market solution*[2]. *Second*, and alternatively, a firm can attempt to gain ownership and control over the whole spectrum of specialized skills and resources in order to secure their rapid deployment and potential cost advantages, to reduce risks, or to exclude potential rivals. We will call this the *integrated solution*[3].

---

1   For this distinction into three generic modes of coordination see Richardson (1972), Teece (1991), Williamson (1980, 1990), Bidlingmaier (1967), Grochla (1982), Schneider (1973), as well as our more extensive analysis in chapter 4.
2   The market solution requires interactions between autonomous, legally independent agents ("independence"), with free choice to select other market participants ("exit"). An extreme form of market solution is the atomistic spot market emphasized in neoclassical economics. Other forms differ in terms of frequency of transactions, type of negotiations, intensity of information exchanged, etc. Networks, as they are analyzed within the Swedish investment literature (see section 4.3) can be regarded as market forms of exchange with a high frequency of transactions between the same agents, who rely on very intense forms of communication. Networks can be transformed into collaborative forms of interaction if the relationships between independent agents involves more binding contracts, the build-up of informal (e. g. trust) or formal ties (e. g. exclusive arrangements for machinery or human capital).
3   Again, we can differentiate between different degrees of integration which may be measured by the extent to which it relies on ownership and control rights for specific assets and activities. A certain degree of integrated ownership and management will often be crucial, and has to be differentiated from the concept of the firm as a simple bundle of contracts maintained in order to secure re sources owned by others. Typically, an *integrated* firm will attempt to *own* at least a major part of the key resources and assets needed for its operation and will integrate major management functions.

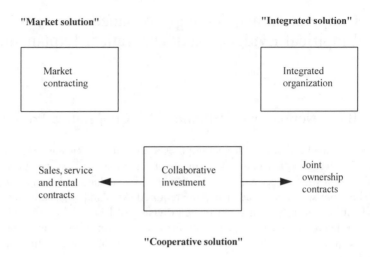

Fig. 1.1:   Alternative Modes of Governance and Organization

A *third* way of securing access to specialized skills and assets involves cooperation between two or more independent firms. These firms will join forces for a specific project, but will remain legally independent organizations. Ownership and management of the cooperating firms will not be fully integrated[4]. This *cooperative solution* can be interpreted as a hybrid or intermediate form of the other two strategies (see Fig. 1.1)[5]. There are a variety of different forms of cooperation; some will primarily emphasize longer-term (renegotiable) contracts with independent market participants (*cooperation without joint ownership*); alternatively, two or more firms may decide to set up a *joint-ownership* collaborative project for a certain activity or function while remaining legally and organizationally independent for most other activities.

Whatever form of cooperation may be sought, the participating agents will have to commit resources and make investments, the return on which will depend on the functioning of the collaborative venture. For some of these investments which are specific to the coalition, the return for each partner will be higher than the return on investment he could realize elsewhere. Such specific investments run a high risk of expropriation of quasi-rents, if resource-owners are just loosely

---

4   The very definition of cooperation requires separate ownership and separate management by the cooperating firms, even though some separable activities can be jointly owned and managed. See Bidlingmaier (1967, 355) and Schneider (1973, 35).

5   The idea of cooperation as an intermediate and "alternative form of transactional relationship between firms" has been most consequently emphasized by Richardson (1972); a similar concep tualization can already be found in Knight (1965).

inter-connected. In order to protect themselves from expropriation, owners of specific resources will seek pre-investment contractual arrangements[6]. The level of investments committed, the degree to which quasi-rents may be expropriated, as well as the kind of reciprocity and interdependence between agents will influence the appropriate contract modes and the particular form of collaboration to be chosen. If investments committed and the risks of expropriation are low, a rather loose structure may be appropriate and protective contractual arrangements must not neccessarily be formalized[7]. If, by contrast, large investments must be committed, and if there is a high risk of expropriation, agents will select a formalized structure with strong emphasis on reciprocal protective contractual arrangements, often in the form of joint equity, and with clearly specified liabilities.

An *economic theory of cooperation* must explain what kind of investment projects are selected by participating agents, what the risk and return profile will be in dependence of the coalition's performance, what kind of protective contractual arrangements are being sought, and how agents can secure themselves through joint equity and through the specification of liabilities. This requires a more "rigid view" of cooperation, which explicitly takes into account cost-benefit comparisons for alternative institutional settings. Most existing studies on cooperation focus *either* on benefits *or* on the costs of collaborative ventures[8]. Hardly any studies try to simultaneously evaluate benefits *and* costs, and to analyze cooperation relative to all alternative modes of governance and organization.

Benefits of collaboration to participating agents are related to more effective achievement of objectives as compared to both integration and the market solution. The formulation of *joint objectives* is the major element of any cooperative strategy. The meaning of the Latin word *"cooperare"* involves a goal-oriented joint activity of two or more persons. Accordingly, Eschenburg (1971, 4) defines cooperation as conscious activity directed towards a joint target. When these goals have been clarified, participating agents set up collaborative associations to achieve certain objectives which they could *not* attain through other strategies. The pooling of activities and resources must lead to improvements which will result in increased revenues, in lower joint costs, in a reduction of risk and/or in greater speed and flexibility. These improvements can be attained through four *generic strategies* which also define the *primary objectives* of cooperation, including:

---

6   See Alchian (1984, 36) and our analysis in section 2.5.
7   In this case, the distinction between collaboration and market networks may be vanishing. For a clearer distinction between open network arrangements and more formalized contractual arrangements see section 2.5 and chapter 4.
8   While contributions to the *business administration* literature as well as *management studies* often appear to be biased towards *benefits* of collaboration, *economists* tend to view this phenomenon from a more critical angle, emphasizing the *costs* of collaboration and potential anti-competitive threats.

- the access or greater penetration of a particular market or customer group;
- the access of a new technology or knowledge base;
- the achievement of a greater (joint) degree of efficiency;
- as well as the pursuance of a joint political or social goal.

To illustrate this, two or more companies can decide to cooperate (1) in order to jointly build up their market presence in Eastern Europe. (2) They can pool resources to develop sophisticated new materials. (3) They can jointly exploit activities at minimum efficient scale, such as the construction of a large manufacturing plant, or they can agree on a joint standard. Finally, they can (4) decide to participate in collaborative campaigns directed towards urban development or environmental control[9].

For any of these objectives, two or more firms will have to pool complementary resources and will have to cover certain *functions* jointly: these functions can include research and development (R&D), inbound logistics or procurement, manufacturing, marketing and sales, as well as service or after-sales service[10]. They can cooperate within a particular function, or they can divide up their activities and find a suitable match of complementary strengths across different functions. *Strategic alliances* of firms are defined as a pooling of separable functions, activities or business units, which are directed at a specific objective. Strategic alliances are often of a temporary nature and do not affect the primary missions and the ownership and control rights of the participating firms.

The variety of alternative cooperative arrangements can be illustrated by the matrix in *Fig. 1.2*: the *rows* show the four primary objectives, while the functions to be covered are shown in the *columns*. Two or more partners can decide to jointly *penetrate a new market* (e. g. the automotive supply market in France). The specific line of business pursued and the level of activity to be achieved will then imply which functions ought to be covered by the cooperative venture[11]. Similarly, if the prime objective is *access to new technology*, R & D will typically be essential while cooperation in manufacturing (to jointly explore new, related process technologies), as well as marketing and sales (to learn from lead customers) may be important supplementary functions.

---

9 This last, more political type of collaboration is described in more detail in chapter 8 and in Gerybadze (1992).

10 For this differentation into functions or elements of the value chain, see Porter (1985). Different firms and industries may require the use of different classifications of functions. Our approach is most flexible with respect to such differences.

11 The typical sequence for developing a presence in a foreign market often starts with setting up a sales, service and distribution network. As the volume of business builds up, local procurement and manufacturing is considered. In later stages, design and R & D are added. Foreign investment strategies of Japanese firms in Europe (be it single-firm or collaborative), which follow a tightly-controlled logical sequence, are very illustrative in this respect.

Function ⟍ Objective	R&D	Procurement	Manu-facturing	Marketing & sales	After-sales-service
1. New market	█				
2. New technology	█	█	█	█	█
3. Greater efficiency	█				
4. Joint political & social goals	█				

 Area to be covered by technology-related collaborative projects

Fig. 1.2: Objectives and Functions of Cooparative Investment Projects

Most research on cooperation and strategic alliances tends to classify along the horizontal dimension in Fig. 1.2: cooperative ventures are distinguished according to the function on which the joint activity of two companies is focused. Firms often cooperate exclusively in R&D, while they remain rivals for marketing and in manufacturing. Other types of cooperative projects focus on joint procurement, joint manufacturing, or on cooperative activities in marketing, sales and services.

We will show in the following section 1.2 that the emphasis of collaborative investment activity has changed over the last decades. Prime objectives of the past were the penetration of new markets and the intent to achieve greater efficiency through the joint use of fixed investment. Accordingly, joint marketing and sales, as well as collaborative manufacturing were the functions most strongly emphasized. More recent developments seem to indicate that *access to new technology* receives much greater attention; consequently, research, design and development together with new ways of jointly marketing and servicing specific customer groups[12] have received much greater attention in recent descriptions of cooperative activity.

To reflect these changing patterns, we will concentrate our following investigations on those types of cooperative investment activities which emphasize the objective to jointly access new technologies and knowledge bases, and which are directed at pooling R&D and product development. If two or more partners want access to new technology, they can proceed by jointly pursuing different functions, with R&D certainly often being the core function (see row 2 in Fig. 1.2). Similarly, if they want to pool R&D activities, all four objectives can be of relevance, although access to new technology is often listed as the prime objective (column 1 in Fig. 1.2). We will use the term *technology-related cooperative projects* for all types of arrangements between two or more firms for which access to new technology is the prime objective, and/or for which R&D is the key function (see shaded area in Fig. 1.2). Our following models will concentrate on technology-related cooperative investment projects, even though the methodology used can similarly be applied to other types of cooperative ventures.

Any economic analysis of cooperation must comprehensively compare benefits *and* costs related to collaborative activities, and has to ask whether intended improvements are achieved in an efficient way. Do collaborative activities fulfill the aspirations of participating agents and do they really lead to the desired results? Which potential hazards have to be considered and are the full costs incurred through collaboration really lower than the expected benefits, particularly if we take all cost elements and all alternative organizational solutions into consideration?

Problems associated with such a comprehensive evaluation are related to the fact that collaborative investment projects are often very time-consuming, and that they

---

12 This also means that the functions of marketing, sales and service cannot be interpreted in the same way within the newly arising "pattern of collaboration". While the old form of jointly accessing a new market was more a kind of "one way street" of servicing a more or less predifined customer need, the new form involves an interactive approach of joint learning between customers and suppliers, and close coordination between sales, design, R&D and manufacturing.

involve many hidden, often unforeseeable cost elements. It may often take five to ten years until a technology related joint-venture leads to the desired results. During that time, considerable expenditures must be taken into consideration including outlays for capital equipment, manpower and management time. Particularly the management costs of initiating, stabilizing and maintaining a cooperation project are most often underestimated. Empirical studies of cooperation are often based on announced objectives at the time of formation of a new collaborative program. Post-contractual difficulties and management costs are regularly underestimated[13]. These include costs related to difficulties of agreeing on compatible goals, management inefficiencies in coordinating loose alliances, repetitive contractual difficulties and "haggling problems"[14]. All in all, this results in an *ex-ante* overestimation of benefits during the formation of cooperative associations. *Ex-post*, realized benefits often turn out lower, while costs tend to be much higher than anticipated. This will frequently lead to "frustration" among the partners, and will often undermine the sustainability of a cooperative venture[15].

Similar to this divergence between ex-ante and ex-post calculations of costs and benefits, we also have to distinguish between effects on collaborating agents and those accruing to non-coalition members. The effectiveness of coalitions is often correlated to their degree of exclusiveness[16]. Members of an effective coalition may find their objectives, such as the attempted access to a new market or to a new technology suitably fulfilled, but this is often achieved by excluding other firms from being active in this market or from exploiting a new technological opportunity (Lorange 1985, 11 f). Members of the coalition will gain while non-members will be worse off. Such *external costs of cooperation* must necessarily be considered in an overall evaluation of advantages and disadvantages of collaborative programs. Accordingly, an economic theory of cooperation has to approach a balance between dynamic allocation and static distribution effects. Supporters of the "new cooperative paradigm" tend to argue for a greater enhancement of collaborative activities in order to maintain a high level of innovation and dynamic efficiency. Their view is heavily contested by proponents of

---

13 These management costs are often intrinsically unpredictable since new partners interact with no "joint history of collaboration". Cooperative associations imply that partners can "move in all directions" and that there is ample of room for strategic behavior. Resulting interactions cannot be predicted in the same way as within a tightly managed firm, except when partners can rely on a long chain of past cooperative activities.

14 Lorange (1985, 11 f) and Bleicher (1987, 11) show that this often causes the top management of the parent companies to be involved in solving subordinate problems, with the effect that top management has less time available for solving strategic issues related to the core business.

15 Not surprisingly, empirical surveys of management consulting companies show that seven out of ten joint ventures do not fulfill the expectations of their parent companies. See Coopers & Lybrand (1986).

16 See Olson (1968) and our own investigations in chapters 6 and 7.

a free market system, who argue that the new forms of cooperation are just disguised variants of old anti-competitive practices. They refer to Adam Smith's (1776) warnings, that "people of the same trade seldom meet together, even for merriment and diversion, but that the conversation ends in a conspiracy against the public or in some contrivance to raise prices".

1.2 Empirical Evidence for Increases and Changes in Cooperative Investment Activity

There are many empirical studies on cooperation, joint ventures and international strategic alliances. For the following summary of the most important studies and for our assessment of the more recent empirical trends, we have reviewed the following sources:

- research on direct foreign investment and economic studies of investment strategies of multinational firms[17];
- business administration studies on joint ventures and strategic alliances[18];
- statistical databases on collaborative investment and international strategic alliances[19];
- as well as surveys and case descriptions within the management consulting literature[20].

The large number of studies on this subject appears to reflect the growing importance of cooperative investment and international strategic alliances. Most studies come to the conclusion that the quantity and frequency of cooperative agreements between firms has risen considerably during the last ten to fifteen years. There is widespread and ubiquitous belief that the growing world market integration, the intensified degree of international competition and the increasing importance of new technologies have led to the evolution of a different pattern

---

17 See Buckley and Casson (1985), Bartlett and Ghoshal (1989), Dunning (1988) and UNCTC (1988).

18 See Contractor and Lorange (1987, 1988), Lorange (1985), Harrigan (1985, 1986 and 1988), Buckley and Casson (1985), Porter (1986), Porter and Fuller (1986).

19 Joint-venture activities are regularly monitored within the U.S.-based report Mergers and Acquisitions. The United Nations (UNCTC 1988) and OECD (1986) publish statistical surveys on this subject. A detailed database on technology-related cooperation projects has been established within MERIT (see Hagedorn and Schakenraad 1989a and 1989b).

20 See Ohmae (1985), Business International Corporation (1987), as well as studies by Arthur D. Little, Booz, Allen & Hamilton, Boston Consulting Group, Coopers & Lybrand and McKinsey.

of transnational business, thus emphasizing new forms of collaborative associations (Ohmae 1985, 14, Bleicher 1987, 2, and Dunning 1988, 377 ff).

One of the features of the mid 1980s has been a dramatic escalation in the number of strategic and 'first-best' cooperative ventures concluded between large enterprises that are often domiciled in different countries, with the expressed purpose of either exploiting production synergies or reducing transaction costs of activities at different stages of the value-adding chain; or to capture strategic and economic gains by pooling resources among enterprises engaged in similar value-adding activities. Both these types of coalitions are very different in kind and purpose from the joint-ventures and non-equity arrangements of the earlier postwar period which more often than not were made for defensive or second-best reasons, e.g. in response to the exhortations of host governments (Dunning 1988, 328).

These changes seem to indicate a movement away from the pure market mode of exchange. Unidirectional flows in the forms of licensing agreements tend to be replaced by reciprocal arrangements between partners of equivalent strengths and with complementary capabilities. As a result, a dominant share of the new international alliances is *concentrated within the so-called Triad countries* U.S., Japan, and in Western Europe (Ohmae 1985, Bleicher 1987, and Lorange 1985). Within these countries, a large and growing share of cooperative activities is pursued by the 500 largest enterprises which increasingly consider that "a company's competitive situation no longer depends on itself alone but on the quality of the alliances it is able to form"[21]. Large corporations are thus basically transforming their nature and searching for new ways for competitive differentiation and strategic repositioning

From behaving largely as a confederation of loosely knit foreign affiliates, . . . the multinational enterprise is now increasingly assuming the role of an orchestrator of production and transactions within a cluster or network of cross-border internal and external relationships. . . . The decision-taking nexus of the multinational enterprise in the late 1980s has come to resemble the central nervous system of a much larger group of interdependent but less formally governed activities, whose function is primarily to advance the global competitive strategy and position of the core organization. This it does, not only by, or even chiefly, organizing its internal production and transactions in the most efficient way, or by its technology, product and marketing strategies, but by the nature and form of alliances it concludes with other firms (Dunning (1988, 327).

Partly because of this new emphasis that large international firms place on cooperative investment activities[22], but also for a number of other reasons which will be explored later, joint ventures and strategic alliances are strongly *concen-*

---

21 Bruno Lamborghini, Director of Olivetti, cited in Coopers & Lybrand (1986, 99).
22 As an example, Philips has concluded more than 800 separate alliances with other firms all over the world. Companies like IBM, Siemens or Olivetti can report similar numbers.

trated within a few industries. These include motor vehicles, aerospace, electronics and telecommunications, factory automation equipment and information technology, as well as chemicals and pharmaceuticals. A large average firm size, a high level of capital intensity and rapidly growing capital expenditures, as well as a strong dependence on large R & D expenditures are among the most important explanatory factors[23].

Apart from being very R & D-intensive, these industries tend to be the most important generators and users of a certain class of new technologies which are of an encompassing nature in that they affect both products and production methods of a wide range of industrial sectors (Dunning 1988, 334). Such *generic and encompassing technologies*, or "fusion technologies" (Kodama 1992) include microelectronics, computers and telecommunication, robotics and factory automation, new materials and biotechnology. All these technologies can be characterized as *"chain linked"* (Kline and Rosenberg 1986 and Teece 1991) on both the user and the supplier side. On the *user side*, these technologies can only be fully exploited and disseminated by making full use of extensive links to customer firms in a wide range of application areas. On the *supply side*, generic new technologies often have to be combined with complementary technologies which are made available by *different* groups of firms, often from other industries. Both types of "chain links" lead to a growing interdependence between firms comprising a wide range of complementary skills and know-how areas. It is said that the full spectrum of required skills extends the capabilities of even the largest international companies, and that this explains their "openness" in negotiating with other firms, and their readiness to cast doubts upon their traditional organizational boundaries[24].

More recent studies on new types of inter-company alliances do in fact pronounce this influence of generic and "chain linked" technologies. A United Nations survey on cooperative agreements between European, Japanese and U.S. based firms showed that a large majority of such agreements were centered around information technology and biotechnology[25]. The MERIT based CATI

---

23 See Berg, Duncan, and Friedman (1982), Marity and Smiley (1983), Porter and Fuller (1986) and UNCTC (1988).

24 See for example Imai and Baba (1991) and Teece (1991). It will be argued later (in sections 1.3 and 1.4, as well as in chapters 4 and 5) that these "chain links" as such cannot always be used as a sufficient argument for the superiority of collaboration over other modes of governance and organization.

25 See UNCTC (1988); in information technolgy alone, the study identified 618 new inter-firm alliances between 1984 and 1986. In biotechnolgy, U.S. firms reported 227 agreements between 1981 and early 1986, while Japanese firms concluded 203 agreements during the same period.

database has identified almost 7000 cooperative agreements of which 2700 were concluded in information technology, 1200 in biotechnology and 700 in new materials (Hagedoorn and Schakenraad 1989b, 2).

This growing importance of generic new technologies, together with the reported changes in international business practices appears to have induced a considerable *qualititive change* in collaborative investment activity relating to:

- different *objectives* for the more recent cooperation agreements;
- a changing emphasis on *specific functions* to be covered by collaboration;
- a reconsideration of new *organizational modes* of cooperation;
- the appearance of a new form of *division of labour* between firms;
- and a crossing of traditional *boundaries* between firms and industry sectors.

With respect to *changing objectives*, cooperative investment activities "are becoming more strategic through linking major competitors together to compete worldwide. More traditional coalitions were often tactical, involving tie-ups with local firms to gain market access or to transfer technology passively to regions where a firm did not want to compete directly" (Porter and Fuller 1986, 315f). Whereas in the past, cooperative investment activities were often pursued at the business unit level, aiming primarily at cost advantages through the use of joint production facilities, or towards penetrating a well-defined and narrow market segment, more recent cooperative agreements are often seen as the only way to get access to strategic new technologies or to develop new marketing and service functions, often at a global level. This attracts the attention of corporate management and even tends to get intertwined with political and social goals[26].

With respect to business *functions* covered by international cooperative agreements, there is a strongly growing emphasis on R&D, on technology-related agreements in manufacturing (directed towards the introduction of flexible manufacturing and new logistic concepts) and on distribution (new forms of communicating with customers and lead-user). Cooperative ventures are more and more directed towards jointly exploring new areas of expertise, and less towards exploiting simple economies of scale in manufacturing or distribution.

As a result, new modes of *governance and organization* are being sought that bring partners of more equal stature together. There appears to be a movement away from one-way transfer and pure market-mediated licensing agreements. A growing importance is placed on joint projects between firms and on the establishment of joint ventures, particularly in the field of R & D. The analysis of data

---

26 More and more of the very large cooperative programs in areas seen as strategic for national development are pursued in line with strong political arguments. This is, for instance, the case for European projects (Jessi, Esprit, Eureka).

from the MERIT-CATI database shows that joint R & D accounts for the largest share of all cooperative agreements in biotechnology (30 %), in information technology (27 %) and in new materials (25 %). Joint ventures and research corporations are established in 17 % of all the cases documented (Hagedoorn and Schakenraad 1989 b, 8 f). In the course of time, both forms of collaboration tend to increase in importance both with respect to more market-mediated forms such as customer-supplier relationships and one-directional licensing agreements, and also in comparison to more integrated solutions such as direct investment, mergers and acquisitions.

This goes hand in hand with a *changing division of labor* between firms participating in cooperative ventures. Traditional forms of segregation according to products or markets are more and more being replaced by new forms of cooperation between two firms both producing a similar product or serving the same customer group, while each partner focuses on specific sub-segments of economic activities. Cooperative agreements are thus molded around a very sophisticated segmentation, around functions and around specific steps within the value chain (Porter 1985 and 1990).

Parallel to this, we observe a *bridging of traditional boundaries* between sectors which were in the past only characterized by minor interrelatedness. Since more emphasis is placed on the access to new technologies, and because many new technologies are of a synergistic nature with a wide application potential (information technology, biotechnology, new materials), firms from very distinct sectors tend to tie up (Kodama 1992). Typical examples are collaborative arrangements between firms in food processing and pharmaceuticals, between automotives and electronics, aerospace and new materials, as well as between the electronics and machinery sectors.

Both quantitative and qualitative changes seem to imply at first sight that a greater degree of openness and cooperation is continuously being approached. Empirical evidence, however, is not as straightforward and unambiguous as it might appear. Since reported success rates for inter-firm alliances are rather low[27], the described proliferation of joint ventures over the last ten years may be interpreted as a temporary phenomenon. In this case, it would be a mistake to over-emphasize the relative advantage of cooperation as opposed to both market transactions and vertical integration, and "to swing the pendulum too far and obscure the cooperative merits" (Kogut 1988, 50). Some empirical signs already indicate a selective reversal: as recent changes in the field of biotechnology show, large companies tend to

---

27 See Harrigan (1988, 53). Kogut (1988, 40f) shows that failure rates of joint ventures are almost as high as failure rates of small start-up firms. Within the first six years of their existence, only about half of all joint ventures survive.

"run sour" of collaborative arrangements with technology-driven start-up companies and prefer to redirect themselves towards more "conventional" forms of integrated control[28].

There are more reported incidences where the pendulum has eventually swung more towards the integrated solution; meanwhile, in other cases, original collaborative efforts may become replaced by more appropriate market-mediated forms of exchange. Empirical evidence that can be found for both cases appears to be rather arbitrary and indecisive. A tendency to favor collaborative forms of investment within the business community of the Triad countries may turn out to be just a temporary move which might have been advantageous to initiate a large wave of globalization and to assimilate new generations of fusion technologies. As soon as a next stage of consolidation is approached, though, and if ex-post performance evaluations of cooperative ventures turn out not to keep up with ex-ante expectations, a significant reversal may occur.

In order to reliably interpret recent changes and to predict future trends, both quantitive and qualitative changes relating to collaboration have to be explained from within a *coherent theoretical framework*. We need to understand better under which particular conditions cooperative investment can really be regarded as superior and sustainable. The large and growing literature on the subject, however, falls short of consistent theoretical explanations. Empirical data analysis concentrates on a rather simple list of explanatory factors, the most important of which cover:

– the argument of *growing investment outlays* (particularly for R & D);
– the *greater speed* of development and technological change;
– the *greater risks* involved in technology development;
– as well as the *synergy* opened up through a number of generic new technologies (microelectronics, biotechnology, etc.)[29].

While many of these reasons appear to be plausible on a case by case basis, there is no convincing and general answer to the following question: why is it that firms choose the *cooperative solution* as the most prefered option; and why, if so, is this strategy really superior to both the market solution *and* the integrated solution? There are two lines of reasoning which try to solve this question, one

---

28 Hagedorn and Schakenraad (1989b, 8f) show, that "in the years 1975 to 1985, . . . many small R & D intensive biotechnology firms were established in which a number of large companies took minority stakes". However, "for many companies in biotechnology, minority stakes did not provide them with the technological and company information they expected and therefore many large companies were abandoning this particular mode of cooperation".
29 See, for instance, Ohmae (1985), Porter and Fuller (1986) as well as Contractor and Lorange (1987).

being the "classical explanation" which is most often found in economic textbooks, and which will be explained in section 1.3. This will be contrasted with more recent economic explanations (see sections 1.4 and 1.5, and chapters 3 and 4). We will show that both lines of reasoning can provide some answers, but that there remains a missing theoretical link still waiting for discovery.

1.3   "Classical" Explanations for Cooperation

There are a number of reasons for cooperation reported in the empirical and theoretical literature. Fusfeld (1958) has argued that cooperation at horizontal level serves primarily to reduce competition, while it may also allow for more efficient sourcing and an improved cost structure. In addition, it is seen as a vehicle for accessing new markets, primarily for diversifying large companies. West (1959) has identified four reasons for cooperation: (1) diversification, (2) capital constraints, (3) government pressure (primarily related to overseas operation) and (4) pooling of know-how. A slightly different interpretation can be found in Mariti and Smiley's (1983) empirical study: (1) marketing agreements, (2) economies of scale, (3) risk-sharing and (4) technology transfer resp. technology complementarity. Ohmae (1985) has argued that the accelerated diffusion of new technology and the need to establish a position in a region of the world market where a firm is so far under-represented serve as principal motives for collaborative investment activity and for strategic alliances. More recently, Contractor and Lorange (1988), Ghemawat, Porter and Rawlinson (1986), and Dunning (1988) have argued that the following five reasons have become most important for explaining joint ventures and cooperation activities: (1) sharing of capital risks, (2) sharing of R&D costs, (3) acquisition of complementary technology and skills, (4) the need to capture economies of scale, (5) and overcoming entry barriers to new markets.

Given this multifarious list of reasons or motives which is often neither very well structured nor logically consistent, one should proceed in deriving a few generic objectives. *First*, agents want to access a *new market* or a new line of business activity and they consider it worthwhile to do this with some other partner. *Second*, they may want to get access to a *specific input*, a certain technology or skill being one example. And *third*, they want to achieve a more appropriate risk-return profile for their transformation of inputs into outputs. Finally, they may also consider other, often more long-term oriented or "intangible" social and political objectives. In the following, we will concentrate on the *first three generic objectives*: access to markets, access to specific inputs and improvements in the risk-return profile. These generic objectives have to be distinguished according to:
– whether they just explain *inducement effects* which can lead to cooperative activities if we start from within a given institutional setting;

– or whether they can really explain under which conditions cooperative institutional arrangements will be *sustainable and efficient* in comparison to other forms of organization.

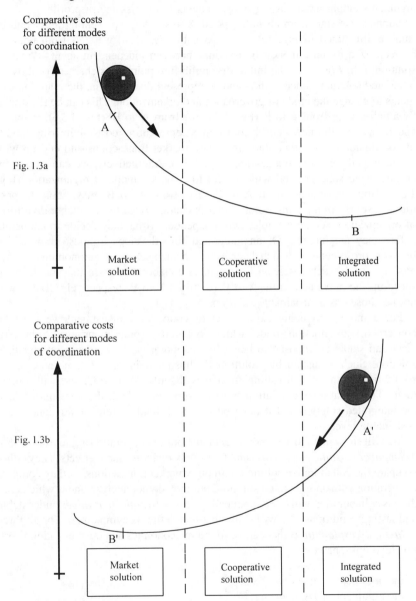

Fig 1.3:   Non-Sustaniable Collaboration

We will argue that access to markets and specific inputs will most often serve only as an explanation for *temporary inducement effects*. Explanations for the sustainability and efficiency of cooperation, by contrast, have to be built around arguments emphasizing lasting improvements in the risk-return profile.

Suppose we start from an initial point A (resp. A'), representing a disequilibrium as illustrated in Fig. 1.3a and 1.3b. In *Fig. 1.3a*, we start from point A characterized by pure market transactions between independent agents ("market solution"). In *Fig. 1.3b*, the initial disequilibrium point A' is characterized by an integrated solution. Since both A and A' represent disequilibria, there are inducements to change the mode of governance and organization. This can be illustrated by a ball rolling from A to B (Fig. 1.3a), or from A' to B' (Fig. 1.3b). Points B and B' will be the new equilibrium points representing cost-minimizing modes of coordination. We either start from pure market transactions and end up with an integrated form of organization (Fig. 1.3a). Alternatively, we can start from an integrated solution, and will transfer to a market mode of organization (Fig. 1.3b). Both movements from A to B resp. from A' to B' may imply to pass through some *intermediate* point which is characterized by a collaborative form of organization. As an example, two independent firms may decide to cooperate before they are merged. Or an integrated firm develops in-house transactions between profit-centers, which later establish themselves as autonomous market participants. In such cases, an intermediate collaborative form may facilitate or speed up the movement from A to B (or from A' to B' respectively), but it will not be chosen as a sustainable solution.

For a more convincing explanation of cooperative investment we must be concerned with situations under which cooperative solutions promise to be efficient and stable as opposed to being just temporarily chosen as an intermediate solution. Such a sustainable solution is illustrated in *Fig. 1.4*: point C is an equilibrium point. A ball rolling from A will settle down in C, and will remain there. The collaborative solution must be superior to both the pure market and the integrated solution and it must be able to defend its relative advantage at a sustainable level.

We will show that most economic explanations of cooperation argue from within a *comparative-static framework*, and focus only on inducement effects. They either compare the collaborative solution with pure market transactions, or they compare cooperation with an integrated solution, but they do not analyze under which conditions collaboration will be economically superior to *both alternatives* under stable and lasting conditions. We will show that this deficit is symptomatic for all three *"classical" explanations* that can be found in economics and business administration textbooks, namely:

– the argument of *investment size*;
– the argument of *risk-sharing*;
– and the argument of *synergy*.

We will explain each argument separately and will show that each can explain a specific form of inducement effect, while none of them is a valid argument for the sustainability and efficiency of cooperation.

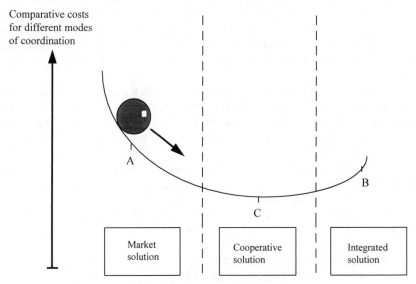

Fig. 1.4:   Cooperative Investment as Sustainable Solution

1.3.1   The Argument of Investment Size

The argument most often used in the cooperation literature emphasizes investment indivisibilities which lead to the consideration of joint activities of two or more independent partners who want to attain minimum efficient size. *Investment indivisibilities* can be relevant for all functions including:

– large laboratories and test facilities required for *R & D*;
– large investments for logistics and inspection related to *procurement*;
– expensive factory automation systems for *manufacturing*;
– as well as large investments for *marketing and sales* (distribution channels, brand names, advertising, etc.).

In markets with many small suppliers all below the minimum efficient size, there are strong inducement effects for firms to cooperate. But independent companies might as well merge and exploit scale effects within a *single, integrated firm*[30].

Even in industries with very large suppliers, scale effects may require a level of operation which cannot be maintained efficiently within the largest firm. Several big companies can decide to pool their resources for a particular activity (e. g. a collaborative R & D program or a materials test facility). Again, there are inducements to cooperation, but will these be sustainable? As soon as one firm (or a few firms) specialize in exploiting large scale effects and in providing that particular service to all firms, *pure market contracting* will turn out to be superior[31].

There may be indivisibilities of a size level beyond the reach of any large firm operating on the world market. Several investors may decide to form consortia to overcome that size barrier. The crucial question will then be, whether the world market is large enough to allow for profitability of such a very large operation. If this is the case, *collaborative* investment and finance may lead to a feasible solution. But there is no generally convincing reason why a collaborative solution should be superior to the setting up of one single, large and integrated firm which raises funds on the capital market.

As a result, *size* in itself does not seem to be a convincing argument for the efficiency and sustainablity of collaboration. If the size of the overall market is large enough to support minimum scale effects, *any* of the three basic modes of governance and organization can lead to the desired results. If all existing firms are small relative to the investment indivisibility there will be an inducement towards integration with collaboration as an intermediate, but ephemeral solution. If even large integrated firms cannot efficiently run an operation characterized by very large indivisibilities while the overall market is large enough to support specialized suppliers, there will be an inducement to out-source that activity and to switch to a market solution. Cooperation can again be one step on this way[32], but it will not be an efficient and long-lasting solution.

Overall, the size of investment *does not* appear to be a convincing argument for the efficiency and sustainability of cooperation over both the pure market and the integrated solution. It may explain temporary inducement effects to

---

30 The food retail cooperatives that provide advantages such as joint procurement or advertising to smaller food stores are a typical example for this. However, large and highly integrated food chains eventually turned out to be more efficient in the long run. See Gerth (1971, 38).

31 Williamson (1985) and Buckley and Casson (1988) argue similarly that very large scale effects work in favor of a market solution.

32 Large firms tend to "nurture" specialized suppliers by providing bilateral purchasing agreements during their early establishment. The prime motive, however, is the establishment of a sustainable, independent supplier infrastructure, not long-term collaboration.

switch to that intermediate form of organization. A strong point for superiority of collaboration, however, cannot be concluded from size and indivisibility considerations.

1.3.2   The Argument of Risk-sharing

An argument often used for explaining cooperation between firms, and which appears plausible at first sight, is based on the idea of diversification and risk-sharing. Two firms that invest considerable amounts of capital for activities with highly uncertain outcome, so the argument, may reduce risks by joining forces. It may be doubted, however, to which extent risks can really be diversified through cooperation. Furthermore, it cannot be assumed that a certain mode of organization is generally superior in dealing with different classes and degrees of uncertainty.

First, we have to distinguish between true, unpredictable uncertainty and risk[33]. Dedicated and organized attempts at risk-sharing appear to be feasible only in situations for which future events and their probability distributions are known ex-ante. *Risk* itself consists of two components: (1) the probability of failure ("original risk"), and (2) the size of potential losses incurred in case of failure ("consequences"). The pooling of resources by independent partners can hardly work in favor of reducing the *original risk*. Quite contrary, it often works in the opposite direction: through pooling activities, independent partners often create additional coordination problems which affect the probability of failure in a detrimental way.

Collaboration may be more helpful in affecting the *second component of risk*: by pooling resources, independent partners can insure themselves against large potential losses that would lead to great hazards of expropriation for any individual partner. Pooled risks can become lower than individual risks if certain assumptions (about probability distributions) are fulfilled. Such an *insurance effect of cooperation* may be very helpful in making some risky projects feasible, particularly if potential losses would endanger each individual partner in case of non-collaboration. This insurance effect will, however, be only significant as long as we compare cooperation with the pure market solution. Compared to the integrated solution, collaboration will often turn out to be inferior, since a large, integrated firm is able to benefit from all possible insurance

---

33 Knight (1965) and Shackle (1955) distinguish between "true", unmeasurable *uncertaintity* and situations of *risk* in which probability distributions for future events are known ex-ante. A similar and generalized conceptualization of predictable and unpredictable processes can be found in Faber and Proops (1990, chapter 2).

effects[34]. There is no reason to believe that collaboration should be the most appropriate way of insurance against potential losses for which probability distributions are known ex-ante.

If, on the other hand, we have to deal with *true uncertainty* for which probability distributions are *not* known ex-ante, it is very difficult to safeguard against potential losses through specific forms of non-market coordination. Integrated solutions can become detrimental to change and very ineffective in reducing risks. The opposite form of market contracting may, under certain conditions, turn out to be the best "discovery procedure" (Hayek 1987)[35]. A competitive market system can even deal with large potential losses if it is supported by efficient capital markets and appropriate insurance arrangements. In any case, it is not clear why a collaborative form of investment should be superior to market solutions, particularly if trust relationships can be established between market participants.

It thus appears that there is no one-to-one relationship between the type and degree of uncertainty and the preferable mode of organization to be chosen in order to deal with this uncertainty. While there are some types of uncertainty best to be coped with through the use of integrated solutions, other types will lead to advantages of markets. Only some very peculiar classes of uncertainty in connection with additional explanatory factors may lead to a superiority of cooperation. The simple notion of risk-sharing, however, cannot be used as a valid argument for explaining why firms pursue collaborative investment projects[36]. There is no reason whatsoever to believe in the differential efficiency of cooperation in absorbing or diversifying risks.

1.3.3   The Argument of Synergy

A third argument used for explaining collaborative investment is based on the notion of *synergy* or *economies-of-scope*. These can involve product-related synergies or input-related synergies. A product-related synergy is characterized

---

34 There may be other problems such as *risk-aversion* correlated positively to the size of firms which we will deal with in later chapters. This problem will, however, become more serious for situations with true uncertaintity and will not necessarily arise for "simple" (measurable) risk.

35 We will show in later chapters that markets are most appropriate to deal with high degrees of uncertainty if the degree of asset specificity is comparatively low. See chapters 3 and 4.

36 We will show in chapters 3 to 5 that the degree of uncertainty may have some influence on the relative advantage of a collaborative solution if it is seen in conjunction with other explanatory factors, such as irreversibility and asset specificity.

by a situation in which two firms produce two separate goods at quantities q_1 and q_2, but for which there is a strictly sub-additive cost function (Tirole 1989,20):

$$C(q_1,0) + C(0,q_2) > C(q_1,q_2).$$

Lower potential costs of producing both products in one facility will result in incentives to two independent firms to pool their activities. Relatedly, *input-related synergies* involve cost reductions through sharing complementary inputs which were hitherto applied separately within two individual firms. Both types of synergies may allow for considerable cost reductions through pooling of activities. However, even though both types of synergy may be of explanatory value from within a comparative-static framework, i.e. if we only compare two isolated institutional arrangements (pure market solution vs. cooperation), synergy does not appear to be a strong argument for the overall merits of collaboration. By contrast, given a strictly subadditive cost function as shown above, an *integrated solution* will be dominant over market transactions between independent suppliers of the two products, and will be at least as effective if not better than collaboration[37].

There are some very specific situations in which synergy may in fact be only exploited within cooperative institutional arrangements: if two independent firms have exclusive access to a specific resource or to an activity needed to exploit synergy. In the case of *input-related-synergy*, this can be based on exclusive access to specific materials, sophisticated capital goods or to highly-skilled labour. In the case of *product-related-synergy*, two firms may have exclusive access to production or marketing of two particular products. Monopolization of critical assets[38], be it temporary or not, can result in a situation in which collaboration may turn out to be the superior mode of organization. While the market solution is disadvantageous because of non-exploitation of synergy (explained by fragmentation), integration may not be feasible if both potential partners want to keep a strategic negotiating position over their exclusive assets.

Such an argumentation in favor of cooperative arrangements, however, can only be convincingly put forth if certain institutional settings (e.g. property rights) and negotiating positions are specified. It is much more this institutional and contractual setting on which arguments in favor of collaboration have to be based than the pure argument of synergy. Synergy in itself cannot explain advantages of cooperation. In most cases, synergy will work in favor of integrated solutions with collaboration being only an ephemeral, intermediate step.

---

37 Collaboration between two independent firms may involve pooling of production to fully exploit economies-of-scope. But there is no advantage of collaboration over merger or over establishing a new, integrated two-product firm. If one considers the typical control problems of collaboration, an integrated solution may turn out to be much more advantageous.

38 This argument of monopolization of critical assets is a cornerstone of Teece's (1986, 1991) explanations of new collaborative institutional forms. See section 4.3.

1.4   Sustainable Differentiation through Alternative Modes of Organization

We have shown in section 1.2 that empirical investment activities are characterized by a growing emphasis on new forms of collaborative institutional arrangements, particularly in industries which require large capital expenditures and which generate rapid rates of technological change. This perceived trend towards new forms of collaboration has so far not been appropriately explained. Existing economic explanations, even though they may seem plausible at first sight, cannot convincingly show under which conditions cooperation can really be regarded as superior to all alternative modes of governance and organization including different forms of market contracting as well as integration. In section 1.3 we have summarized the main arguments put forth by economists to explain collaboration. None of these arguments (investment size, risk-sharing, synergy) can be regarded as valid explanation for the superiority and sustainability of cooperative investment and finance. In most cases, each of these three arguments can be used arbitrarily to opt for either the market or the integrated solution. Collaboration will most often remain a secondary choice, being dominated either by pure market contracting or by the integrated solution. It is only under some very specific conditions which are typically not addressed by the above mentioned "classical arguments", that cooperation will really turn out to be superior to both other modes of governance and organization. These specific conditions will be outlined in detail in this section, and will be used for formulating the basic concepts needed for a theory of cooperative investment and finance which will be elaborated in the following chapters.

1.4.1   Case I: Integration Superior

We consider two independent firms, F_1 and F_2, with an expected return $E(R_i)$ and a risk level σ_i (i = 1,2). Their risk-return combinations are illustrated in *Fig. 1.5*. Both firms operate separately (e.g. separate plants and separate management) but financial investors can buy shares of both firms. If we assume that there is no financial diversification effect[39], an external financial investor will realize risk-return combinations along the linear line connecting $(E(R_1),\sigma_1)$ and $E(R_2),\sigma_2)$.

---

39 This financial diversification effect depends primarily on the statistical correlation between R_1 and R_2. For a correlation coefficient of 1, there is no diversification effect. This assumption of perfectly correlated returns is not necessary for our argumentation, but it helps us to exclude the pure financial consideration from our reasoning.

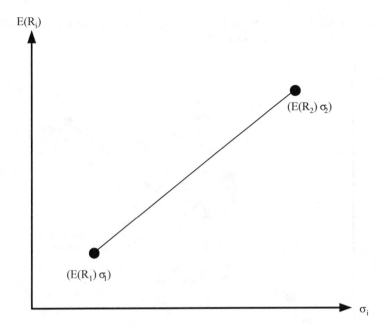

Fig. 1.5:   Risk-Return Combinations for Two Independent Firms

We then consider institutional changes leading to the integration of two firms. Both firms can decide to merge, or an external financial investor can decide to acquire both firms and integrate them. Under certain conditions favorable to integration, the merged firms will realize risk-return combinations lying above the linear line connecting $(E(R_1),\sigma_1)$ and $(E(R_2),\sigma_2)$ in *Fig. 1.6*. Compared to point A (portfolio of independent firms F_1 and F_2), an integrated solution will lead to the realization of a larger expected return and a lower risk level (point B). This improvement can be explained by:

- *reduced cost* through (joint) exploitation of economies-of-scale (vertical arrow in Fig. 1.6);
- reduced cost through exploitation of *synergy* (vertical arrow);
- and by *reduced risks* achievable through integration (horizontal arrow).

Consider that integration must not necessarily lead to both a reduction of cost *and* of risk (as implied in Fig. 1.6). Potential cost reductions through scale and synergy effects must be large enough to compensate for additional management costs of integration. And a reduction of risks will only be achieved if a given risk structure allows for insurance effects. If this is the case, integration will result in a north-west movement in Fig. 1.6 (movement from A to B). Point B will lie on a new efficiency line representing more favorable risk-return combinations that can be attained by an integrated firm, compared to risk-return combinations achievable through a market solution.

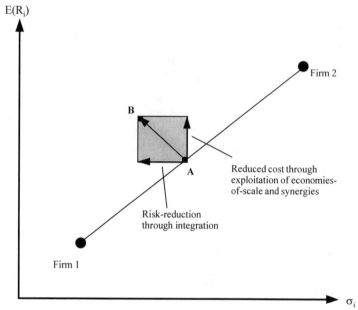

Fig. 1.6:   Risk-Return Combinations Attainable through Integration

Given such favorable conditions for integration, risk-return combinations for an integrated firm can also be expected to lie above the line of risk-return combinations that can be achieved through cooperation. This can be explained by smaller risk-reduction and/or by lower reduced costs achievable through collaboration, as compared to the integrated solution[40]. If we start from point A in *Fig. 1.7*, which represents an initial market solution, there will be incentives for both firms to start collaborative activities and to switch to point C. This solution, however, will be dominated by the integrated solution B. If both firms themselves cannot decide to merge, there will be incentives to financial investors to acquire both of them and to let them merge thereafter. Collaboration will be at best a temporary solution.

---

40 In the case of *risk-reduction*, this can be explained through hazards of coordination between
   independent partners. Similarly, potential *cost reductions* have to take into consideration
   non-negligible management costs of collaboration.

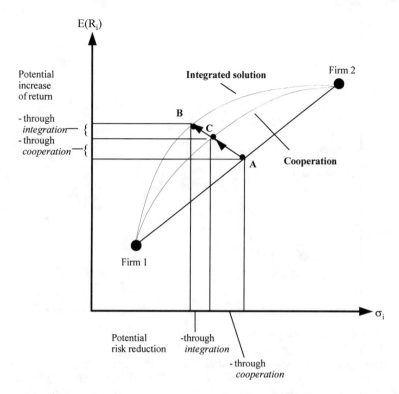

Fig. 1.7:   Comparison of the Integrated Solution with Collaboration

1.4.2   Case II: Market Solution Superior

In contrast to the assumptions outlined in section 1.4.1, there may be certain conditions which work against an integrated solution. These relate to both cost and risk considerations. With respect to cost, we may have to consider decreasing returns-to-scale, and diseconomies-of-scope[41]. Potential production cost advantages of a large, integrated firm may be more than outweighed by high management costs of internal coordination. This detrimental cost effect is illustrated by the vertical arrow in *Fig. 1.8*.

---

41 Diseconomies-of-scope mean that the joint production of q_1 and q_2 leads to higher cost than a separated production in two units, i.e.
$C(q_1,O) + C(q_2,O) < C(q_1,q_2)$.
Decreasing returns-to-scale are equivalent to
$C(q) + C(q) < C(2q)$.

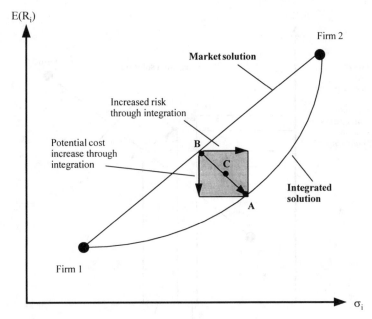

Fig. 1.8:   Potential Disadvantages of Integration

With respect to *risk*, a large firm may benefit from an insurance effect, as long as we deal with predictable future events. If future events are totally *unpredictable* (with the potential choice set and probability distributions changing considerably), the possibility for insurance through size will be limited. Furthermore, a large integrated firm runs a much higher risk of being "locked into" a particular technology or institutional arrangement which may suddenly turn out to be a wrong and burdensome choice. A market solution is more flexible and the potential loss may be reduced if there are many small firms competing with different designs. This is illustrated by the horizontal arrow in Fig. 1.8.

Since cost and risk considerations lead to disadvantages of size, the *market solution* will turn out to be efficient. If we start from an initial, integrated solution (point A in Fig. 1.8), we can attain improved results by disintegrating firms. This can temporarily be attained by forming two cooperating sub-units or firms. However, collaboration will only be an intermediate step, being ultimately replaced by a pure market solution (point B in Fig. 1.8).

1.4.3   Case III: Collaboration Superior

Our investigations have so far not shown any convincing theoretical argument why collaborative investment and finance should offer efficient and sustainable solutions leading to better results compared to to both the market solution and integration. Any theoretical explanation for the alleged empirical trend towards new, collaborative institutional arrangements must be built around a combination of reverse risk and return effects. Collaborative arrangements can combine the virtues of size and flexibility. In most instances, though, collaboration must be regarded as "second-best solution", being outperformed by either markets or by the integrated solution. Only for some very peculiar situations, collaboration can help to benefit from size effects, while simultaneously allowing for a high degree of flexibility. Given this peculiar *combination of scale and flexibility advantages*, collaboration can turn out to be ultimately superior to both the market and the integrated solution.

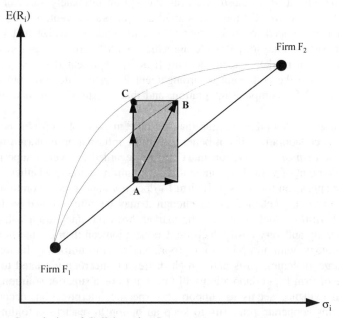

Fig. 1.9:   Superiority of Collaborative Investment

This is illustrated in *Fig. 1.9*: starting from an initial market solution (point A), the two firms F_1 and F_2 can decide to integrate, which will result in a larger expected return, but also in a larger risk level. There are large uncertainties as to whether integration of firms F_1 and F_2 will turn out to be the right choice. The new risk-return combination that can be achieved is represented by point B. Now consider a collaborative solution: it will result in larger expected returns due to the exploitation of scale effects or synergies, even though these advantages may be smaller than for complete integration. These size disadvantages relative to integration are more than compensated for by very low switching costs related to collaboration: if the choice to pool certain activities between firms F_1 and F_2 at a cooperative level turns out to be false, it can be reversed at much lower cost than if the two firms were integrated. Through collaboration we can thus attain point C, lying on the "collaborative line" north-west of the line of risk-return combinations that can be achieved through integration.

Such advantages of cooperative investment over integration are particularly important in situations in which there are turbulent changes affecting the consequences of a particular institutional choice. A firm F_1 may decide to "go along" with firm F_2 to develop a particular technology. Risk-return combinations, as they are evaluated in period t_1, are represented by the two points $(E(R_1),\sigma_1)$ and $(E(R_2),\sigma_2)$ in *Fig. 1.10*. This evaluation may be completely revised in period t_2, due to the advent of a *new firm* F_3 introducing an ultimately superior technological design. A firm F_1, that has started a collaborative venture with firm F_2, and which has hoped to attain point C, has to suddenly realize that F_2 is not the right partner. Due to a flexible agreement with F_2, firm F_1 can switch and attain at least a market agreement with firm F_3 (represented by A'). The firm that has chosen the collaborative arrangement is much better off than the firm that has opted for complete integration, and that is "stuck" with one particular partner.

One might be tempted to argue that the pure market solution will be at least as good as collaboration, if not better, given the information in period t_2. While this is true *ex-post*, cooperation must still be regarded as overall superior from an *ex-ante* point of view. It is inherently uncertain in period t_1 whether a firm F_3 will *ever* appear on the market. If firm F_3 does *not* appear, collaboration will be superior to the market mode, even though it may be outperformed by full integration. If firm F_3 *does* appear on the market, however, integration will turn out to be a wrong and very costly decision. Cooperation can then be interpreted as a mixed strategy, with an option to appropriately react to unfolding future events. Given large switching costs and a high degree of uncertainty related to the appearance of firm F_3, collaboration will turn out to be a superior solution. Recent empirical evidence seems to support this specific interpretation, according to which firms cooperate primarily to keep an option to react to unfolding future events. They join cooperative associations and strategic alliances not primarily to reduce costs or to pool risk, but to screen a wide array of opportunities with different potential partners. According to the empirical studies completed by Mariti and Smiley (1983) and by Hagedoorn and Schakenraad (1989b), it is primarily the need to monitor technological opportunities and to get access to complementary skills which drives firms into cooperative ventures, especially in technology related collaboration activities. Contrary to "classical" economic wisdom, economies-of-scale or risk-sharing were mentioned as a more subordinate motive (see Mariti and Smiley 1983, 440ff, and Hagedorn and Schakenraad 1989b, 18f).

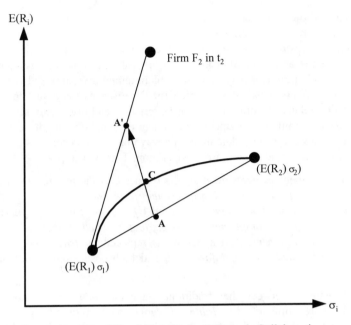

Fig. 1.10: Greater Degree of Flexibility Attained through Collaboration

1.5   Summary

Empirical evidence as well as a growing number of publications seem to indicate that the importance of cooperative investment and finance is increasing. At least there is a growing emphasis on new forms of alliances between firms which are directed towards exploring new market and product opportunities, and for which joint technology development and R&D is a core activity. This *new pattern of cooperation*, however, has so far not been appropriately reflected in economic theory.

The reason for such an *explanatory gap* may be sought in the fact that empirical changes are analyzed within a framework of traditional textbook economics. Economic explanations which center around a comparative-static, manufacturing-oriented view were certainly helpful in explaining *old* patterns of specialization and *old* forms of coalitions (particularly the ones focused on factor-price related specialization in manufacturing). These "traditional" explanations, however, are increasingly becoming invalid for the analysis of *new* forms of the international division of labor, and for *new* types of collaborative associations, which are based on sophisticated complementary skills, on temporary know-how advantages, and on differentiated technology-related search activities.

We have shown in section 1.3 that "traditional" textbook explanations for coalition activity cannot convincingly be used for analyzing the *new pattern of cooperative investment*, since neither the arguments of investment size or synergy, nor the argument of risk-sharing are valid reasons for sustainable cooperation. Each argument may serve to explain temporary gains and inducement effects, but it is not a valid explanation for the efficiency and sustainability of collaboration relative to other modes of governance and organization.

In order to formulate convincing theoretical explanations, we have to extend these arguments and reformulate them in a way that they can serve as appropriate explanations for the new pattern of cooperation. This will imply:

- that the argument of investment size is replaced by the argument of *specific, irreversible and time-consuming investment processes*;
- that the argument of synergy is replaced by *specific forms of synergy with exclusive access to complementary assets and knowledge pools*;
- and that the argument of risk-sharing is replaced by *true uncertainty with asymmetric distribution of information* and high costs of information transmission.

These differences between the "traditional" and the "new" explanatory framework which are summarized in *Table 1.1*, cannot be overcome by just replacing one element of theory by another. It requires a distinctly different theoretical approach which is characterized by:

- the consideration of *disequilibrium dynamics* as opposed to simple comparative-static models;
- the explicit consideration of *time and long gestation processes* leading to irreversibilities and temporary restraints for the access to specific resources;
- the explicit development of a theory which explains the *generation, storage and transmission of knowledge* between independent economic agents;
- and the explanation of relative advantages of different modes of governance and organization by *neo-institutional analysis*, which is embedded into a dynamic economic framework.

In the following chapters we will try to develop such a new theoretical framework for the analysis of cooperative investment. We will begin our approach in *chapter 2*, by formulating a general methodology for defining *joint investment strategies* and for mapping the related processes and activities required to attain strategic objectives. In *chapter 3* we will introduce *capital theoretical concepts* for the analysis of investment processes involving time and long gestation periods. We will then show in *chapter 4*, which new developments in *neo-institutional economics* are suitable for explaining sustainable economic advantages of cooperative modes of governance and organization. *Chapter 5* will include a generalized model for structuring and implementing cooperative investment projects. *Chapters 6 and 7* contain selected case studies of cooperative investment and finance projects.

Table 1.1: Traditional versus New Explorations of Collaborative Investment and Finance

"Traditional" explanations	"New" explanations
• Investment size	• Specific, irreversible and time-consuming investment processes
• Synergy	• Synergy with exclusive access to complementary assets and knowledge pools
• Risk-sharing	• True uncertainty with assymetric distribution of information and very high costs of information transmission

Part II: Theoretical Building Blocs

2   Strategy, Process Redesign, and Organization

In this chapter, we want to develop a generic concept for strategic investment decisions, process redesign and institutional choice. We begin in sections 2.1 and 2.2 by showing that *economic theory* can most suitably be applied to conceptualize strategic types of investment decisions, but that most models of investment theory have reduced the scope merely to simple and routine-types of investments. In sections 2.3 we describe the relationship between strategic objectives and processes, and how tasks are selected. In section 2.4 and 2.5 we discuss which process characteristics and tasks will have an influence on the selection of specific organizational structures. Our aim is to develop a generic framework which can help to identify under which conditions cooperative solutions are efficient and sustainable.

2.1   Economic Theory and Strategic Investment Decisions

Most economic theories operate in a fictitious world in which economic activities are pursued within a predetermined institutional setting. One extreme form is the perfectly *competitive market*, in which large numbers of independent traders interact through spot contracts. The complex separation of labor and the large number of agents required for such a "perfect market solution" are assumed as given. It is neither reflected how market structures evolve, nor how agents learn their profession, how they become specialized and how they interact with each other. Investment decisions are pursued in an isolated and decentralized way, and they are just a minor activity required to smoothen out technical indivisibilities and life-time differentials for intermediate capital goods. Agents react to changes in exogenous parameters in the form of stimulus-response, and their investment-decisions can never be considered as strategic[1].

The other extreme form is the *integrated corporation*, which operates in a given industry, or in several business segments, and which benefits from internalization economics based on production or transaction cost advantages[2]. The genesis of this institutional structure is most often neglected, and changes related to the boundaries of the firm are not explicitly considered. Investment decisions to be studied within this context of predetermined institutional structures are

---

1   Since all agents act in polypolistic markets, there is no room for strategic choices.
2   The reason for the existence of large corporations is analyzed in Coase (1937), Stigler (1968), Chandler (1977), and Williamson (1975, 1985). See also chapter 4.

primarily of an operational kind. *Operational investments* will be defined as those types of incremental changes which are needed to perform the day-to-day activities of an existing institution, but which do not affect the scope of its business, its organizational structure or its institutional boundaries. *Strategic investments*, by contrast, lead to major changes in the scope of activities, they often lead to considerable restructuring processes, and they will affect the institutional boundaries, and sometimes even the very existence of a firm.

There is a clear *bias in investment theory* to preferably deal with the more operational types of decisions. Investment theorists have concentrated their efforts on developing many sophisticated methods for analyzing *operational decisions*. Analytical sophistication of these models, however, has led to a reduction in their scope and applicability. The wide array of real-life investment decisions cannot be modeled in an appropriate way, particularly if we have to deal with more strategic types of investment. In contrast to such strategic decisions, investment theory has concentrated on a narrow range of (solvable) investment situations which are characterized by:

– well-defined and simple *objectives*;
– clearly-defined and unchanging *choice alternatives*;
– a given organizational *structure* within which decisions are pursued;
– and, typically, the involvement of one *single agent*[3].

A more *dynamic theory of investment and change* would have to interpret economic activities as chains of events, through which agents and firms relentlessly interact and build up relationships and institutional arrangements. Complex arrays of activities and institutions will be permanently rearranged and restructured[4]. Small firms enter new forms of market arrangements and customer-supplier relationships, while large firms are restructured repetitively. Investment decisions related to such entrepreneurial activities are typically of a strategic kind. Compared to the above-mentioned operational decisions, *strategic investment decisions* are different with respect to at least one of the following characteristics:

– *objectives* are often not very well-defined, and can sometimes be very complex (long range, multi-purpose, involving large and complex achievements);
– the *choice set* changes in the course of time, and available choice alternatives have to be discovered and searched for;
– *institutional structures* are flexible and may be developed only after the investment decisions have been completed;
– furthermore, many investment decisions require *multi-agent* involvement.

---

3   This single agent is either regarded as an individual (e.g., the CEO of a large firm), or as a team which in fact acts as one agent.
4   This view is promoted by Richardson (1972), and by several authors arguing from the "dynamic network" perspective. See Jarillo (1988), Håkansson (1987), and Lundgren and Björklund (1989), whose arguments will be summarized in section 4.4.

These changes are increasingly reflected in the modern theory of investment and finance (Brealey and Myers 1988, Schmidt 1986, and Spremann 1986), and in the recent publications on strategic management and corporate renewal (Chakravarthy and Doz 1992, Chakravarthy and Lorange 1991, Davenport 1993, and Hammer and Champy 1993). The more *traditional* view of the investment process, by contrast, was emphasizing investment decisions within well-established firms with given objectives related to products and technologies. Very specific business targets led to a formulation of investment plans, to a calculation of capital budgets, and to appropriate financial decisions. According to this view, decision-makers were primarily concerned with financial cash-flow considerations, and with the smooth maintenance of technical process flows (operational procurement, manufacturing and sales). (See the left hand side in *Fig. 2.1.*)

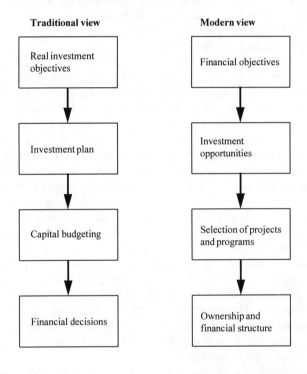

Fig. 2.1:   Traditional and Modern Theory of Investment and Finance

The *modern view* of investment and institutional redesign is distinctly different in that it does not start from a given organizational entity. By contrast, it starts from a set of objectives formulated by different, often institutionally separated agents. These agents can be investors, financiers, or managers; they may decide to form coalitions in order to reach their objectives. These coalitions can be characterized by quite distinctive modes of coordination, with an integrated, hierarchically organized firm being only one of these alternatives. According to this modern view, corporations are not seen as predetermined institutional structures. Instead, they are seen as an "instrument" which is chosen by agents in order to jointly attain their objectives (Schmidt 1986, chapter 2). According to this *"agency concept"*, institutions are optimized forms of contractual arrangements, through which different agents try to best achieve their goals; the goals pursued can include both real objectives (e. g. to penetrate a certain new market), as well as purely financial targets (e. g. a return on investment above x%).

This modern view of investment and institutional redesign is illustrated by the sequence on the right hand side in Fig. 2.1. Financial objectives influence the choice of investment opportunities. Investment projects and programs are selected accordingly, and will lead to a reconsideration of the ownership pattern and the appropriate financial structure.

Such a flexible institutional design related to strategic investment processes, however, is very difficult to conceptualize and to model in an analytically convincing way. It is recommendable to relax only one of the above four assumptions while strictly keeping to the other three. As an example, *technological change*, involving changing choice sets and the discovery of unknown technical solutions, is often analyzed within models for which objectives and structures are well-defined, and in which investment decisions are pursued by a single agent. Similarly, investment decisions for more than one agent are most often analyzed with models for which the first three assumptions are strictly valid.

In this second chapter, we want to develop a framework which is generic and flexible enough to conceptualize a wide array of investment decisions covering both "simple" and routine-type investments, as well as "complicated" and more strategic ones. The term *strategic investment decision* is used for decisions for which rather ambitious and more long-term objectives are pursued. Strategic objectives and goals will, under favorable conditions lead to the discovery of the suitable choice opportunities, and to the formation of the most appropriate institutional arrangement. The institutional structure to be chosen can involve one single agent or many independent agents; these agents can either be loosely associated or they may decide to become tightly organized, depending on their objectives and the related tasks to be achieved.

The process of strategic investment and institutional redesign, which is illustrated in *Fig. 2.2*, starts with the determination of strategic objectives. These strategic objectives influence choice alternatives. To cope with certain choice alternatives and to perform certain tasks, institutional structures will be designed on a "contingency" basis. Environmental forces continuously influence and shape strategic objectives, choice alternatives, as well institutional structures. In consideration of these ongoing changes in their environment, institutions are forced to reconsider and adapt their strategic objectives (as illustrated by the upward moving arrow in Fig. 2.2). This last influence of organizational structure on strategic objectives, however, will be considered as secondary. The more important and primary influence will be that organizational structure follows from, and is guided by strategic decisions (Chandler 1962, Lawrence and Lorsch 1967).

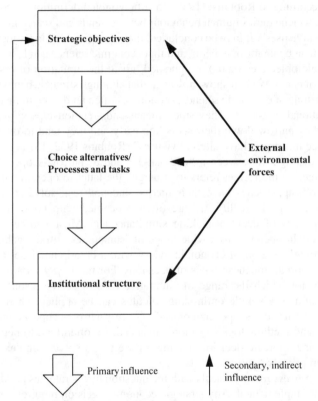

Fig. 2.2:   Strategic Investment Decision Processes

2.2   Wide-scope versus Narrow-scope Economics

Recent studies on strategic management differentiate between "strategy content" and "strategy process" (Chakravarthy and Doz 1992, Chakravarty and Lorange 1991, Pettigrew 1988). Within *strategy content research*, a *strategy* pursued by one single agent or a group of agents can be defined as:

- a selection of *objectives* with a minimum degree of stability and future orientation;
- the consideration of *resource limitations*;
- and the selection of a *course of action* to achieve these objectives under given resource limitations[5].

This definition of strategy is quite closely related to the *general scope of economic science*. According to Robbins' (1932, 15) often quoted definition, "economics is the science which studies human behaviour between ends and scarce means which have alternative uses". It may be concluded, that strategic behavior is just a special form of human behavior in general, and that economic science can help to explain how strategic objectives (ends) are pursued, given the limitation of resource endowments (means). We will show, however, that although strategic behavior should be a cornerstone of economic science, economists often tend to be more concerned with operational questions. They study means-ends-relationships within a given field, but they narrow down their scope too early and they tend to overlook that most "scarce means . . . have alternative uses" (Robbins 1932, 15)[6].

We can distinguish between a "wide-angle" and a "narrow-scope" version of economic theory; the former refers to strategic, the latter to operational decision-making. Both approaches have their merits, and both can solve some specific types of problems. In reality, we are often concerned with both strategic and operational types of decision-making simultaneously. Most *strategic decisions* require a certain openness to a wide range of (sometimes unforeseeable) events. A *"wide-angle" version* of economic theory with a broad choice set considered is most appropriate for these types of decisions. For most *operational decisions*, by contrast, for which the range of alternative uses of scarce resources can be narrowly defined, a simple optimizing calculus can be applied which is within the realm of "narrow-scope economics". Since "narrow-scope economics" is technically and methodologically more advanced, we often tend to neglect problems requiring strategic decision-making, or we try to solve complex problems with inappropriately "narrow" tools.

Strategy process research deals with the question how strategies are developed, changed and implemented. Any strategic economic decision requires a sequential *problem-solving process* which can be broken down into the following phases[7]:

---

5   See Ansoff (1968), Hax and Majluf (1985), and Porter (1980, 1985).
6   If we take alternative uses of resources into consideration, we "widen our scope" and allow for the discovery of a wide array of application areas and for different courses of action. Our economic agent is *not* the simple optimizer but the entrepreneur, as distinguished by v. Mises (1963) and Kirzner (1973).
7   This distinction of phases is consistent with the general problem-solving process described by Simon (1960) and Ansoff (1968). The fifth phase of implementation, which according to our view belongs to problem solving, is added.

- the *intelligence phase* during which opportunities and objectives as well as the scope of activities are more narrowly defined[8];
- the *formulation* of alternative courses of action;
- the *evaluation* of alternatives;
- the *choice* of one or more alternatives;
- and the final phase of *implementation.*

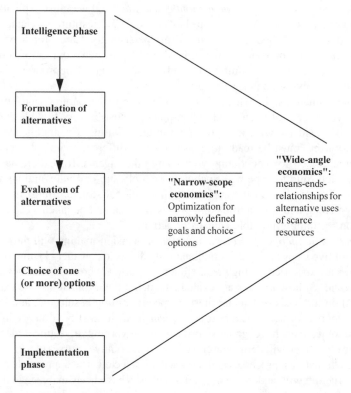

Fig. 2.3: The Wide-Angle and Narrow Scope View of the Problem-Solving Process

Economic theory and most formal methods of business decision-making, which concentrate more on strategy content than on strategy processes, usually leave out the first two phases and offer solutions to phase 3 and 4 only (see *Fig. 2.3*).

---

8   This can be interpreted as a "zooming-in" from a wide angle perspective to a narrow-scope view.

This narrow view is helpful for analyzing *routine economic activities*, and can help to solve problems in situations in which the choise set is well known, where the probability distribution of outcomes is given, and where a rather stable group of agents pursues well-agreed objectives. In particular, this will be the case if all agents are members of institutions for which the above phases 1 (intelligence) and 2 (formulation of alternatives) have already been completed[9].

For most problems related to strategic management, by contrast, we are concerned with *non-routine types of economic activities*, and we must explicitly deal with strategy processes. Markets will be "created" and institutions change. New firms will be established and existing firms persistently search for new opportunities. Intelligent behavior leads to the discovery of new courses of action, to the extension of resource limitations, and to the design of appropriate new institutions for solving complex problems.

In such situations, in which there is considerable economic and structural change, the process of strategic decision-making must be very flexible and open enough to consider a wide array of opportunities. During the intelligence phase, decision-makers must be ready to consider many different chains of events, and must remain open for negotiating with many other agents. If institutional boundaries are too rigid to cope with such a phase, only sub-optimal solutions will be attained. The selection of the appropriate institutional structure must be a *result* of the screening and decision-making process, and cannot be taken as a boundary condition restraining possible courses of action.

An *economic theory of strategic investment* decision-making will thus have to include all five steps in Fig. 2.3 simultaneously. It has to consider (1) how *strategic objectives* are specified during the intelligence phase, (2) how *alternatives* are formulated and (3) how *options* are evaluated; such a theory must also be explicitly show (4) on the basis of which criteria a specific *option* is selected, and (5) how selected courses of action can best be *implemented*. It must be a theory in which strategic objectives have greatest priority in governing investment decisions. Strategic objectives will define the choice set for alternative courses of action; based on these alternatives, processes and tasks will be selected. The appropriate organizational structure will be derived only after the tasks have been analyzed in detail[10].

In the following sections we will concentrate on such a "wide-scope" approach to investment decisions, process redesign and institutional choice. We will first describe how strategic objectives are formulated and selected (section 2.3.1). We

---

9 This is the case for all models of competition between firms, which operate in a given industry, and for which products and technologies are well-defined.

10 This sequence is reversed in most approaches to investment theory, in which a specific structure (organization of a firm, market or industry structure) is taken as given. In contrast to such an approach, older process-oriented organization theories (Nordsieck 1934, Kosiol 1962) have pointed out the priority of detailed process and task analysis. See section 2.4.

will then go on to show how strategic objectives will define the processes and tasks to be selected (section 2.3.2). After the principle characteristics of processes and tasks have been described, we will show how economic agents can select the most appropriate institutional structure, and under which conditions they will tend to seek cooperative solutions.

2.3 The Relationship between Strategic Objectives and Processes

2.3.1 Strategic Objectives as a Starting-point

Any strategy has certain goals or objectives as its constituent element[11]. Objectives pursued in connection with investment projects include (1) the *directional* or strategic objectives of decision-makers, which define where an investor wants to go and what he wants to achieve. These can be differentiated from (2) *instrumental objectives* which describe the principles or rules to be considered for attaining the desired strategic objectives. In the following, we will concentrate on a description of strategic objectives, and on how these influence the choice of processes, and, indirectly, the selection of institutional structures. Instrumental objectives will not be considered in detail; they have some influence on operational decisions during the process selection phase, and will thus be mentioned in section 2.3.2. However, we will not consider instrumental objectives as a core element of the strategic investment decision process.

Strategic objectives can be described in both financial as well as in real terms. *Financial objectives* of investors typically involve:

– the overall *level of achievement* of financial targets (such as return on investment, net present value or other indicators);
– the *time preference*; and
– the *risk-preference*[12].

The overall *level of achievement* corresponds to a certain income level within a predetermined time period. Within that period, annual income levels may be constant, or they may fluctuate. The *time preference* of investors describes their preferred time-profile: some investors are willing to wait for income generated

---

11 We will use the terms "goals" and "objectives" in a synonymous way, even though "goals" are often defined much more specifically than "strategic objectives" For a more precise distinction between the two terms see Chakravarthy and Lorange (1991, chap. 2).
12 See Schmidt (1986, chapter 2), Schneider (1980), and Ballwieser and Schmidt (1981).

in the distant future, while others are more interested in present income. Furthermore, annual income levels may fluctuate stochastically. The *risk-preference* of
investors describes their willingness to bear risk in exchange for a high enough
level of expected income. These financial objectives, which are described purely
in terms of income (level, time profile, stochastic distribution), can only be
attained by pursuing some *real objectives*; these real objectives specify how the
desired income pattern should be generated. We can distinguish between:

- the expected *level of achievement*: "do we want to make a large move forward,
  or are we more modest in our expectations?";
- the underlying *time-horizon* (short-term vs. long-term oriented goals);
- and the *specificity* of goals: "do we want to pursue targets, which are highly-
  specific to a certain area, product or technology, or are we more general and
  flexible in our orientation?"[13].

Any investment project can be described by these three characteristics of strategic
objectives: an investor must specify the time horizon of investment, the size of
investment and the level of its expected outcome, as well as the area or domain of
activity. This is illustrated in *Fig. 2.4*: on the left hand side, marked by the profile
x, we find a very short-term oriented investment project with a low level of achievement, and a very low degree of specificity. Investments in short-term financial
assets with a high degree of liquidity are an example for this. On the other hand,
we can pursue a large and long-term oriented investment project which is highly-
specific to a certain area, and which is illustrated by the profile y in Fig. 2.4. An
example for the second type are investments for energy production and distribution,
which typically require large activity levels, a very long time horizon, and the
willingness to invest in highly-specific assets with relatedly high risks.

This differentiation according to generic characteristics of strategic goals
allows for a wide spectrum of investment decisions to be considered. At one end
of the spectrum, we find more routine-type decisions for the replacement of
standard machinery with a relatively short life-time. Diversification decisions of
firms are related to higher levels of achievement with a longer time horizon (often
5—10 years). Even still larger and long-term-oriented are public policy decisions
on technological innovation, environmental policy, or for the infrastructure. An
extreme case of investment decision is related to space policy, with a necessary
time horizon of 30—50 years, the solution of very complex missions, and an
extreme degree of specificity (see, for instance, our case description of satellite
investment projects in chapter 6).

---

13 The degree of specificity describing *real* objectives must be related to the risk-preference
   describing financial objectives. The more someone invests in highly-specific assets, the
   higher is the risk of not attaining expected income levels.

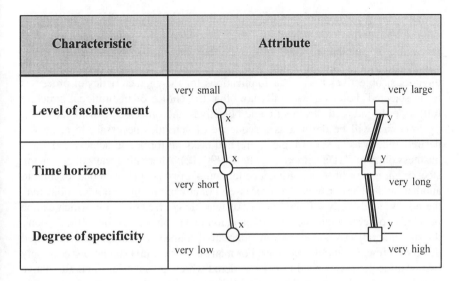

Characteristic	Attribute
Level of achievement	very small · · · · · · · · · · · · · · · very large
Time horizon	very short · · · · · · · · · · · · · · · very long
Degree of specificity	very low · · · · · · · · · · · · · · · very high

Fig. 2.4:   Generic Characteristics of Strategic Objectives

Strategic objectives are the cornerstone and the starting point for the investment process; the specification of strategic objectives leads to the consideration
of a set of feasible processes. In a later stage, a specific process will be selected,
and the appropriate institutional arrangement will be chosen. The advantage of
this proposed new approach for investment theory, which starts from an identification of strategic objectives, lies in its flexibility and openness to consider a
wide spectrum of different investment decisions and a large array of different
institutional arrangements. By contrast, "traditional" economic theory is usually
more concerned with the more "mundane" type of investment decisions (routine-
type, relatively short time horizons, low achievement levels). However, it is the
more long-term-oriented, large and highly-specific type of investment, which
poses the greatest problems for decision-makers, and for which economic theory
should develop appropriate solutions.

2.3.2   Relationship between Objectives and Process Characteristics

The second major element of an investment strategy as defined in the preceding
section 2.2 is a *course of action* needed to achieve strategic objectives[14]. The

---

14 Based on our definition in section 2.2, a strategy is represented by a set of objectives, a
   course of action, and the consideration of resource limitations.

terms *"course of action"* or *"process"* will be used synonymously. In order to achieve the desired objectives, we have to select and pursue certain types of processes. To implement these processes, they have to be organized and maintained within a certain structure. We will first argue that the characteristics of directional objectives have clear implications for the characteristics of processes to be selected. Later on, we will show that the choice of institutional structure follows only indirectly from strategic objectives and processes considered.

Processes will be defined as a sequence of activities necessary to achieve a desired end, or as "a set of logically related tasks performed to achieve a defined business outcome" (Davenport and Short 1990, 12). Alternative ways of producing steel or energy, or of transporting a certain number of people from one location to another, will all be considered as processes. For any pre-defined strategic objective, there is typically only a finite number of feasible courses of action which can be pursued in order to attain the goals of an individual or an organization. If we specify the strategic objectives, the relevant alternative courses of action can be narrowed down to a few *dominant processes*. For many empirical investment projects, only two or three processes need to be considered which are superior to all alternative courses of action[15]. Similar to the basic characteristics of objectives described in Fig. 2.4, different processes can be characterized by:

- their *time profile* ("long" versus "short" processes);
- their degree of *complexity* (measured by the number and sophistication of intermediate steps);
- and by the degree of *irreversibility* (size and asset specificity of investment).

Capital theoretical models usually approach investment choice situations by comparing two processes P_1 and P_2. Let P_1 be the less time-consuming process which is characterized by lower degrees of complexity and irreversibility. The example illustrated in *Fig. 2.5* compares a rather simple, one-period process, P_1, through which labor (L) and natural resources (R) are transformed into product Y, with a two-stage process, P_2, using labor and resources to produce an intermediate capital good, which is then applied for the production of Y.

Process P_1 is short (one period), non-complex (only one step), and characterized by a very low degree of irreversibility, since labor and resources can be easily used for other processes. Compared to P_1, process P_2 is "longer", more complex and irreversible. The degree of irreversibility depends on whether the (intermediate) capital good can easily be applied for other processes[16].

---

15 As an example, for travelling from town A to town B, there may be hundreds of alternative paths, only one or two of which will be dominant, given a certain budget of time and travel expenses.
16 See also our definition of the degree of *asset specificity* in section 3.2.

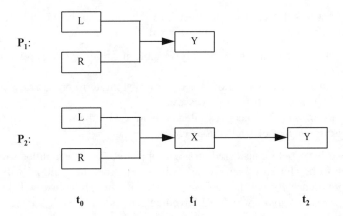

Fig. 2.5:   Processes With and Without Intermediate Capital Goods

More complex processes involving several intermediate capital goods produced in parallel or at several consecutive intervals can be analyzed and compared in a similar way (see *Fig. 2.6*). The *degree of complexity* of each process is directly related to the number of (intermediate) process steps, and to their type of interconnectedness. The degree of *irreversibility* is dependent on whether capital goods produced at intermediate stages can be easily transferred to other processes or not.

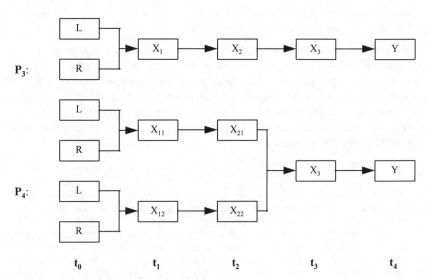

Fig. 2.6:   Sequential and Complex Processes

The characteristics of strategic objectives described above are closely related to the types of processes that an investor will focus on, since:

- large achievements are usually only feasible if *large and complex* processes are used;
- a *long time horizon* will allow for the use of long-term processes, which are often superior to short-term processes;
- the focus on *specific* objectives often coincides with the selection of processes with a high degree of *irreversibility*.

So far, we have only considered strategic objectives and their influence on the processes to be chosen by an investor. Many investors, in addition, will have a certain preference for specific courses of action. This preference will influence their *instrumental goals*, which we have neglected so far. While strategic objectives define "where an investor wants to go", instrumental objectives describe the "way through which he wants to achieve his targets". Typical *characteristics of instrumental objectives* include:

- a preference for processes involving *large activity levels* as opposed to small tasks;
- a preference for processes involving *complex tasks*, as opposed to simple activities;
- the preference for *mission-oriented* approaches for achieving goals vs. more *incremental* or experimental approaches[17];
- the degree of *risk-acceptance* and the willingness to bear risk;
- the emphasis on *innovativeness* (preference for more traditional "ways of doing things" vs. the emphasis on novelty);
- the emphasis on *flexibility* and *adaptiveness*.

We propose a two-step approach of finding one (or more) appropriate process(es) which best correspond(s) to the objectives to be achieved. According to this approach, *strategic objectives* help to identify a subset of dominant processes (strategic decision). Within this subset, *instrumental objectives* will then influence the choice of a specific process (operational decision)[18]. Characteristics of instrumental objectives will influence the operational selection of processes in the following ways:

---

17 Mission-oriented approaches relate to cases where one investor defines a prestigious, often very large and expensive investment project "once and for all". The opposite case would be more sequential, evolutionary decision-making involving many independent agents, which develop the best approach only as an outcome of experimentation and mutual learning.

18 This hierarchy of strategic and instrumental objectives may not be unanimously accepted; "fundamentalists" will argue more in favor of instrumental goals, saying that certain ways of doing things should be forbidden from the first beginning.

- a predisposition for *large size* and for *complexity* typically leads to the preferential selection of large, complex processes;
- a *mission-orientation* is most often related to long, complex processes with a high degree of irreversibility;
- *low risk-acceptance* usually corresponds with a preference for short-term oriented processes, which are relatively non-complex and characterized by a low degree of specificity;
- high *innovativeness* often corresponds with a longer time horizon and a high degree of specificity related to research, human capital and equipment required for the latest state of technological evolution;
- the emphasis on *flexibility and adaptiveness* leads to a preference for processes involving less complex tasks and a lower degree of irreversibility.

We summarize our goal-oriented approach to the analysis of the strategic investment decisions in the following way: objectives of investors have implications on the choice of processes. Strategic objectives get a first-order ranking, while instrumental objectives get a second-order ranking[19]. Strategic objectives define the relevant choice set for processes to be considered by an investor. Instrumental objectives will influence the selection of specific processes within this subset of relevant choices.

2.3.3   Implications on Organizational Structure

While objectives influence the selection of processes, the relationship between objectives and organizational structure is not as simple as one might expect. Similar objectives can be achieved with quite different types of organizational structures. This is particularly the case for the following *strategic objectives*:

- *long-term objectives* can sometimes only be achieved by relying on institutions with a tight organizational structure and with a long lifetime. But pure market coordination or flexible structures (collaboration agreements) can also make sure that participating agents pursue long-range plans;
- *large and complex* tasks can be solved by large organizations, but also by rather flexible project organizations, or through appropriate contractual arrangements between independent market participants;
- very *specific goals* can sometimes most appropriately be achieved within a firm specifically set up for this purpose; this need not imply, however, to fully

---

19 If directional goals involve the production of a consumer good, this view corresponds to the Austrian method of "targeting" final production: "Das Endziel aller Produktion ist die Herstellung der Dinge, mit denen wir unsere Bedürfnisse befriedigen können, also von Genußgütern oder Gütern erster Ordnung" (Böhm-Bawerk 1921, 11).

integrate all activities. Market contracting within a decentralized system of specialized agents can often be a very efficient solution, at least for sourcing-in complementary, though less critical resources.

Although some *instrumental objectives* will coincide with a certain preference for specific types of organizational structure (with flexibility and adaptiveness typically working against integrated solutions), there is no one-to-one correspondance: similar objectives can be achieved through different institutional structures. A high degree of risk-acceptance and innovativeness can under some circumstances be made feasible only within a large firm pursuing a mission-oriented policy; but integration within a large firm will often also lead to risk-aversion, low innovativeness and incrementalism (see our description of the limits of integration in section 4.2).

In spite of the fact that similar objectives can be achieved through different institutional arrangements, "institutional openness" should not imply structural ambiguity. Objectives often have an indirect influence on the choice of institutional structure. Particular objectives have clear implications on the selection of processes and on the types of resources needed. As soon as we know the details of the process and the characteristics of resources to be selected, we can draw conclusions about the appropriate organizational structure. This indirect relationship, which helps to solve the riddle between strategic objectives and organizational structure, requires a mapping and a detailed analysis of the relevant processes, through which specific objectives can be attained. This will be explored further in the next section.

2.4 The Relationship between Processes and Organizational Structure

In this section, we will formulate an analytical approach for the endogenous design of institutional structures. *Strategic objectives* are determined at a first stage of an investment program and will lead to the selection of processes at a second stage. Based on these strategic objectives and on the related selection of processes, institutional structures have to be chosen such that the whole sequence of activities needed to attain the predetermined objectives can be "optimized"[20], or at least re-arranged in a more efficient way. As illustrated in Fig. 2.7, strategic

---

20 The term "optimization" is used in parantheses, because it cannot be compared to the typical optimization approach used in neoclassical economics. In contrast to the last, "optimization" in our terms also involves time-consuming adaptation processes, bounded rationality, and sequential learning.

objectives influence processes, while institutional structures cannot be derived directly from neither objectives nor processes. There is a "missing link", which must be explored and analyzed first, before appropriate institutional structures can be designed.

This *"missing link"* is further specified on the right hand side in Fig. 2.7. Processes have to be sub-divided into tasks, or sequential process steps. Detailed *task analysis* allows for the *specification of resources* needed. The longer, the more complex, and the more irreversible the considered processes are, the more specific resources must be combined in a coordinated way. This coordination is dependent upon the appropriate *specification of contracts*, which represent a basic element for institutional structures to become established.

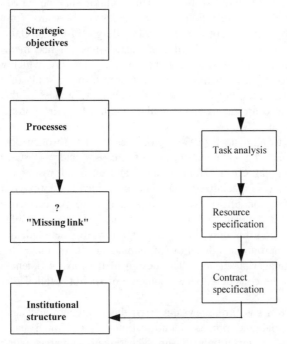

Fig. 2.7: Endogenous Design of Institutional Structures

The design and establishment of appropriate institutional structures must be a result of these three steps, namely of (1) task analysis, (2) resource specification, and (3) contract specification. It is our intent, to outline the logic behind these three steps. This will be done through reference to three distinct schools of thought:

- older concepts of *process-oriented organization theory* (process and task analysis in section 2.4.1);
- the *Austrian* explanation for the value of complementary resources (resource specification in section 2.4.2);
- and modern *contract theory* (contract specification in section 2.5).

2.4.1   Process and Task Analysis

Organization theory has been overly concerned with the functioning of existing institutional structures, but has somewhat neglected to analyze how institutions evolve. There is an older tradition of organization theory originally developed in German-speaking countries, which used processes and tasks as starting-points for the analysis and design of institutions. This tradition shall be called the *"process-oriented theory of organization"*. Major representatives are Nordsieck (1934), Kosiol (1962), Ulrich (1968), Frese (1988), Berg (1981) and Gaitanides (1983). Their approach to the analysis of organization has not become widely known within the business administration and economics literature, which was for a long time dominated by a "structure-oriented approach to the study of organization". During the last years, however, there is growing awareness of these older concepts, which also appear to be particularly suited for our approach to business process redesign.

According to Nordsieck (1934), processes must be broken down into *tasks*, which represent the elementary unit of analysis and the starting point for any organizational effort. Human labor and material resources which have become extremely specialized, must be combined, and this requires an extensive coordination effort. Since diverse tasks are typically distributed over many agents, a detailed and precise task analysis is inevitable for resource allocation and coordination. Task analysis allows for detailed job descriptions, and for the appropriate allocation of human talent, of material resources, as well as of managerial services. The design of the most efficient organizational structure must be considered as an outcome of such a detailed process and task analysis.

Kosiol (1962) has further systematized this approach, and has differentiated between (1) goal and process identification, (2) task analysis, (3) task synthesis, and (4) organizational design. The organizational structure is designed in a way to achieve predetermined goals in a most efficient way. Kosiol (1962, 58 f) distinguishes between primary tasks and secondary tasks: *primary tasks* are directed at performing activities directly related to predetermined goals (such as "serving the customer"); *secondary tasks* are supplementary activities needed to coordinate and maintain these primary activities at an efficient level. Primary tasks most often correspond to *core functions* or *value-adding activities* (e.g. procurement, manufacturing, sales);

secondary tasks often relate to supplementary functions (e.g. management, administration, finance)[21].

It is the aim of process-oriented theories of organizational design, to start from primary tasks and core functions, and to derive secondary tasks and supplementary functions accordingly. Primary goals and processes should have a "first-order" influence on the organizational structure; the evolving structure should be suitably adapted to the requirements of primary tasks and core functions. Complex interdependencies between resources needed for primary tasks should then be taken as starting-point for establishing coordination mechanisms at a secondary, administrative level.

Frese (1988) and Gaitanides (1983) have further specified the types of interdependencies related to primary tasks. These can be distinguished into (1) interdependencies between tasks, and (2) interdependencies between resources[22]. Both types of interdependencies are analyzed in detail in order to develop some principles for organizational design. Appropriate coordination mechanisms such as hierarchy, rules and programs, and markets (see Frese 1988, 95) are derived according to primary task requirements, and in consideration of the specific types of primary, task-related interdependencies.

These older concepts of a *process-oriented theory of organization*, which have become somewhat neglected in the meantime, seem to be promising for both a theory of strategic investment decisions, as well as for analyzing the advantages and limits of collaborative investment. Two critical arguments must be raised against them, however. First, existing approaches must still be considered as too *static* and as *non-entrepreneurial*. Second, they still appear to be overly analytical, and do not succeed at a stringent synthesis of appropriate institutional structures[23].

---

21 With respect to this distinction between primary and secondary tasks, and between core functions and supplementary functions, older authors like Schramm (1936, 28), Mellerowicz (1958, 27 resp. 204) and Kosiol (1962, 58 f) were much more precise than Porter (1985) and other modern authors. The *value-chain concept* appears as a mere re-invention, having been adapted to new types of economic activities such as services, R&D and logistics. It is important to note, that the question of whether a certain function is to be considered as *"core"* or *"value-adding"*, is dependent on the very nature and the primary purpose of a firm. The description of Kosiol, Schramm and Mellerowicz is thus valid only for manufacturing firms, while for other, more service-oriented organizations, systems management or finance may be considered as core functions.

22 For a more detailed analysis of *interdependencies* see Thompson (1967), Khandwalla (1977) and our capital theoretical interpretation in sections 3.1 and 3.2.

23 They are still embedded into an older organization theoretical line of reasoning, which can be characterized by the term "mechanistic organization", and which emphasizes the "chain-of-command"-type, authoritarian governance structure. For a critique see Burns and Stalker (1961) and Lawrence and Lorsch (1967). Our proposed framework of endogenous organizational design is aimed at a synthesis of these new concepts with older methods of process-oriented organization theories.

For both reasons, the final step from task synthesis to organizational design still offers too many degrees of freedom. Only if processes are well-defined, if goals are predetermined, if there is not much change, and if a rather stable group of resource owners can be delineated, will task analysis and task synthesis determine institutional structure in an unambiguous way. Management within an integrated, hierarchical firm will under these conditions represent the most appropriate mode of governance and organization.

If, by contrast, goals and processes change frequently, if complex tasks require highly-specific resources with a wide distribution of ownership, appropriate institutional structures cannot be easily and unambiguously derived. Appropriate institutional structures can only be determined on a project-by project basis, often in an "ad-hoc" way, and different modes of governance and organization will often overlap[24].

If we are concerned with investment decisions in a dynamic environment, which demands a high degree of entrepreneurial activity, and in which institutional structures must remain rather open and flexible, the *agency concept of organizations* will be much more appropriate than the entity concept of the firm (see Schmidt 1986). Most existing theories of organization, however, are still restrained to the entity concept: they view the primary tasks of "a firm" as predetermined. In order to derive appropriate institutional structures endogenously and on a "contingency" basis, proposed methods of task analysis and task synthesis must therefore be complemented by a further specification of resources and their ownership structure (see section 2.4.2), and by a specification of alternative contractual arrangements (section 2.5).

2.4.2   Resource Specification and Ownership

Resource complementarity must be seen in conjunction with resource ownership if organizational solutions are to be derived from process and task analysis. It is helpful to refer to the concepts of the value of complementary resources developed by Austrian economists. According to Menger (1871), production is always a "time-consuming process through which intermediate goods of higher order (upstream activities) are transformed into goods of first order (consumer goods/downstream activities). It is the peculiarity of goods of higher order, that they cannot usually produce goods of lower order without the cooperation of other 'complementary' goods of the same order"[25].

---

24 Burns and Stalker (1961), Lawrence and Lorsch (1967), Mintzberg (1979, 1983) and Kanter (1983) have extensively analyzed structural requirements of organizations which have to cope with the "management of change".

25 Stigler (1948, 157) in summarizing Menger (1871, 11 ff). The Austrian capital theoretical foundations to the institutional choice problem will be analyzed in more detail in chapter 3.

Advanced economic systems with an extensive division of labor and a sophisticated distribution of resource ownership will offer potential hazards for resource owners, which cannot easily secure the coordination of other complementary goods required for the same stage of production. This is particularly difficult for complex and irreversible processes, requiring many different, highly-specific resources for every stage of production. The quality and the value of resources owned by one agent are dependent on resources provided by other agents, and this dependence is greater, the more a resource is dedicated to one particular good of first order. Differential dependence affects distribution, and may result in coordination problems and social friction[26].

These coordination problems and the resulting distributional effects were further analyzed by Böhm-Bawerk (1921). He assumed that resouces $R_1, \ldots, R_R$, which are needed for one production stage, are owned by different agents, and he distinguished between four generic cases:

> *Case 1: (rigidly fixed proportions):* None of the factors of a combination can be used without the cooperation of the other combination members, and none of the factors is replaceable.

In this extreme case of *rigidly fixed proportions,* "one single member has the full value of the group, and the other members are entirely valueless" (Böhm-Bawerk 1921, 171). In such a case, there is no stable mode of coordination and distribution other than integrating all agents within a firm and distributing equivalent shares to them. Any other mode would lead to strategic behavior, through which each agent would try to withhold the "Schlußstück" (Menger 1871), i. e. the last factor needed to complete a combination.

Böhm-Bawerk is not dealing with an economic problem; in the case of rigidly fixed proportions between member-factors . . ., the totality of the members is one commodity, and the individual member-goods apart from one another have no economic significance. In the case of production goods, specifically, no imputation would be possible under this condition. The owner of each member could and obviously would demand the full product of the factor group, and there is no economic principle by which this dispute could be settled. . . . In actual economic life, which Böhm-Bawerk purports to describe, chaos would result, if 'circumstances' dictated a variable reward for a factor — most obviously

---

26 Menger (1871, 25) describes that these complex coordination mechanisms are almost taken for granted in advanced industrial societies, and that most producers are never aware of their dependence on other members of society. Only in periods of sudden structural change and crisis will people become aware of this tremendous, though typically unconsciously performed coordination task. This problem characterizes the transition process in Eastern Europe, where we can observe the dis-integration of the old coordination mechanism, while the new, market-mediated coordination mechanism is not yet in place.

almost all economic activity would be devoted to altering the 'circumstances' (Stigler 1948, 149)[27].

Fig.2.8 illustrates these four generic cases of complementary resource ownership; case 1 is illustrated by the set of resources contained in the upper square. Böhm-Bawerk's *case 2* is described as an intermediate case with partial opportunities for factor owners to use their resources elsewhere:

> *Case 2 (factors irreplaceable, but positive alternative value):* Member agents are irreplaceable, and have other, though less profitable employment opportunities for their resources outside the combination.

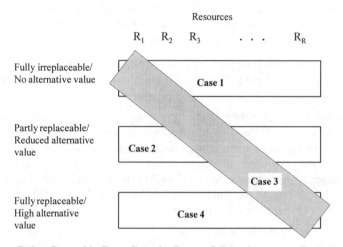

Fig. 2.8:   Böhm-Bawerk's Four Generic Cases of Complementary Resource Ownership

Agents can choose to leave the combination, but have an incentive to cooperate with the other owners of complementary resources, since their remuneration would be lower elsewhere. The lower 'isolated' value for each resource owner forms his *minimum* compensation; the *maximum* value is equal to the total product of the combination minus the sum of the 'isolated' values of the cooperating members (Böhm-Bawerk 1921, 208). Members of the combination will stick to the association, as long as their value within the group is considerably higher than their 'isolated' value outside the group. This will be particularly the case, if

---

27 This case is structurally equivalent to Williamson's (1985) explanation of integration as a helpful institutional device, which will be introduced in order to prevent "haggling" between resource owners, and which will lead to a related reduction in transaction costs.

external conditions (which affect their value alternatives) remain rather stable, and if agents can agree on a "fair" distribution of surplus values. Stable collaboration agreements are feasible and may be advantageous to full integration modes.

Case 3 (some factors replaceable): It is assumed that resources owned by some agents are replaceable, while resources owned by others are irreplaceable. The sub-group of agents holding irreplaceable resources can then be described by either case 1 or case 2.

In this third case, replaceable agents will be first remunerated on the basis of their value outside the combination. The remainder of the joint product will then be divided by the irreplaceable agent, based on the distribution procedures described for cases 1 and 2. The most familiar application of case 3 is the distribution between the owner-manager of a firm, and its workers. Similar distribution patterns apply for all resources which are easily substitutable. The appropriate coordination mode would involve market exchange for replaceable resources, and either cooperation or integration for owners of irreplaceable resources.

Case 4 (full replaceability): All member are freely replaceable and remunerations for resources earned ouside the combination are equal or comparable to their values generated within the combination.

This last case corresponds to the conditions of fully competitive markets with unrestricted entry and exit conditions; it is illustrated by the lower square in Fig. 2.8. The joint value of the combination will equal the sum of the replacement or substitution costs, and each factor will earn its market value. Price signals represent reliable indicators of value, and transaction costs can be considered as negligible. The market mode of coordination is the most suitable institutional arrangement for this case.

Key explanatory factors, on which the appropriate choice of coordination mechanisms should be built, are thus:

- the *degree* of *replaceability* for the resources required for a combination;
- and the *alternative value* to be generated by each resource in its second-best application outside the combination[28].

The described Austrian method for the evaluation of complementary resources provides a good basis for the endogenous design of institutional structures, which are suitably adapted to task requirements, and to the specification and ownership structure of resources. This is particularly the case, if the older Austrian theory is complemented by more recent developments of contract theory to which we turn in the following section 2.5.

---

28 In chapter 3, we will relate these key eplanatory factors relevant for distributive shares and organizational choices to the time structure of production, and to entry and exit times for particular assets.

2.5   Contract Specification and Endogenous Design of Institutional Structures

The last missing element in the sequence of decision-making processes needed for the endogenous design of institutional structures, which was outlined in Fig. 2.7, is *contract specification*. Tasks have been analyzed and lead to the specification of resources with distributed ownership. In order to secure the co-ordination of resource flows and to arrange for combinations of complementary resources, contractual arrangements must be specified. The types of contracts and the ways in which they are executed must be derived endogenously; economic contract theory offers a helpful methodological framework.

Modern contract theory is closely related to the Austrian concepts of the value of complementary resources as outlined in section 2.4.2, even though without explicit reference. Resource complementarity and resource specificity play a central role. Resources can be complementary and specific to goals, processes, tasks, combinations and coalitions. The *Austrian method* analyzes complementarity and specificity for a combination of resources which are required for a certain activity such as the production of an intermediate capital good. *Contract theory* is interested in a coalition of agents (and resource owners) as an institutional arrangement needed to make a certain combination of resources feasible. Contractual issues and complications arise if resources are complementary and specific with respect to this particular coalition.

If resources R_1 and R_2 are complementary, agents owning only R_1 will be induced to form a coalition with the owner of resource R_2. Both resources can be unilaterally or reciprocally specific to a coalition[29]. These characteristics are closely related to the notion of replaceability emphasized by Austrian economists. The inducement to form coalitions is particularly strong if resources are reciprocally specific, and if there is low potential for replaceability.

Resource complementarity and replaceability explains why coalitions are formed, but not which contracts will be chosen. The specification of contracts is dependent on the second characteristic of specific resources, namely value differentials of resources used within and outside of a coalition

In forming a coalition, some members will make investments the value of which elsewhere will be less than the value in the coalition (and also less than its costs). If its value in the coalition is higher than elsewhere, it is defined to be specific to the coalition. Some of the resources have values independent of the coalition. They will be able to earn just as much elsewhere. They are nonspecific to this coalition. If the coalition fails, they loose nothing.

---

29 For a more detailed analysis of different types of complementarities and their organizational implications see sections 3.2.2 and 4.3.3.

But resources that are specific to the coalition are those that loose the excess of the investment cost over the salvage value (Alchian 1984, 36).

Value differentials of specific resources used within and outside of a coaliton are defined as *coalition-specific quasi-rents*. In other words: "the return on the investment cost that is non-salvageable if the resource to which it is specifically dependent disappears, is called the specific quasi-rent" (Alchian 1984, 36). If the value of resources owned by one agent is considerably lower elsewhere than within the coalition, this agent runs a high risk of expropriation of quasi-rents due to the behavior of other, independent agents[30].

Anticipation of expropriability of quasi-rent will motivate pre-investment protective contractual arrangements. The owner of a resource whose value is alterable or affected by specific other people will have an interest in controlling or restricting their acts. If arrangements are made between the several resource owners to restrict or control the future actions, the several are said to be a coalition. Even if the acts of one party can effect the value of another, if no arrangements are made to influence the future acts, the two are not in a coalition (Alchian 1984, 37).

Potential coalition members will search for protective contractual arrangements which can be "fine-tuned" to the tasks and resource characteristics. In general, more binding and tightly controlled contracts will be selected the larger the size of investments involved, the longer the investment activity and the more specific the resources are.

Any institutional structure, and any mode of governance and organization can be described as a *nexus of contracts* (Aoki, Gustafsson, and Williamson 1989). An integrated firm is one extreme form of such a nexus of contracts characterized by "specialization, continuity of association, and reliance on direction" (Demsetz 1988, 157). Delineation of boundaries of the firm will require to raise the following two questions: (1) When should coordination preferredly be achieved *within firms* as opposed to coordination achieved through *markets* (comparison of integrated solutions and market solution)? (2) When should a nexus of contracts which is "firm-like" be preferred to coordination *within* a firm (comparison of collaboration with an integrated solution)?

The second question with which we are most concerned in our investigation of the superiority and sustainability of cooperative investment, can thus be reformulated in the following way: under which conditions is it economically advantageous to maintain a nexus of contracts which is characterized by:

- *joint objectives:* the collaborative association has to formulate a clear mission; goals pursued by the association must be comparible with the goals pursued by each participating member;

---

30 This argument of expropriation of quasi-rents was formulated by Klein, Crawford and Alchian (1978). In chapter 3, we will introduce a capital theoretical interpretation of exit costs related to sunk investments for highly-specific capital goods.

- *complementary specialization:* each party specializes in specific activities and resources which are complementary in a reciprocal way;
- *medium duration:* contractual arrangements and their duration and persistence is located "somewhere between firms and markets".

For cooperative institutional arrangements, contracts can be more easily renegotiated and are less binding than the nexus of contracts representing an integrated firm. The stability of collaborative association is maintained through trust relationships and through expected gains from joint activity (Demsetz 1988, 160f).

Any nexus of contracts can be described as an amalgam of three generic contract modes:

- *Ownership* contracts with related control rights;
- *sales, service* and *rental* contracts; and finally
- *cooperative* contract modes.

Ownership contracts regulate the property rights of agents. These property rights of an agent include (1) his determination of use of a resource (or a bundle of resources owned by him), (2) the bearing of the market value of his resources, and (3) the exchangeability of rights to (1) and (2) (Alchian 1984, 34; 1977, 129ff). Property rights require a certain state of the evolution of an economic system, and they are often influenced and constrained by the regulating power of the state as well as by private institutions[31].

The institution of private property is interconnected with a clear specification of control rights. *Control rights* regulate the control of complex bundles of resources. They include (1) the right to choose uses that affect the values of specialized resources in a combination, (2) monitoring rights for measuring the performance of resources and the outcome of a resource combination. Finally, (3) control rights allow to select and dismiss managers as persons with a rather wide "constrained, conditional distribution of effects on values of resources in the coalition" (Alchian 1984, 44)[32].

---

31 For some contractual arrangements such as franchising, general contractorship, and for the analysis of public regulation, it is important to distinguish between the ownership of resources and the right to regulate or constrain the use of these resources. See also our analysis of regulation and public policy in chapter 8.

32 Alchian (1984, 43f) defines "management as 'choosing' uses that affect the values of the specialized resources in the coalition ... Let the *range* of selectable uses be specialized for each person for each resource. Given the range of authorized optional actions, there will be some probability distribution of value effects called the 'conditional' (or constrained) value distribution, conditional on the range of selectable uses and the amount of monitoring of that person's behaviour. Any person whose constrained, conditional distribution of effects on values of resources in the coalition is wider, is more of a manager". For a critique of this definition of a manager see Picot (1984).

Sales, service and rental contracts regulate compensated transfers of resources between agents on a "quid pro quo" basis. For more durable resources, *service and rental contracts* specify the use of resources over a particular time period. The most important type of service contract is the *labor contract* which has been extensively studied in contract theory (Alchian and Demsetz 1972, and Williamson, Wachter and Harris 1975). Non-equity financial contracts are another special form which regulate the provision of services for one particular form of resource, i. e. for money. Service contracts are typically applied for those durable resources which often cannot be easily traded, be it for legal reasons (in the case of labor), or because of indivisibilities or wealth concentration. By contrast, *sales contracts* regulate transactions of resources between agents. A buys a resource R_1 from B in exchange for a certain amount of money. Sales contracts are the most common and least problematic form of contracts; they will be easiliy applicable, as long as the resources traded are rather homogenous, divisible, and sufficiently standardized.

There are specific types of resources, or certain combinations of resources, for which it is very difficult to determine values, prices, and a clear specification of ownership rights. The right of use of these resources and certain control rights may be agreed upon *before* ownership rights or sales, service and rental agreements can be clearly specified. A certain combination of resources is then often only feasible through distinctive *cooperative contract modes*, which correspond to "quoad usum" and "quoad sortem" type contracts. Agents participating in such a legal arrangement grant the right to use a resource to a project organization, while they remain the legal owners of that particular resource; the resource is not provided through a "quid pro quo" type service or rental agreement, but through a collaborative contribution[33].

Task analysis for a particular investment project will lead to the specification of resources needed, and to a description of the resource ownership pattern. Appropriate contractual arrangements can be designed thereafter. For all resources which are not too specific, for which there is a sufficient number of suppliers, and which are not critical in the sense that supply shortages would lead to considerable expropriations of quasi-rents, sales, service or rental agreements will suffice. The *market mode* of governance and organization will then be the most appropriate coordination mechanism.

Contractual arrangements will become tighter and more codified for all tasks which require the utilization of specific resources, which are more closely held by a few agents, and which are more critical as regards the feasibility and success of an investment program. *Cooperation* may suffice if members of an "open"

---

33 For a more detailed analysis of collaborative contract modes, and the specific conditions under which they are advantageous see section 3.3.

coalition can rely on "quoad usum" and quoad sortem" type contract modes, which must be supported by reciprocity and trust. The greater the complexity of the tasks pursued, and the larger the required investments for coalition-specific resources, the more must a collaborative association be supported by tighter control rights, and, if possible, by joint ownership contracts.

Finally, if the level of investment is very high, if highly-specific resources are supplied in rigidly-fixed proportions, and if supply shortages for particular resources would lead to considerable expropriations of quasi-rents, tight ownership and control rights must be secured. *Full integration* and a 100% ownership and control within a single firm will then be the most appropriate mode of governance and organization.

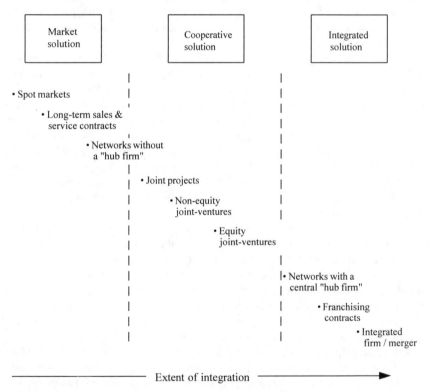

Fig. 2.9:   Alternative Contractual Arrangements and Coordination Mechanisms

Depending on the results of task analysis, resource specification and contract specification, we may choose from a large variety of alternative contractual arrangements. These can encompass market contracting (negotiations, customer-supplier networks without a central coordinator), or collaborative associations (joint projects, non-equity joint ventures, equity joint ventures). Finally, more integrated contractual arrangements would include networks with a central coordinator (a hub firm), franchising contracts, and the full integration within a hierarchical firm[34] (see *Fig. 2.9*).

These alternative contractual arrangements can be suitably adapted in mixed forms, which can be differentiated for each specific task and function. As an example, two firms can participate in rather open networks for basic R&D, and can pursue more exclusive joint projects for applied R&D; they can decide to establish a joint-equity based firm, or they can even merge for manufacturing and sales. A wide spectrum of contractual arrangements can be imagined. However, to perform a wide array of complex activities efficiently and profitably, sooner or later firms must adapt their organizational structure in a way most suitable to the underlying tasks and resource requirements. Structural optimization may, under some very specific conditions, lead to the superiority of, as well as to the necessity for cooperation. Such specific conditions leading to the superiority of collaboration must be explained by the time structure of investments, and by specific types of resource complementarities which will be further explained in chapters 3 and 4.

---

34 We prefer to interpret customer-supplier relationships with a hub firm, as well as franchising arrangements as vertical quasi-integration. Even though resources in both cases are often owned by suppliers or by franchisees, the "hub firm" tightly controls the scope of resources used and exercises a strong influence on their values.

3 Capital, Time, and Cooperative Contract Modes

In this chapter we want to focus on a capital theoretical interpretation of the institutional choice problem, which has been analyzed in chapter 2. Under which conditions is it necessary to form cooperative or integrated institutions? What are the specific conditions under which cooperative modes of governance and organization are superior to integration within a single firm? The answers to both questions require a detailed understanding of *capital* and *time*. Capital goods, knowledge and skills must be accumulated over longer periods of time; they are owned and controlled by individual agents or particular institutions. Capital goods and knowledge bases are durable and generate a multi-period income stream. The maintenance of a complex investment project requires that a multitude of assets of different maturity classes be deployed and combined. Market coordination will only be feasible for certain classes and combinations of assets, i.e. for easily redeployable goods with a short time profile related to production and application. For capital goods with a relatively long period of production and utilization, more formalized institutional arrangements will be necessary.

Institutions as such, will also be interpreted as capital goods that take a long time to become established and a long time to dissolve. Institutions are established during certain historical periods, in order to govern and control the smooth coordination of capital goods. While the projects and particular combinations of capital goods, for which an institution has become established may have been phased out, the institution itself will often still be in place. Institutional inertia will often reverse the choice problem outlined in the preceding: it does not consist of "projects in search for institutions" as has been proposed in chapter 2; quite the opposite is often the case, which means that "institutions are in search of projects". Most investment planning and strategic management pursued in the business world is primarily a quest for projects and growth opportunities required to sustain the life of existing institutions[1].

For many types of projects requiring particular combinations of capital goods and institutional assets, existing institutional structures will not be appropriate. New reconfigurations of institutional assets, that run counter to the integrated mode of governance and organization within established institutional structures, will be necessary. The superiority of cooperative institutional arrangements and

---

1 These considerations lead to a new capital theoretical interpretation of the growth and diversification of the business firm in section 3.4.

networks is explained by the character of assets to be used for a particular investment project. These basic characteristics will be introduced in *sections 3.1 and
3.2*. A strong emphasis is laid on *knowledge*-related assets which are seen as a
focal point for the capital theoretical explanation of institutions.

Section 3.3 contains an analysis of contract modes and institutional arrangements being adapted to the properties of *capital goods* which are used for an
investment project. Collaborative contract modes "between markets and hierarchies" are analyzed as superior institutional arrangements needed to maximize the
value of projects for which the required assets are characterized by *long time
profiles* and a high degree of asset specificity.

In *section 3.4*, we will interpret the growth and diversification process of
business firms as a *sequential chain of investment activities*. Strategic development, growth and innovation are guided and constrained by the *portfolio of capital goods*; a strong emphasis is laid on *path-dependencies* related to firm-specific
investments in knowledge.

The portfolio of assets will, under certain conditions, also constrain further
expansion. Collaboration will help to solve this dilemma. *Section 3.5* concludes
with a capital theoretical interpretation of collaboration as a *call option*[2] on "complicated assets" which are owned by different agents, and the true value of which
needs to be explored through a joint project.

3.1   The Time-profile of Project-related Assets

3.1.1   Some Basic Characteristics of Capital Goods

In this section we will define some basic characteristics of assets that have a
strong influence on institutional choices and on the way in which combinations
of assets are coordinated. Contrary to neo-institutional theory which will be outlined in chapter 4, and which introduces asset characteristics in a rather arbitrary

---

2   A *call option* gives its owner the right to buy assets at a predetermined future date. *Financial
call options* are applied to stock, for which the "exercise" or "striking price" is specified
ex-ante (Brealey and Myers 1988, 471). Financial call options have been extensively explored in the literature (Black and Scholes 1973, 637ff, Haley and Schall 1979, 247ff, and
Spremann 1986, 264ff). While option trading is also very important for certain classes
of *real assets*, no similarly stringent theory for *real call options* has so far been
developed. Our work will be directed at a new interpretation of collaboration as a
contractual agreement being very closely related to a call option.

way, we will derive these asset characteristics from some elementary notions of capital theory.

Austrian capital theory analyzes chains of activities and processes within time. Assets to be used for a process cannot easily be separated. Capital goods are strongly connected to other capital goods, and *complementarities* between assets play an important role. *Neoclassical economics* tries to circumvent this complication by focusing on market transactions for separable homogenous goods, for which values and prices can easily be determined. Complementarities between goods are instantaneously resolved through the price mechanism and within the set of well-defined production techniques.

The opposing view was pronounced by Menger (1871), who argued that "it appears to be of pre-eminent importance to our science that we should become clear about the causal connections between goods". In accordance with this view, we will define causal connections between goods as *complementarities*, which can be analyzed in three dimensions:

- complementarities in *time*;
- complementarities related to particular *project objectives*; and
- complementarities *between different capital goods*.

Complementarities in time describe the time sequence of inputs and outputs for one particular capital good. This capital good is developed and produced by employing different inputs during s periods; it generates a multi-period stream of services during the following n-s periods. This type of complementarity is illustrated by the two shaded horizontal squares in *Fig. 3.1*. The construction period (Hicks 1973, 15) will be interpreted as entry time; It is illustrated by the light shaded zone within these squares, and will be described in more detail in section 3.1.3. The period of utilization of the capital good (Hicks 1973, 15) will be related to the term exit time; this period of utilization is illustrated by the dark shaded area on the right side of the two squares, and will be analyzed in section 3.1.4.

The capital good may be related to one particular objective, for example the production of one certain type of final consumer good. In Fig. 3.1, this is illustrated by the arrows on the right hand side: a stream of outputs of the capital good is transformed into one specific consumer good. Alternatively, a capital good may serve different objectives, and may become transformed into a variety of different final consumer goods. This type of *complementarity between capital goods and project objectives* will serve as a capital theoretical explanation for the notion of *asset specificity*, and will be described in more detail in section 3.2.1.

Finally, two or more *different capital goods* may be characterized by strong complementarities. In Fig. 3.1, the final consumer good is produced through a combination of services from two capital goods G_1 and G_2. This type of interrelatedness will be defined as asset complementarity, and will be described in section 3.2.2

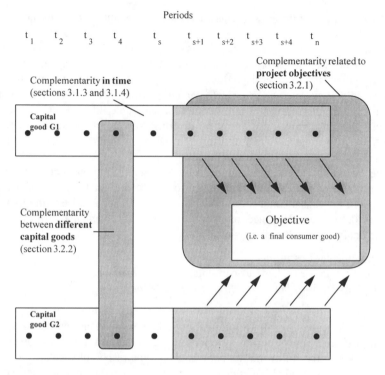

Fig. 3.1:   Types of Complementarities

Our capital theoretical interpretation of complementarities is closely related to notions of *interdependence* used in process theories of organization. These notions of interdependence have been extensively studied by Kosiol (1962), Thompson (1967), Khandwalla (1977), Frese (1988) and Gaitanides (1983). However, these authors have so far analyzed interdependence merely in technical terms. An economic and capital theoretical analysis of resource interdependence appears to be necessary.

3.1.2   The Consideration of Time in Capital Theory

Böhm-Bawerk (1921) has emphasized the strong role of the *period of production* for capital goods. Multi-period inputs represent an inextricable complementarity in time. Waiting is required before a new capital good can become readily utilized. Since different classes of capital goods are characterized by different waiting periods, and since any portfolio of assets consists of capital goods of different maturity classes, the representation of capital in value terms depends crucially on the various assumptions necessary to compute its value. In particular, these assumptions depend on the time horizon, the rate of depreciation, and on the type of intertemporal price system used at large. Since the value of each single capital good is contingent on these assumptions, there is a danger of arbitrariness related to the evaluation of investment projects. It is therefore expedient to consider the real side of the investment process, with careful selection of the underlying assumptions for each single project. A capital theoretical interpretation that is concerned with the *real side* of the investment process implies, that it is explicitly concerned with time-consuming formation processes, and vice versa.

The Austrian emphasis on the real side of the investment process and on time-related complementarities was introduced by Menger (1871, 130f), who defined capital as a "set of economic goods of higher order". This view of capital as a set of material goods is distinctively different from the neoclassical perspective, which concentrates on a *financial* representation of capital[3]. This financial and timeless interpretation was introduced by Clark (1893, 302f), who argued that *"true capital"* ought to be distinguished from the particular material goods by which it is formed. "True capital", according to Clark, is a permanent fund of productive wealth, or a fund of value that has a permanent and continuous existence in spite of the underlying creation and destruction of material goods.

The opposing view of capital as a "set of economic goods" emphasized by Menger and Böhm-Bawerk which implies explicit concern for the formation process, and for the underlying real side of the investment process, will lead to a different balance between formal elegance and empirical relevance. Formal modelling is made very difficult if one wants to be concerned with heterogeneous capital goods being produced and utilized in different periods (see Hahn 1966, 1970). The neoclassical paradigm emphasizing formal capital theoretical models has gained a widespread acceptance; meanwhile, Austrian capital theoretical concepts have not attained strong influence, partly due to formal problems related to Böhm-Bawerk's concept of the *production period*. Notional difficulties in defining the scope and the boundaries of this period of production have led to its refutation by economists such as Clark (1893), Knight (1965) and Stigler (1948).

---

3   Such an emphasis on a financial representation of capital has been a characteristic of *mainstream* developments within the neoclassical theory of capital, growth and finance up to the present. We admit that a more explicit consideration of time can be found in more recent publications by neoclassical authors, who have introduced adjustment costs, delivery lags and irreversibilities into their *"special-purpose-models"*. The mainstream line of reasoning and model building, however, has not been reversed by these "special purpose models" (see Faber 1986).

Their critique has pointed at the "infinite regress problem" of tracing back the origins of the capital formation process[4].

As the development of neo-Austrian capital theory has shown, these kinds of methodological shortcomings may be more easily solved if the problem is decomposed appropriately. For many empirical investment processes, explicit consideration of the time profile and of the real side is very important, and these can even be analyzed in a more formal way (see Bernholz 1971, v. Weizsäcker 1971, Hicks 1973, and Faber 1979, 1986). Böhm-Bawerk himself has attempted to solve this methodological problem by introducing the concept of the *average production period* which, unfortunately, has aroused even stronger refutation. For investment theoretical applications, in contrast, we suggest use of the concept of a *project-related production* period: an investment project is started in period t_o; all factors of production which are readily available at the beginning of that period, will be mobilized without any consideration of their historical gestation process. The project-related production period will be defined by the time required to develop and process a new capital good, given the set of readily available factors.

3.1.3   Entry Time and Entry Cost

The construction period of a capital good can be decomposed into several substages such as research, development and manufacturing. An increasingly large percentage of resources and time spent during the formative periods must be attributed to research and development, while the pure period of manufacturing will, in many cases, shrink considerably. For several highly-developed industries, an increasingly large part of value added must be attributed to development and design, while production itself will become more and more of a peripheral activity, being "squeezed" between R&D, inbound and outbound logistics. Time considerations for R&D are increasingly critical, while time considerations related to the production period can often be considered as negligible. As an example, a new car is designed and developed over a period of 50 to 60 months, while the

---

4   The "infinite regress problem" and related problems were adressed by Clark (1893, 302f) in his critique to Böhm-Bawerk: "Production periods begin with civilization and never end. It is not possible to lengthen them". Formal deficiencies related to the concept of the production period have led, among other reasons, to a dismissal of Austrian economics during the 1930s. See Faber (1979, 10ff) and Stigler (1948, 201ff). Only when it became apparent at the end of the 1960s that neoclassical capital theory was not able to explain important features of reality, revival of Austrian capital theory occured. For a summary of the development of neo-Austrian capital theory see Faber (1986).

manufacturing of automotive components and their assembly is a matter of a few weeks. Automation and new logistics concepts ("just-in-time") lead to a continous reduction of the manufacturing period, while research and development periods cannot be reduced in a related way, and may often be increased due to the complexity of products and regulatory processes. In accordance with these trends, we will use the term *project-related gestation period*, which covers research and development as well as the production period, but for which the development period is strongly emphasized.

During this project-related gestation period, complementarities between multi-period-inputs are used to develop and manufacture a new capital good G_i, which will become readily available at the end of period s. The interval $[t_o, s]$ will be defined as *entry time*, which corresponds to the construction period. The expenditures required to buy the inputs during that period will be defined as *entry cost*. As long as time can be considered a *less critical factor*, which is the case if the gestation period is relatively short and/or if the timing of the new capital good does not matter much, it may be sufficient to only be concerned with the wealth aspect. Entry time and entry cost can then be compounded into the cumulated value of expenditures, which represents an element of the "permanent fund of productive wealth" (Clark 1893).

$$(1) \qquad C_{is} = \sum_{t=1}^{s} E_{it}(1+r)^{s-t}, \quad t = 1, \ldots, s,$$

where C_{is} denotes the cumulated value of expenditures for capital good G_i at the end of the gestation period s, and where r is the rate of interest; E_{it} represents the expenditures for capital good G_i in period t.

If the timing of the new capital good *does* matter, and if its gestation period is relatively long, it will be important to consider both aspects of the investment project simultaneously, but separately. Each investment project is then more appropriately represented by two parameters, namely by entry time and by entry cost.

$$(2) \qquad [\text{Entry time; entry cost}] = [s; C_{is}].$$

For many investment projects in an increasing number of competitive industries for which new technologies are a critical asset, the timing of new capital goods is the most crucial parameter, and potential reductions of gestation periods will be a decisive factor for competitiveness. For those industries it will be increasingly important to consider the real side of the investment process and the time sequence of development in particular.

In *Fig. 3.2*, the entry time for an early entrant that starts the development process in time to, is illustrated by the interval $[t_o, s]$. Entry costs are represented by the cumulated value of expenditures at the end of period s. A firm that decides to enter at a later date, at time t', will either have to replicate the entire development process, or will have to aquire intermediate results from the development work performed by the early entrant. Since the semi-completed capital good represents a highly-specific asset, the value of which is very difficult to determine, the aquiror will have to bear transaction costs related to product inspection and contracting. In addition, the contract must be negotiated, and this leads to further delays during the ongoing development process. Entry time for the late entrant will be delayed to s', and entry costs will be considerably increased.

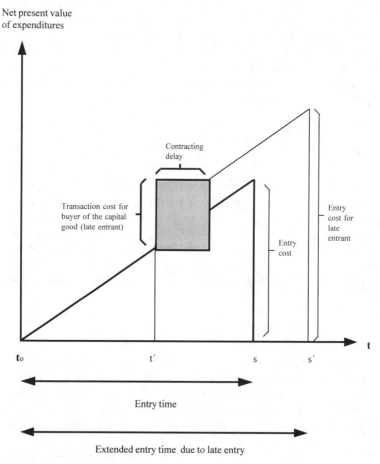

Fig. 3.2   Entry Time and Entry Cost

3.1.4   Exit Time and Exit Cost

Another very important characteristic is the *durability* of project-related assets: capital goods generate multiperiod outputs; utilization periods cannot eaily be shortened and they represent barriers to the circulation of goods and to inter-institutional transfers. The durable nature of capital goods is one of the main reasons why institutions become established and why they gain comparative advantages over other institutions. In order to exploit the multi-period services of capital goods, investors have to make sacrifices in terms of exit time and exit cost.

Faber (1979) has interpreted the *durability problem* as a special case of joint production, or as complementarity in time:

The main reason why fix capital is so difficult to analyze, is that its use in the production of other goods is a special case of joint production, namely, over time. After they have been produced, capital goods yield a flow of usages which can be distributed variously over the individual time periods (Faber 1979, 42).

We will analyze the use of a capital good that is readily available at the end of period s. This capital good generates a service over k periods, after which it will be fully depreciated. The *depreciated value* D_{it} at the end of each period during the utilization period will be defined as:

$$(3) \qquad D_{it} = C_{is}[1 - c (t - s)], \quad t = s + 1, \ldots, n,$$

where c is the rate of depreciation and n represents the time period until which the capital good will be utilized. The depreciated value of the capital good is illustrated by the upper linear line in *Fig. 3.3*. It will be zero at the end of the utilization period $(t = n)$. During the interval $s < t \leq n$, the capital good is assumed to generate a constant stream of revenues Rit. The cumulated value of services Vit generated from the capital good in period t will be:

$$(4) \qquad V_{it} = \sum_{t=s+1}^{t} R_{it} (1 + r)^{s-t}, \quad t = s + 1, \ldots, n.$$

Annual revenues generated by the capital good over k periods are assumed to be at least as great as the annual level of depreciation. As a result, the dotted line in Fig. 3.3, which represents the *amortization value*, i.e. the net present value of expenditures minus the net present value of services, will lie below the line of the depreciated value.

$$(5) \qquad C_{is} - V_{it} < D_{it} \text{ for } s < t \leq n.$$

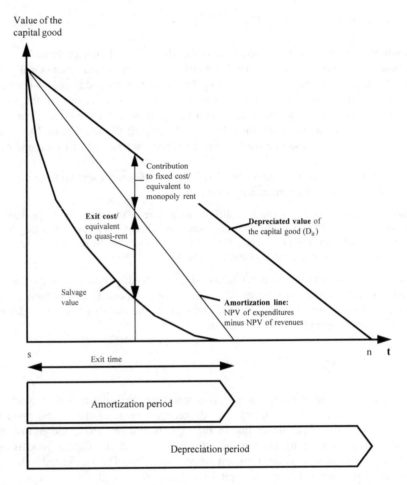

Fig. 3.3:   Exit Time and Exit Cost

The vertical distance between the amortization line and the line of the depreciated value represents an additional contribution to fixed cost; it can be interpreted as the *monopoly rent* earned by the capital good. The more difficult the entry conditions (in terms of entry cost and entry time), and the more proprietary the ownership of the capital good, the larger will be the annual revenues generated in excess of annual depreciation.

The *exit time* related to the investment for a capital good G_i will be defined as the minimum amount of time needed to recover the net present value of expenditures for the capital good.

(6)   Exit time $= \min_{t}\{C_{is} - V_{it} \le 0\} - s.$

In Fig. 3.3, the exit time is illustrated by the horizontal arrow; it is equal to the amortization period.

Exit costs must be born if an investor wants to terminate the use of a durable capital good *before* it has become amortized. Before amortization, the capital good can be scrapped or it can be sold in a second-hand market. In both cases, its *salvage value* will be considerably lower than both its depreciated value (represented by the upper line) and the difference between the net present value of cost and the net present value of services (represented by the lower line).

Depending on the degree of specificity of the capital good, the salvage value will typically be lower than the depreciated value (represented by the upper linear line in Fig. 3.3), and lower than the net present value of expenditures minus the net present value of revenues (represented by the lower linear line). Exit costs for an investor who wants to terminate the utilization of a capital good in period t" $<<$ n will be defined by the vertical distance between the amortization line in Fig. 3.3 and the line of the salvage value. These exit costs are equivalent to the quasi-rent which a resource-owner would earn if he decided to continue the utilization of the capital good (Klein, Crawford and Alchian 1978, and Alchian 1984). Quasi-rents respective exit costs are a function of the durability of the capital good and of its degree of specificity, which will be explained in the following section.

3.2   Asset Specificity and Asset Complementarity

3.2.1   Asset Specificity

Asset specificity will be defined as another type of complementarity that restrains the application and transfer of capital goods[5]. Capital goods of higher order are used to produce goods of lower order. If a particular capital good can be used to produce a *wide* array of goods of lower order, as is illustrated by the upper case A in *Fig. 3.4*, it will be called *generic*. If, by contrast, a capital good can only be used to produce one particular good of lower order, it will be defined as *specific* (illustrated by case B in the lower part of *Fig. 3.4*). The degree of complementarity between goods of lower order and goods of higher order can be measured on a continuous scale ranging from completely generic to completely specific capital goods.

---

5   The degree of *specificity* of assets is the most important determinant in Williamson's (1985) theory of institutional choice, which will be described in more detail in section 4.2.

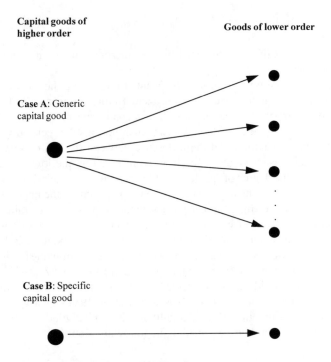

Fig. 3.4:   Generic and Specific Capital Goods

The degree of specificity has a strong influence on the valuation of assets and on exit conditions. If an asset is completely *generic*, its value will not be dependent on one particular application. If agents change their objectives, and if they decide to replace one good of lower order by another one, a generic capital good of higher order can be easily transferred to the new application. Exit costs will be relatively low during both the gestation and the utilization period. In the extreme case of *completely generic assets*, the salvage or resale value of a capital good during its *gestation period* will be equal to the cumulated costs of development and production (as illustrated by the linear line on the left hand side in *Fig. 3.5*).

During the *utilization period* of a completely generic asset, i.e. after the capital good has been completed and become utilized for producing a particular good of lower order, its resale value will be equal to its depreciated value (illustrated by the linear line on the right hand side in Fig. 3.5). Easy redeployability of assets allows for competitive markets for capital goods of all maturity classes, and this reduces variations between prices, depreciated values, and amortization values.

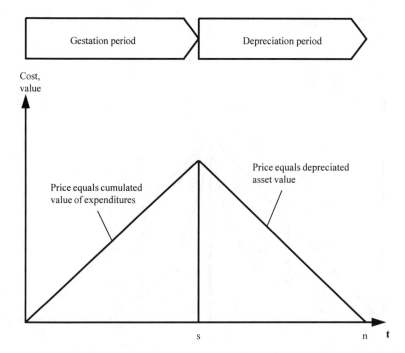

Fig. 3.5:   The Value of Generic Assets

This situation is completely different if capital goods are *highly-specific*. During the gestation period, it will be extremely difficult to sell unmature capital goods, and this results in low salvage values for those types of assets (as illustrated on the left hand side in *Fig. 3.6*). The greater the degree of asset specificity, the larger are the *exit costs*, which are measured by the vertical distance between the line of cumulated expenditures and the line of the salvage value, similar as before in Fig. 3.3. An investor involved in the development of a new capital good may be forced to terminate the project and sell the semi-completed asset. As an example, a house that has not been readily built can be sold relatively easily if its architecture and construction is not too specific. If the architecture of the house, by contrast, is esoteric and if its construction is custom-made for very specific needs, the builder will have great difficulty in selling the uncompleted house, and his exit costs will thus be considerable. In the extreme case, the total investment has to be written off at once: this is often the case for highly-specific engineering plants and for terminated R&D projects[6].

---

6   An extreme example is the development of the fast breeder reactor in Kalkar in Germany; development and construction was terminated in 1990. Total costs amounting to six billion Deutschmark had to be written off.

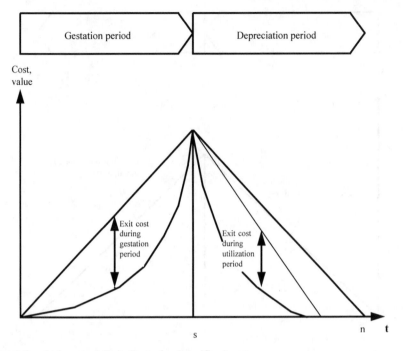

Fig. 3.6:   Values and Exit Costs for Specific Assets

In Fig. 3.6, we have assumed that a highly-specific capital good will be easily tradeable only during a very short period, and that its price at the end of period s will equal the cumulated value of expenditures. *Before* the end of the gestation period, the investor has to bear exit costs, which may only be reduced shortly before the capital good becomes tradeable on the market. There are other classes of highly-specific assets which will always remain captive, and for which the line of the salvage value will always lie below the line of cumulated expenditures and the amortization line.

After a highly-specific capital good has been completed and utilized for the production of a particular good of lower order, it will also become very difficult to transfer it to another application. Producers will have to wait until it is fully amortized, or they will have to incur losses by realizing low salvage values. The greater the degree of asset specificity, the steeper will be the function of the salvage value as is illustrated on the right hand side in Fig. 3.6. Exit costs during the utilization period are measured by the vertical distance between the amortization line and the function of the salvage value. The larger the degree of asset specificity, the lower will be the resale value of capital goods and the greater will be the losses incurred.

3.2.2   Asset Complementarity

So far, we have only considered the characteristics of *single* capital goods. Additional problems of coordination arise if two or more capital goods have to be used in a joint process. Two capital goods G_i and G_j are said to be complementary if their net present value in a combination is greater than the sum of their net present values in single use:

$$(7) \qquad NPV_s[G_i, G_j] > NPV_s[G_i] + NPV_s[G_j].$$

If the two capital goods are *non-specific* and if entry and exit times are relatively short, the value of the two goods can be reliably assessed by prices determined in every single period. Price signals will induce entrepreneurs to compare values of separated capital goods with the value of new combinations of resources[7]. It is relatively easy to determine whether condition (7) is fulfilled in the entrepreneur's advantage; easy entry and exit conditions will allow for rapid adaptation processes.

In contrast, entrepreneurial processes and new combinations of complementary assets are made more difficult, if entry and exit lags are long and if capital goods are highly-specific. Prices for specific capital goods of different maturity classes cannot easily be determined and are only unreliable indicators of asset values. From this follows that plans of independent agents will not be coordinated through the price mechanism, and the result will tend to be malinvestment and a failure to calibrate entry and exit lags for two or more complementary assets[8]. In order to prevent malinvestment and to secure positive quasi-rents for specific capital goods, agents interested in a project must become involved in dense contractual arrangements.

Alternative modes of coordination other than market contracting do not necessarily offer an easy solution to these problems, particularly if property rights have to be transferred. This will be explored in detail in chapter 4. At this stage, we will just briefly mention the organizational implications of asset specificity and

---

7   The *entrepreneurial function*, according to Say (1802) and Kirzner (1973), consists primarily of a relentless effort of comparing prices of separated inputs with the value of combinations of these inputs.

8   This role of *malinvestment* for complementary capital goods has been emphasized by Lachmann (1977, 330). "Every capital good exists in a specific form which limits the range of its possible uses: it has limited versatility. Each capital good therefore depends for its efficient use on the support of other capital goods, complementary to it. Malinvestment may arise in many ways through faulty expectations, but failure of complementary goods to become available is one of them."

asset complementarity. If the two capital goods G_i and G_j are highly-specific and characterized by long entry and exit lags, it is very difficult to transfer assets across institutional boundaries. Two agents that have specialized in the development and production of assets G_i and G_j respectively, will find difficulties in coordinating resource-flows, and of exploiting asset complementarities. The condition that the net present value of the combination is higher than the sum of the net present values of the two assets in single use may serve as an *inducement* to enter a coalition. It is not certain, however, whether the two agents can agree on distributive shares, and whether they will maintain a stable institutional arrangement.

Favorable conditions for a coalition require that *assets are co-specific* for a particular project and application. If both capital goods G_i and G_j have a significantly higher value *within* a particular combination than for any other use, there will be strong inducements to enter a coalition *and* to maintain it at a stable level[9].

The situation is different for *unilateral dependence* between capital goods G_i and G_j. One capital good, G_i, may have a considerably higher value within the combination than outside. The other capital good G_j, by contrast, can realize more or less similar values inside and outside the combination. The owner of asset G_i will become extremely dependent on G_j, while the owner of G_j is less dependent on G_i. In this last case of unilateral dependence, the owner of asset G_j will gain a strategic position, and will change distributive shares in his favor.

If complementarities between goods are unbalanced, no coordination problems arise as long as the degree of specificity is not too high, and if asset prices can more or less easily be determined. If this is not the case, i.e. if highly-specific capital goods with long entry and exit lags have to be combined, serious coordination problems will arise. New combinations of capital goods with a high added value for the joint project will not be realized, or will lead to very high transaction costs and/or contracting delays. To find an agreement over distributive shares may be so costly and time-consuming, that the added value of a coalition becomes neutralized. To realize new combinations of capital goods will require involvement with new types of organizations which are outlined in the following sections.

---

9   This argument of symmetrical vs. non-symmetrical relationships between resource owners
    has been emphasized by Teece (1986 and 1991). He uses the term *"co-specialization"*,
    which has a slightly different meaning than *"co-specificity"*. For a more detailed descrip-
    tion of Teece's arguments for cospecialization vs. unilateral dependence see section 4.3.

3.3 Generic Contract Modes and Institutional Arrangements

The time structure of production and the complementarities between bundles of specific goods, which have been outlined in sections 3.1 and 3.2, are very important for explaining institutional choices and the design of institutional structures. In spite of this strong explanatory value, these capital theoretical concepts have been neglected both in the neoclassical and in the neo-institutional literature. A main reason for this neglect is that most of neoclassical capital theory employs the concepts of the production function (see Burmeister 1980, Hirshleifer 1970, and Faber 1979). The concept of the production function, however, is ill-suited for an analysis of production in time (Faber and Proops 1990, 110ff). Neo-institutional theorists, on the other hand, do not explicitly consider time and intertemporal resource allocation processes. Business-oriented economics and neo-institutional theories could be improved considerably through explicit consideration of capital and time (see chapter 4).

In the following analyisis, we will interpret *institutional arrangements* as a nexus of contracts, i.e. a particular combination of generic contract modes specifying and governing the coordination of assets[10]. According to our definition in section 2.5, we distinguish between *three generic contract modes:* (1) property rights, (2) sales and rental contracts, and (3) cooperative contractual arrangements. The first two types are extensively studied in contract theoretical and neo-institutional literature, while the third, cooperative contract mode has rarely been analyzed and defined precisely enough. In the following, we will define all three generic contract modes from a capital theoretical perspective: contracts are institutional devices that can themselves be interpreted as a special sort of capital good. After this capital theoretical interpretation of generic contract modes has been completed in section 3.3.1, we will interpret alternative institutional arrangements as a nexus of contracts needed to govern time-consuming resource allocation processes.

---

10 This interpretation of *institutional arrangements* as a particular combination of generic contract modes is closely related to the "nexus of contracts" interpretation of the business firm (see the following section 3.4). It is our intent to emphasize the *capital theoretical foundations of these neo-institutional concepts. Contracts* are interpreted as generic or modular capital goods, that can be combined in a "tool-kit" like procedure. A *few generic or modular types of contracts* can be combined for a large variety of institutional arrangements, that can be "custom-tailored" to the underlying tasks and resource requirements (see also sections 2.5 and 5.2 to 5.4).

3.3.1   A Capital Theoretical Interpretation of Generic Contract Modes

We will interpret *contracts* as highly-specific types of capital goods, which are necessary for governing the coordinated use of other highly-specific capital goods. Institutional arrangements will be composed of three types of *generic contract modes*:

– *property rights* or ownership contracts ("quoad dominium");
– *sales, service or rental* contracts ("quid pro quo");
– and *cooperation agreements* as a distinctive contract mode ("quoad usum" and "quoad sortem").

Property rights specify ownership titles of agents to particular capital goods. The owner of the capital good will have (1) full control over its use, he will (2) bear the market value of his capital good, and (3) he is entitled to transfer his rights (1) and (2) to other agents (Alchian 1984, 34). Transfer of property rights can be comprehensive, i.e. by transfering ownership titles to other agents, or constrained, such as is the case if the owner delegates some control rights of his resource to other agents.

Property rights to highly-specific capital goods are themselves characterized by *long entry* and *long exit*, and imply considerable complications for exchange. Ownership titles are often acquired through a time-consuming accumulation process. Capital goods that have once been accumulated are of a durable nature, and property rights remain in place for considerable periods of time. The greater the degree of asset specificity, and the longer entry and exit times for specific capital goods, the more difficult will be the transfer of property rights: to reach an agreement on the price for a highly-specific capital good will itself be very time-consuming and will incur considerable *costs*. The costs of transfering ownership to a specific good will be a non-negligible fraction of its total value[11]. The *time* it takes to come to an agreement may often be a considerable fraction of the lifetime of the capital good in question. Contracting costs and delays may be so high that ownership titles for highly-specific capital goods cannot be transferred in an economical way.

Sales, service and rental contracts are devices to govern the use of resources of a less specific nature. They closely correspond to the market mode of coordination. Prices for a good, or for its rental service can easily be determined. Negotiation processes, i.e. *entry times* for a contract, are relatively short and

---

11 Klein, Crawford and Alchian (1978, 300) distinguish between the "costs of reaching an agreement" and the "costs involved in assuring compliance with an agreement". Both cost elements may be considerable for highly-specific and durable capital goods.

entry costs are often negligible. *Exit* is relatively easy and inexpensive, depending on the durability of the commodity in question, and on the length of the contract. Sales, service and rental agreements will, however, only work effectively for a very narrow range of resources[12], and these must be embedded in a well-functioning, generic legal and institutional framework[13].

Cooperative contract modes ("quoad usum" and "quoad sortem") are legal devices governing the use of "critical" capital goods for which the use of the other generic contract modes would not be feasible, too costly or not flexible enough. In a *"quoad usum"* type of agreement, a resource owner, A, provides capital goods for a project. He keeps the ownership title of the resource, but (1) he grants the "right of use" to a separate project organization. He will not receive rental income from his resource, but will (2) be entitled to a certain fraction of the future income stream related to the project, even though distributive shares do *not* have to be determined ex-ante. *"Quoad sortem"* type contracts represent a stronger form, which involves a "right of use" plus a considerable transfer of control rights from A to the project organization, while ownership rights will not necessarily be transferred (see also our definition in the introduction).

Both types of agreement facilitate the coordination of "critical" assets for which prices are difficult to determine. Resources can be contributed to a project without precisely defining asset values and project equity shares. If the project fails, resource owners will often keep their ownership titles to the asset contributed (particularly in the case of "quoad usum" contracts); if the project leads to success, they can still find time to agree on a fair sharing of the added value. The underlying real tasks for the time-consuming investment process are implemented, while the partners can still negotiate contractual conditions and distributive shares. The behavioral pattern can be described by the principle "wait and see how things develop, and contribute as much as possible to the project in the meantime". Such a behavior would not be feasible, if agreements over property rights and prices had to be terminated at the beginning of the project.

---

12 Sales, service and rental agreements are only applicable to non-specific resources with relatively short entry and exit times. The greater the extent of complementarity and connectedness as defined in sections 3.1 and 3.2, the greater the necessity for other types of contracts to govern the coordination of resource flows.

13 The ongoing transformation problems in Eastern Europe can be explained by the fact that (1) the legal and institutional framework required for governing market forces is not effectively in place, and (2) that self-regulating market forces are expected to function for highly-specific capital goods for which other types of contracts and institutions would be needed.

3.3.2   A Capital Theoretical Interpretation of Institutions

The theoretical literature on the choice of institutions has so far emphasized a simplified, "bipolar" perspective, i.e., the stylized choice between markets and hierarchies. This alternative between market contracting and integrated control was shown to be a matter of differences in the *costs of operating institutions*:

The main reason why it is profitable to establish a firm would seem to be that there is a cost of using the price mechanism. The most obvious cost of organizing production through the price mechanism is that of discovering what the relevant prices are (Coase 1937, 390).

As long as all products and inputs are characterized by (1) short entry and exit lags, by (2) a low degree of specificity, and (3) by easy separability, prices can easily be determined and the *cost of operating markets* is low. The more we are concerned with specific capital goods, long entry and exit lags, and with complex asset complementarities, the costs of operating markets will be increased considerably, primarily due to high *costs of discovering prices*. The information cost of knowing a product will rise considerably, and the number of binary transactions between market participants must increase accordingly. High information costs of knowing a product, complicated measurement problems, and considerable problems for separating individual contributions will lead to the economic advantages of those institutions which supplement or substitute market contracting: the setting up of intermediaries, integration within a firm and collaborative contract agreements.

In his classical article, Coase (1937) focused on a "bipolar" differentiation into two basic types of institutions through which equilibria can be reached; markets will be supplemented by integrated hierarchies for all transactions which are related to highly-specific capital goods: "a firm will tend to expand until the costs of organizing an extra transaction within the firm become equal to the costs of carrying out the same transaction by means of an exchange on the open market" (Coase 1937, 305). A dual institutional structure will evolve as an equilibrium state, in which "firms might be envisaged as islands of planned coordination in a sea of market relations" (Richardson 1972, 883).

This simple "bipolar view" requires, however, that the underlying assets display certain characteristics allowing for institutional separation on the one hand, and for easy tradeability of products and inputs on the other side. These conditions are illustrated in *Fig. 3.7*: (1) producers sell directly to consumers though sales contracts (*nexus 1* on the right hand side); (2) input owners provide their inputs on a wage or rental basis to producers (*nexus 2* on the left hand side). Production processes are integrated within "black boxes" of firms (producers A, B, and C), whose production activities can

be easily separated. Even if producers depend on each other for intermediate products or inputs, they can agree on simple sales, wage or rental
contracts.

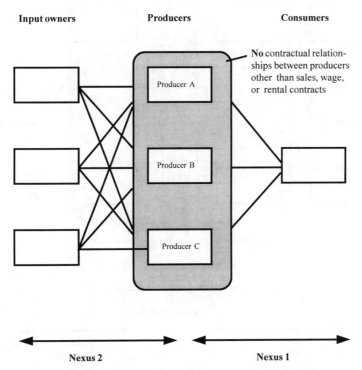

Fig. 3.7:   The Neoclassical Production Structure

This simple, "bipolar" institutional setting corresponds most closely to neoclassical assumptions about the resource allocation process: all products and inputs are tradeable in every single period, property rights for inputs and firms are
clearly specified, firms are characterized as separable production sets, and they
do not have to interact with other producers except on the basis of simple sales
or service contracts. This simple, "bipolar" view is challenged both by Austrian
capital theorists (Pellengahr 1986a, 1986b, Reekie 1984, Shand 1984) and by
modern contract theory:

The world is more complex. The polar cases are complicated by middle men and subcon-
tractors; agents contract among themselves; and any type of input may support a variety
of contractual arrangements. We surmise that these complications which render the 'firm'
ambiguous, have arisen from attempts to save transaction costs that are not avoidable in
the polar cases (Cheung (1983, 19).

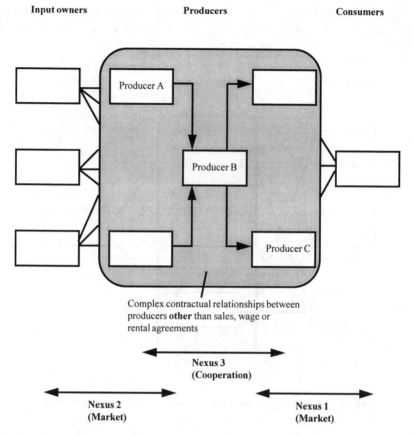

Fig. 3.8:   The Austrian Structure of Production

If the structure of the resource allocation process is characterized by strong, time-dependent *complementarities within the production sector*, the costs of operating institutions may become prohibitive for *both* markets and hierarchies. In *Fig. 3.8*, the shaded zone represents transactions between producers (*nexus 3*), which cannot appropriately be coordinated through sales, rental or equity owner-ship contracts. Each single producer will have to rely on a complex bundle of highly-specific capital goods, only some of which he will own directly. Because of *long entry lags* and high degrees of specificity, the *costs of operating markets* for bringing plans of independent producers into alignment will be too high. *Long exit lags*, on the other hand, and the need to remain flexible with respect to new combinations of assets, will lead to overly high *costs of operating firms*. As a result, more differentiated, "tripartite" institutional arrangements will evolve in which:

- *cooperative agreements* other than sales, wage or rental contracts govern complex interactions between producers. These agreements are primarily related to specific, non-transferable assets;
- *firms* will be established and will expand for those activities for which central ownership of assets offers economic advantages;
- finally, *markets* will govern those activities for which sales and service contracts are sufficient.

3.3.3   The Role of "Quoad Usum" and "Quoad Sortem" Contracts

In an Austrian capital theoretical perspective, we have to consider strong complementarities in time, and we have to concern ourselves with strong complementarities between highly-specific capital goods which are often owned by different agents. Capital goods distributed amongst independent agents are not easily transferable. As a result, agents interested in coordinating resource-flows of highly-specific capital goods will have to find suitable collaborative agreements between themselves. These agreements cannot be coordinated through simple product or service markets; nor does the transfer of ownership titles and the coordination of activities within an integrated firm offer a solution.

Sales, service or rental contracts are not feasible legal devices for the coordination of different maturity classes of highly-specific capital goods. The costs and time required to explore and agree on a price, to reach a market agreement and to assure compliance with this agreement would be prohibitive. As a result, there will simply be no market for certain types of capital goods such as semi-finished R&D projects, expensive single-purpose machinery, highly-specialized expert teams, or for similar classes of "highly-critical" assets.

On the other hand, the character of capital goods will often preclude a clear specification of *property rights*, as well as the transfer of ownership titles. If the properties and relative values of assets cannot easily be determined, it is difficult to come to an agreement on each agent's share in the equity of a joint project. Due to strong project-related complementarities, the value of each asset may be crucially dependent on strategic behavior of other asset owners. The time and cost needed to agree on contractual arrangements within a single, integrated firm, may be prohibitive.

Meanwhile, agents may find it attractive to agree on a joint project and to start a productive new activitiy *without* being able to agree on prices, rental terms or ownership titles. Cooperative agreements ("quoad usum" and "quoad sortem" contracts) allow for the flexible combination of productive new bundles of capital goods for which ownership titles need not necessarily be transferred, and for which prices need not be determined ex-ante. Time-consuming and controversial evaluation processes are postponed, while the partners can concentrate on the productive, physical side of the resource-coordination process.

"Quoad usum" and "quoad sortem" type contracts thus appear to be most useful in coordinating resource-flows for which both the cost of operating markets *and* the cost of operating integrated firms would be prohibitive. This is particularly the case for highly-specific, non-transferable assets for which prices cannot easily be determined and for which information about "true values" is asymetrically distributed. In addition, if assets are linked to other assets. it may be very difficult to disconnect combinations and to agree on project organizations other than those of a collaborative type. These considerations are particularly important for the following types of assets:

- for knowledge and human capital;
- for institutional assets;
- and for highly-specific physical capital goods often required for R&D.

Assets related to *knowledge* and *human capital* are often extremely difficult to evaluate[14]. Ownership titles are difficult to specify, to appropriate or to transfer. Knowledge is often linked to people, for which ownership titles are not "tradeable"[15]. Knowledge-related assets are rarely of a "stand alone" character, the productivity of knowledge bases depends on the efficiency of teams, and many specific skills can only be mobilized within a particular, "fertile" environment.

Institutional assets are often non-transferable and inextricably linked to a particular portfolio of activities within existing firms. A particular new project may require a temporary recombination of assets owned by separate firms without "carving these assets out" of exisiting productive linkages within these firms. As an example, two firms can agree on allowing each other temporary access to their respective distribution networks without necessarily integrating the two.

Similarly, if two firms control large fixed investments in durable *physical capital goods* that are linked to various different activities within each single firm, collaborative agreements may be the only feasible solution. This is particularly the case for fixed investments in R&D such as large laboratories, or expensive test equipment (e.g. wind tunnels). Separating these from the firm's other activities for the sake of a particular project would not be feasible. Agreeing on appropriate rental prices for services between different partners would be too costly and time-consuming. Collaborative agreements of a "quoad sortem" type will turn out to be more appropriate. Each partner will appreciate the other partners contributions of knowledge, institutional assets, and their services of specific physical capital goods. They agree that contribu-

---

14 This can be paraphrased by "you can't look into someone's head". The difficulty of assessing individual capabilities is often aggravated if one wants to assess capabilities within a team.

15 While skilled persons can provide their talents to an employer during a service contract, complete transfer of embodied knowledge is not feasible in a free society where slavery is prohibited.

tions are "more or less equivalent", but do not have to undergo unproductive negotiation processes to determine rental prices and equity ownership shares.

3.4   A Capital Theoretical Interpretation of the Business Firm

In this section we will develop a generalized concept of the business firm, of its competitive advantage and its growth, which is explicitly based on the ownership and control of specific capital goods. The economic theory of the firm offers four different interpretations to the question of what it is that constitutes a business firm. It is seen, first of all, as a *bundle of resources* held together by an entrepreneurial function[16]. *Second*, the firm is seen as a nexus of *contracts* (see Cheung 1983, Klein, Crawford and Alchian 1978, and Demsetz 1988). A third concept emphasizes the knowledge aspect and views the firm as a *repository of knowledge* (Winter 1982, and Nelson and Winter 1982). Fourth, behavioral theories view the firm as a *set of routines* and of standard operating procedures (Simon 1957, March and Simon 1958, and Cyert and March 1963). Our capital theoretical interpretation tries to integrate these separate strands. Firms are seen:

– as a *bundle of complementary assets* of varying maturity classes;
– and as a *nexus of contracts* assuring the coordination of these assets.

The bundle of complementary assets comprises knowledge and skills, a wide array of physical capital goods, as well as institutional assets. Institutional assets are defined by the nexus of contracts, and by the set of routines and standard operating procedures that govern and constrain a firm's activities. In order to get a true understanding of institutions, one has to be concerned with the physical and time-related interdependecies between capital goods. An *Austrian capital theory* is more appropriate than neoclassical concepts since:

– physical properties and time profiles of capital goods matter and cannot easily be transformed into value terms;
– specific combinations of assets are often inextricably interconnected;
– specific assets are inextricably linked with institutions and are thus non-transferable;
– certain combinations and production techniques are only known to individual firms[17];

---

16 In this interpretation of the entrepreneurial function, which was first formulated by SAY (1802) and Cantillon (1905), and which forms the basis of theoretical concepts in business adminstration literature (e.g. see Gutenberg 1983), we do not find the necessary distinction between different classes of resources (capital goods vs. consumer goods, durables vs. non-durables).

17 This view is distinctively different from the conceptualization of the *production set* in neoclassical economics. For a comparison of the neoclassical concept of the production set and the evolutionary concept of firms-specific technologies and skills see Nelson and Winter (1982, chapters 3 and 4).

- the knowledge base represents the core assets of a firm, and this knowledge base has to be persistently used, replicated and memorized;
- because highly-specific assets and knowledge bases have to be accumulated through history, every single firm is unique[18].

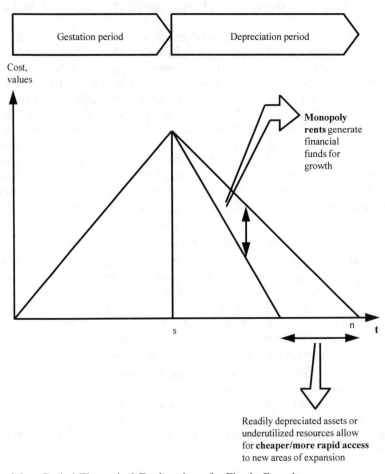

Fig. 3.9:   Capital Theoretical Explanation of a Firm's Growth

---

18 This view is distinctly different from the neoclassical conceptualization of a *market* with many faceless traders.

Our capital theoretical interpretation of the business firm must also be seen as an essential building bloc in the formulation of an *evolutionary theory*. The portfolio of durable assets and contracts represents an element of heritage, and can be interpreted as the set of *genes*. New combinations of assets controlled by the firm often occur as a result of "chance" or of dedicated search efforts, and will then lead to *mutation*[19]. The *selection* environment forces firms relentlessly to find new configurations within their portfolio of assets.

The process of a firm's evolution and growth is thus strongly influenced by its portfolio of durable capital goods, and by institutional assets that have become formalized through its history. Assets with long gestation lags and high entry costs, which a company has accumulated long *before* its rivals, lead to monopoly rents (which we have illustrated by the shaded area in *Fig. 3.9*). These monopoly rents generate financial funds for the growth of the firm. In addition, the firm can rely on capital goods that have already been depreciated, or which are underutilized. These capital goods can be mobilized at variable cost, and they provide much cheaper and more rapid access to new areas of expansion than is available to rival firms. More abundant financial resources and cost advantages through the leveraging of durable assets allow for considerable competitive advantages over other firms (Penrose 1959, chapter 6).

Replicating corporate capabilities works effectively only als long as the portfolio of established business activities and new areas of expansion rely on similar classes of capital goods. As long as companies follow certain trajectories spawned by similar classes of capital goods and related knowledge bases, the exploitation of path-dependencies and of "search in the neighborhood" (Cyert and March 1963) can lead to strong competitive advantages. Disruptive changes in the market or in the technological paradigm, however, may lead to early obsolescence of capital goods, accumulated knowledge bases and institutional assets. In such a situation, decision-makers who want to safeguard their investments in knowledge and specific capital goods often promote inadequate perceptions of the future, and often over-estimate the value of corporate assets and a company's strengths.

Strategic requirements of markets and future business opportunities have to be brought in line with the existing portfolio of assets. While these do have some influence on the selection of strategies, decision-makers are told that "structure should follow strategy" Chandler (1962, 1977). Investment patterns of firms are conditioned by the subjective models of corporate decision-makers and by their interpretations of economic reality and of the future course of events. During the last ten years, strategic management techniques have gained widespread accept-

---

19 Innovation within firms is often a result of *disproportionate combinations of critical assets*. Both bottlenecks and under-utilized assets induce search behavior and mutative forces.

ance throughout the business community[20]. The rapid diffusion of strategic management techniques, however, has not lead to similar developments in economic theory. Existing approaches towards an understanding of strategic management of the business firm have remained rather descriptive and "technical". Even the most recent refinements by Porter (1985, 1990), which are based on the *value-chain concept*[21], have not shown precisley enough, what it is that constitutes the uniqueness and the comparative advantage of firms. His concepts remain descriptive and do not explain why firms have distinctive capabilities, nor do they explain why firms are different with respect to organizational routines and strategies.

To explain differences in firms' capabilities and corporate strategies, one would have to translate Porter's (1985) value chain concept into capital theoretical and evolutionary thinking. Comparative advantages for particular configurations of the value chain would have to be explained by knowledge pools, skills and routines that a firm has accumulated in the past. Such a view is closely related to an understanding of the business firm as a *pool or repository of knowledge*[22]. Firms accummulate a set of technical capabilities and skills and memorize and duplicate these capabilities by applying them in "real time", i.e. during on-going production processes. Because different firms have different histories, and because each firm is involved in differentiated activities and market environments, knowledge bases are unique and specific to the firm. Non-negligible costs of transfering knowledge across institutional boundaries lead to some persistance and stability of firm-specific portfolios of assets.

Strategic differentiation and unique comparative advantages of firms can thus, to a large extent, be explained by *differences in technological asset bases* and by managerial requirements being shaped and restrained by firm-specific knowledge pools. The gradual extension of the firm-specific knowledge base and diversification decisions outside the core business are guided by *technological path dependencies*:

The suitable performance of organizational routines provides the underpinnings for what is commonly thought of as the distinctive competence of an enterprise. 'These people at

---

20 This has, in the meantime, led to a situation in which strategic decision-making has itself almost become a routine-driven activitiy of a special kind. Strategies can be described as a higher-order decision rule, or, as Nelson and Winter (1982, 37) would phrase it, a "change in strategy or policy (that) can be treated in exactly the same way as change in technique".
21 The *value chain concept* is a new method of task-partitioning and strategic differentiation, which has become systematized by Porter (1985, 1990). We have already described older organization theoretical concepts very familiar to the value chain concept in section 2.4.1.
22 This concept of the business firm has been explicitly put forth by Winter (1982, 1987) and by Nelson and Winter (1982).

company X are good at Y' summarizes views which outsiders may develop with respect to these competences. These competences, coupled with a modicum of strategic vision will, in turn, help to define a firm's core business (Teece 1988, 265).

The evolution of the firm, strategic repositioning and corporate change are guided and constrained by its portfolio of assets and by the nexus of contracts which has been developed to coordinate and control these assets. During periods of *continuous and incremental change*, both the portfolio of assets and the nexus of contracts can be jointly adapted in a compatible way. Failures to cope with change, however, are pertinent in connection with technological *discontinuities* and during periods of rapid change. These *discontinuities* often result in a disparity between the portfolio of assets and the nexus of contracts. Rapid changes *"obsolete* major parts of a firm's existing knowledge base and often render investment in complementary assets (production equipment, human capital, distribution channels, etc.) valueless" (Teece 1988, 266). Contractual arrangements within the firm are often directed at safeguarding quasi-rents from assets and knowledge bases of the past. Processes directed at the acquisition of assets as being more conducive to future-oriented activities will be slowed down or even prohibited by the "dominant" nexus of contracts. As a result, if the environment and technologies change rapidly, firms must be able to transcend their own portfolio of assets and must flexibly adapt their nexus of contracts. If entry and exit conditions for specific assets are "difficult", and if new contractual arrangements cannot be implemented within the dominant governance structure of the firm, new network arrangements and strategic alliances will turn out to be the only feasible solution. This will be explained in more detail in the following chapters 4 and 5.

3.5   A New Interpretation of Cooperation as an Option

If resources are characterized by long entry and exit lags and by a high degree of specificity, the asset base of a firm may easily become obsolete, particularly during periods of rapid change. Transition towards a new asset base being more responsive to new environmental conditions will be made difficult because of long entry lags and because the firm-specific nexus of contracts is more oriented towards compliance with exit lags of past investments. New investment projects and innovations require new combinations of assets, which are held by different firms and which are not easily transferable between institutions. The costs of agreeing on prices and values for closely-held, highly-specific resources are prohibitive. Neither the market mode nor the integrated mode will be appropriate for securing the coordination of resources-flows for investment projects.

In order to exploit growth opportunities during phases of strong technological discontinuities and to pursue prospective new investment projects, firms must display "permeable boundaries". New types of *contractual arrangements* between firms such as R&D networks, joint ventures and various forms of strategic alliances will be sought. These consist of a new combination of portfolios of assets which are owned by two or more different firms, and which cannot be transferred across institutional boundaries other than through "quoad usum" and "quoad sortem" type contracts as described in section 3.3.

The incentives for independent agents to participate in a collaborative arrangement are:

- to *reduce entry time and entry cost* related to a new project (*time* considerations);
- and to *reduce exit time and exit cost* if a certain new combination of assets turns out to be more appropriate (*flexibility* considerations).

The *first* argument emphasizing *time* can be illustrated by the example of two agents A and B, who have invested in the development of two complementary capital goods. Either one of the two would have to replicate time-consuming development processes which the other agent has already completed, and would therefore have to wait longer. The transfer of semi-completed capital goods would not be feasible because the time and cost of agreeing on prices are prohibitive. Both agents will, instead, sign a collaboration agreement: agent A will get access to assets accumulated by B and, in turn offers acces to his portfolio of assets. The development cycle will be shortened and the net present value for the joint project will be increased[23].

The *second* argument of *flexibility* is important for assets with long entry and exit lags, for which information about asset values and about the most appropriate combination of resources will be unfolded only during an ongoing investment process. Evaluations on which investment choices will be based, must rely on option values as opposed to "traditional" net present value calculations. Net present value calculations typically rely on information of an investment project in one single period, in which an irreversible decision is made (see the illustration in the upper section in *Fig. 3.10*). Many investment projects, particularly those with long entry and exit lags and a high degree of asset specificity, however, seem to defy such straightforward net present value calculations, since "they are but the first link in a long chain of subsequent investment decisions. . . . Precisely how and when subsequent investment decisions will be made is dependent on future events" (Kester 1980, 3f).

---

23 There may be some dispute over the sharing of profits.The negotiation process over distributive shares, however, can continue parallel to the joint development process, and does not have to be completed *before* the entry decision has been taken, which would be the case for both the market and the integrated mode.

The calculation of *option values* involves a repetitive, iterative evaluation process: a development process is started in time t_o, while the participating agents are still able to reconsider choices about the continuation of the project and its precise specification in the successive periods. In the lower section in Fig. 3.10, we have assumed that an investor can easily switch to a modified type of capital good, or to a new combination of assets at the end of each period during the gestation process. Information about the true value of the project is unfolding during the gestation process, and relevant new information can successively be considered for project design and selection.

A collaborative arrangement between firms can accordingly be interpreted as a *reciprocal call option*: agents A and B start with the exploration and development of two separable, though complementary asset bases. Both offer each other a call option on their resource base. They do not have to agree ex-ante on prices of the respective resources, that will only become known during the ongoing development process. Nor do they have to enter into joint equity agreements which would restrict the flexibility of the arrangement. The reciprocal call option allows both partners to participate in a joint discovery procedure; as information unfolds, they may decide to rent or to jointly own the relevant complementary resource base, but they are free to choose other options as well. *Economic advantages* of the reciprocal call option can be explained by:

- relatively low costs and short delays for *agreeing on prices and values*;
- effectively *reduced* risks since only few resources are committed in early phases;
- a high degree of *flexibility* and responsiveness to ongoing new developments;
- and the *adaptive design and implementation* of the nexus of contracts which will be most suitable for the project at hand.

Our interpretation of a call option to be applied for transactions related to real assets, is slightly different from the institutional arrangements which have evolved in the market for *financial call options* in Western Europe and in the U.S. In both markets, it has become institutionalized to specify the "exercise or "striking price" ex-ante, while the date of the transaction can be differentiated. For the "European call", the option can be exercised only on one particular day, while in the case of an "American call", the option can be exercised on or before that day (see Brealey and Myers 1988, 472). In a related way, the "exercise price" must not necessarily be specified ex-ante. Depending on conventions to be developed within a market for call options, partners can agree on transactions at a specified future date, without necessarily specifying the price. All they need to agree on is a particular rule or procedure through which the future price can be determined. Such markets for real call options have evolved for a number of application areas such as for strategic alliances in R&D or in the venture capital business (see particularly our case descriptions in chapter 7). These empirical developments have so far not appropriately been reflected in the theory of capital or in the theory of finance. Further theoretical investigations would provide promising routes to an understanding of new contractual relations between business firms, and for the structuring of collaborative investment projects.

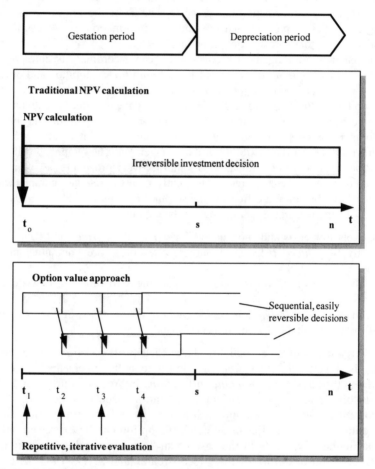

Fig. 3.10: Option Values vs. Traditional NPV Calculations

A convincing economic theory of *cooperation* must emphasize this reciprocal call option approach to the investment decision process. To do this, explicit consideration must be attributed to the time structure of investment and to the sequential character of the decision-making process. Only very few authors have extended option theory, which has primarily been developed for analyzing purely financial decisions, to the analysis of "complicated" real investment projects (see Majd and Pindyck 1987, Roberts and Weitzman 1981, and Weitzman, Newey and Rabin 1981).

4 Neo-institutional Explanations for Cooperative Projects and Networks

We have argued in chapter 2 that institutional structures should logically follow strategic objectives, and that institutions should be designed in such a way that they can best facilitate the processes needed to attain certain objectives. In this chapter, we will concentrate on economic theories explaining choices between different institutions, and we will try to develop a generic neo-institutional framework for comparing the relative efficiency of integrated firms, markets, and different forms of cooperation between firms.

It is the aim of *neo-institutional economics* to explain which types of economic activities can best be governed and organized through markets, within hierarchial firms, or through mixed, cooperative modes of coordination. These three *discrete structural alternatives* (Simon 1978) each appear to offer some advantages for specific tasks, while they may not be the right solution for other tasks. The investigation of discrete structural alternatives was first directed at comparing the differential performance of markets and hierarchies. For certain types of investment projects and innovations, markets will not function appropriately. Some neo-institutional economists thus tend to argue in favor of integration (see particularly the description of Williamson's work in section 4.2).

During the last years, a third category "between markets and hierarchies", the so-called *hybrid form* (Williamson 1985, 1990), has gained increasing attention. To cope with certain types of investment projects, particularly with those characterized by long entry and exit lags, vertical integration will often be just a partial and unbalanced solution. There may be (static or short-term) economic benefits to integrate certain activities, but these may be more than offset by increasing (dynamic and long-term) costs: integrated firms develop inertia and are less flexible to suitably adapt to ongoing change. Even if vertical integration may help to facilitate one innovative project, it may block other, successive projects in the future.

These limits to integration, which have increasingly become a subject of theoretical and empirical analysis, have led to a reconsideration of new and flexible modes of governance and organization. Such *hybrid modes* can be interpreted as more or less formalized organizational solutions "between markets and hierarchies", but somewhere close to the hierarchical spectrum. This stance is represented by Teece (1986 and 1987), who argues in favor of collaborative, equity-based coalitions between firms (see section 4.2). Alternatively, hybrid modes of governance and organization can be interpreted as rather unstructured, informal modes of inter-firm interaction "beyond markets and hierarchies". Along these last lines, a rapidly growing number of researchers try to explore more open network solutions (Jarillo 1988, Håkansson 1987, and others).

So far, most existing neo-institutionalist approaches have remained rather descriptive and static. They operate mostly within a timeless world. Differential costs of operating institutions are analyzed without taking into consideration the complex differences in development, production, and transaction costs *over time*. We thus believe that a fusion of these neo-institutional approaches with some more rigorous capital theoretical explanations may provide a fruitful route to further development. In order to show this, we will first explain the capital theoretical reasons needed to distinguish between *entry and exit time*, and the relevance of these concepts for institutional explanations (see *section 4.1*). In *section 4.2* we will then summarize Williamson's theory of the advantages and limits of integration. *Section 4.3* contains a description of Teece's extension of the market and hierarchy framework to the analysis of cooperation. Finally, in *section 4.4* we will give an outlook on more recent developments related to new, "open" forms of "dynamic" or "strategic networks".

4.1   Entry Times and Exit Times and their Relevance for the Analysis of Institutions

Industrial economists have extensively studied *entry costs* and their impact on prices, market structure and industry performance (Bain 1956, Stigler 1968 and Scherer 1980). They have focused on *entry costs*, and have neglected *entry times*, which, according to our view, are at least as important for the explanation of industrial structure. Scholars of strategic management have emphasized the importance of *exit costs*, i.e. the costs related to leaving a market or giving up an activity, but have often neglected the time dimension[1]. Both concepts of entry and exit costs used by these authors are an amalgam of two distictive elements, if entry to and exit from a market is considered to be a process in time: (1) the *time* it takes to enter or leave a market, and (2) the costs related to this behavior per unit of time. For reasons of simplicity and elegance, economists have tended to aggregate both components into one single term: the net present value of entry, or the net present value of exit, respectively. For institutional decisions, however, it will often be very important to consider both the *time and cost elements separately*. Even if the

---

1   Porter (1980), Hax and Majluf (1984) and Baumol, Panzar and Willig (1982). Again, these autors concentrate on *exit costs*, but do not explicitly consider *exit time*, i.e. the time it takes to give up a certain activity.

net present value of entry for two investment opportunities may be the same, the appropriate institutional solution to deal with an opportunity for instantaneous, expensive entry will be totally different from the institutional solution suitable for a time-consuming entry process.

Similar to many industrial economists and strategic management scholars, Neo-institutionalists argue from a *timeless perspective*: they compare costs and benefits of alternative institutional arrangements from a more or less static point-of-view, and they do not explicitly consider the time it takes to establish, reconstruct or abandon certain institutions. However, we believe that most arguments used in neo-institutional explanations such as irreversibility or specificity, restricted asset ownership, and uncertainty only make sense in a world in which there are considerable time lags related to entry and exit.

In the following chapter, we will thus explicitly consider the time element of investment and will investigate how this time element can explain deficiencies of both markets and hierarchies. We will argue that it is primarily a *combination of long entry and long exit lags* which will induce firms to search for cooperative solutions for certain investment projects. In accordance with the capital theoretical concepts outlined in chapter 3, we will distinguish between:

- *entry time* measured by the gestation period of capital goods (or human capital) needed for an investment project; and
- *exit time*, defined by the time it takes to recapture the value of capital goods used, which can be achieved through depreciation, amortization or resale.

According to our analysis in section 3.1.3, *entry costs* are defined as the costs of developing and building the capital good(s). In *Fig. 4.1*, entry and exit lags are measured along the horizontal axis, while entry costs per unit of time are measured along the vertical axis. The time profile of investment during the gestation as well as the depreciation period can be either characterized by different cost levels per period (Fig. 4.1a), or alternatively it can be transformed into a steady payment (see Fig 4.1b). For reasons of simplicity and clarity, we will transform payments into an equivalent annuity, with a fixed level of expenditures and revenues over the whole period of gestation and depreciation, respectively.

Long entry and exit time will not lead to major problems in the absence of uncertainty if consumption cycles and amortization can be anticipated in a reliable way. This is illustrated by an "orderly solution" (*Case 1*) in *Fig. 4.2*: the life-cycle or consumption period for an activity generated through the investment project is long enough to allow for full amortization, and generated revenues are large enough to allow for a positive net present value. This is somewhat different for *Case 2*: the consumption period is shorter than the expected depreciation period. An investor has to bear the cost of early obsolescence (represented by the shaded area F_2). However, a large enough revenue stream during the shortened consumption period will allow for a compensation of these costs of early obsolescence; the shaded area F_1 is larger than F_2 and the resulting net present value of the investment project is positive.

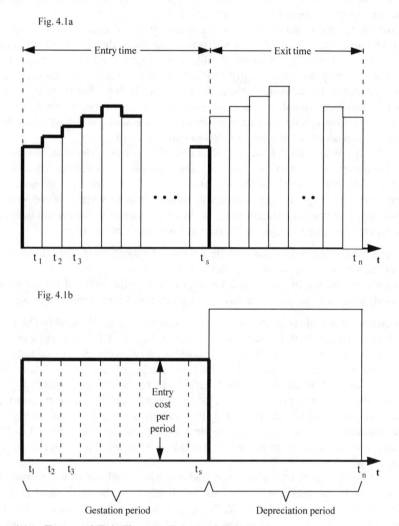

Fig. 4.1a

Fig. 4.1b

Fig. 4.1:   Entry and Exit Time vs. Entry and Exit Cost

There are numerous risks involved in assessing the future revenue stream and the net present value of an investment project, and these risks are greater, the longer the periods of gestation and depreciation. The size of the shaded area F_1

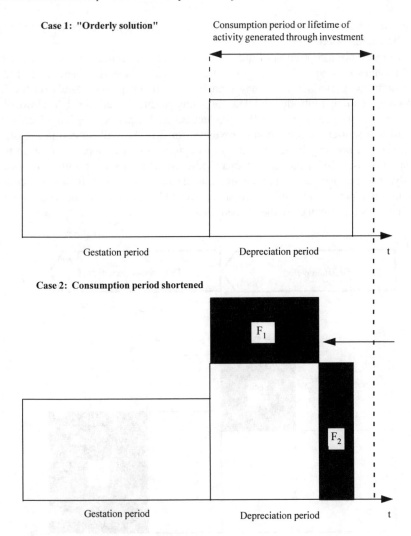

Fig. 4.2:   Entry and Exit Time and Expected Consumption Period

for the introduction of a new product will depend on its expected lifetime, on price fluctuations, and on substitutional effects, all of which are more difficult to predict the longer the gestation period s. Similarly, the loss of early obsolescence, represented by the size of the shaded area F_2 will depend on resale prices of used capital equipment, on price fluctuations for complementary inputs, as well as on the expected consumption period. The hazards of early expropriation of quasi-rents are greater, the longer the exit time and the greater the degree of specificity of the capital good[2].

Dangers of expropriation of quasirents will become particularly high, if external changes lead not only to a shortening, but also to the earlier beginning of the consumption period. Firm A may plan for a gestation period s and and for an appropriate market introduction date for a new product in period s + 1. However, its competitors may introduce this product earlier (in period s' < s), which will result in a shorter appropriation of revenues for firm A, as illustrated in *Fig. 4.3*. Firm A will not only loose revenues to its competitors who appear earlier on the market (illustrated by the shaded area F_3). It will also encounter a greater loss of early obsolescence due to its long anticipated exit time (T − s). It can only count to amortize part of its capital equipment over (T' − s) periods, and will have to bear losses represented by the shaded area F_2.

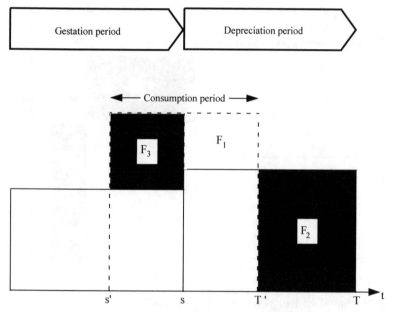

Fig. 4.3:   Early Introduction of Innovations and Shortened Lifecycles

---

2   This is a reason for Williamson's (1985) emphasis on the impact of *specificity*. However, he does not distingish enough between specificity and *exit time*. A high degree of specificity does not lead to great risks for investors, if exit times are short. Implicitly Williamson uses an "amalgam" of specificity and exit time which we suggest to "break up" into its elements.

The magnitude of losses caused by pre-emptive investments of competitors will primarily depend on entry and exit time, entry and exit cost, and on the degree of specificity of capital equipment (or human capital accumulated). Long gestation periods explained by long R&D lead times, and changes of the introduction date from s to s' will result in early obsolescence of those R&D investments that are highly-specific. Only if the results of R&D can be transferred to other processes or to the next generation of products, will the danger of long R&D lead times be reduced. Similarly, if exit times are long and capital equipment is highly-specific, an investor runs a high risk of "being stuck" with dedicated machinery and knowledge that cannot be utilized or sold elsewhere.

If entry and exit lags are long while products and technologies change in an unpredictable way, the *timing of the introduction date* s becomes the foremost important strategic parameter. A firm that introduces a product in period s *after* it has been launched by its competitors, runs a high risk to fail. The net present value that can be captured by the firm will decline and will become negative beyond a certain introduction date. This is illustrated by the function of the net present value in the lower part in *Fig. 4.4*. Relatedly, the net present value will also decline for a firm that introduces a product *too early*. If it enters the market in period s, while the consumption period starts only in period s"(s" < s), it will have to bear waiting costs (interest on R&D expenses and "out-of-pocket-payments" for depreciation). If s" is much greater than the planned introduction date s, the net present value of its investment will become negative.

Given such long entry and exit times, firms will have an incentive to search for new forms of cooperative investment, which allow them to better control the danger of late arrival on the market and early obsolescence, while at the same time remaining flexible enough to adapt to ongoing technological change. They can achieve this through horizontal or technology-oriented cooperation; or they can try to collaborate along a vertical dimension, i.e. by participating in close customer-supplier-relationships. *Horizontal and technology-related alliances* are most often sought if entry time is long, and if there is great uncertainty about the introduction date s. Two firms with complementary R&D skills can then:

- *reduce R&D lead times* by opening each others' repository of knowledge such that each partner can build on existing know-how without having to replicate time-consuming search processes; furthermore, they can
- agree to jointly influence the *realization of introduction date s*, e.g. through setting of standards and through planned timing of product introduction.

Vertical alliances and customer-supplier-relationships will preferredly be formed if entry and exit lags are long, and if there are large uncertainties regarding the introduction date s. Two firms on both the supply and demand side will have strong incentives to establish cooperative agreements in order (1) to prevent that a new product is introduced *before* t = s, because this would be against the interest of the supplier, who wouldn't have R&D completed before that date. If, in that situation, customers are still in the amortization phase for earlier generations of capital goods with long exit lags, both suppliers and customers may mutually benefit from a jointly agreed introduction date s. Similarly, (2) firms on both the demand and supply side for new capital goods may want to cooperate to prevent introduction of the new product *after t = s*. Furthermore, both partners may assure themselves through collaborative agreements that the new product may effectively be consumed and depreciated until period t = T.

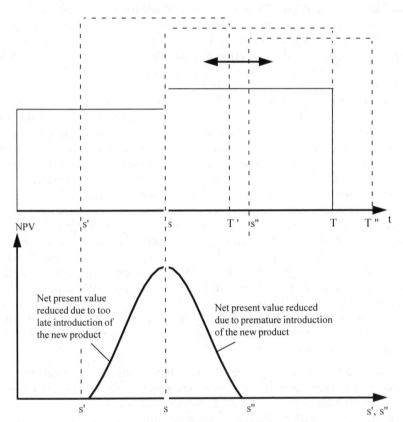

Fig. 4.4:   Impact of Early and Late Introduction Dates

Given these advantages of cooperative forms of investment, one must still raise the question, whether alternative modes of governance and organization will not lead to similarly appropriate results. In *comparison to the integrated solution*, cooperation appears to be a superior mode whenever the frequency of transactions needed to jointly pursue investments is rather low, if there is a high chance that the next generation of products can better be developed within another team, comprising different partners, and if an integrated solution would lead to the pooling of other, rather non-related assets of the companies involved.

On the other hand, collaboration motivated by the desire to shorten R&D lead times, may not easily be *substituted by pure market transactions*. Firm A that wants to buy-in know-how from a company B "further down the road" in R&D, will find this difficult or even impossible, because B has a strategic advantage over A and will prefer to drive A out of the market instead of cooperating. Only if both firms control complementary knowledge bases, the exchange of which would allow each firm to enter the market earlier, will they be prepared to learn from each other, and still behave in a cooperative way. In such a case, however, it is most likely that they would establish some mutual relationship beyond pure market transactions, because there would be too high a risk that one firm would behave opportunistically.

The relative advantages of alternative modes of governance end organization will be explored in more detail in the following sections 4.2 to 4.4 and in chapter 5. Since the neo-institutional framework, on which our reasoning will be based, still operates in a rather timeless world, it was our intent to emphasize the crucial role of the time profile of investment. If entry and exit times are considered more explicitly, some of the questions still unanswered in neo-institutional economics may become more appropriately solved.

4.2   Advantages and Limits of Integration

Neo-institutional scholars have emphasized the role of bounded-rationality, incomplete contracting and asymmetric information, and have studied the influence of these concepts on the evolution of business firms. They have emphasized non-market transactions and the comparative advantages of internal organization within vertically integrated corporations. This *emphasis on integration* has so far resulted in some neglect of the rich diversity of *cooperative* modes of governance and organization; only very recently, neo-institutional scholars have extended their concepts towards the study of cooperation (see sections 4.3 and 4.4).

Neo-institutional economics focuses on the analysis of property rights, and on transactions as basic unit to analyze economic activities[3]. This focus leads to the

---

3   In contrast to neoclassical thinking which concentrates on prices and quantities, Commons (1934, 1970) has emphasized the alternative view of concentrating on *transactions*. His view is related much more closely to a process-oriented analysis of organizations, as outlined in the preceding section 2.4.1.

strong emphasis on transaction costs, a concept which was introduced into the economic debate by Coase (1937). *Transaction costs* can be defined as costs of information and communication needed to find, negotiate, agree upon and monitor contracts[4]. According to Coase, transactions can be pursued within two alternative systems of coordination: (1) through the *market* (equivalent to our "market solution"), or (2) by organizing transactions within *hierarchies* (equivalent to our "integrated solution"). Which system of coordination will be chosen depends primarily on transaction cost considerations. Accordingly, the relative advantage and sustainability of firms or other hierarchial institutions is explained by transaction cost advantages of integrating certain (vertically or horizontally related) activities.

Williamson has extended this *market and hierarchy paradigm* by (1) formulating the specific assumptions under which integration will lead to transaction cost savings, and (2) by considering a larger and more diverse set of alternative systems of coordination[5]. According to his view, shortcomings of markets, and transaction cost related advantages of internal organization must be explained by the following "exogenous factors":

- by *behavioral characteristics* related to all agents participating in transactions, such as *bounded rationality*[6] and *opportunism*[7];
- and by *environmental characteristics*, such as the kind and *degree of uncertainty*, and the *degree of specificity* of capital goods.

In Fig. 4.5, we have illustrated the interrelationship between behavioral and environmental characteristics. For high degrees of uncertainty, bounded rationality will lead to problems in resource allocation and coordination. Similarly, high degrees of asset specificity will be particularly problematic, if agents behave opportunistically. The more the behavioral and environmental characteristics related to a certain investment activity become "complicated", the more will potential conflicts have to be resolved through decisive, clearly regulated and non-spontaneous forms of organization.

---

4   The definition and operationalization of transaction costs has led to endless debates in economics. Picot (1982, 270) has helped to reduce this ambiguity by working out a nomenclature that may serve as a useful basis for further theoretical and empirical work.

5   See Williamson (1975, 1985, 1990) and the summary outline in Frese (1988, 128ff).

6   The assumption of *bounded rationality* describes economic agents as "intendedly rational, but only limitedly so" (Simon 1961, 24). Limitations are caused by restricted cognitive competence. See Williamson 1985, 45f).

7   *Opportunism* describes a type of behavior, in which economic agents exploit opportunities for individual profit which are primarily based on differential access to and disclosure of information. "Opportunism refers to incomplete or distorted disclosure of information, especially to calculated efforts to mislead, distort, disguise, obfuscate, or otherwise confuse. It is responsible for real or contrived conditions of information asymmetry, which vastly complicate problems of economic organization" (Williamson 1985, 47f).

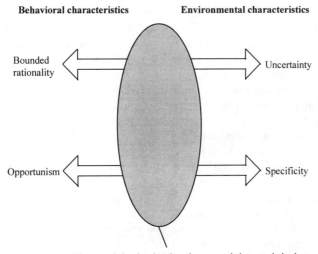

Behavioral characteristics   **Environmental characteristics**

Bounded rationality   Uncertainty

Opportunism   Specificity

The more behavioral and environmental characteristics become "complicated" (measured by the size of this circle), the more of the potential conflict has to be resolved through integrated modes of governance and organization

Fig. 4.5:   Explanatory Factors within the Market and Hierarchy Paradigm

The costs of operating institutions for "complicated" combinations of behavioral and environmental factors will thus work against the *market mode* of governance and organization. If both the degree of specificity and the degree of uncertaintity are considerable, pure market contracting between independent traders will lead to very high transaction costs, given the underlying behavioral characteristics of bounded rationality and opportunism. Transaction-related investments of highly-specific nature must be born, and there is a large risk that other market participants will act in a way which will not allow for the exploitation of quasi-rents from this investment. As a result, the investing firm will try to control transactions as far as possible in-house. If the frequency of in-house transactions is high enough to justify large, transaction-specific fixed costs, the level of transaction cost savings will become considerable, and integrated ownership and control will represent the efficient mode of governance and organization[8].

---

8 Whether integration is superior over market contracting is primarily a matter of leveraging the fixed costs of transactions. See Picot and Dietl (1990) for the analysis of break-even points for transaction-specific investments, and Heidorn (1985) for an analysis of fix-cost leveraging.

Economic *advantages of integration* proposed within the transaction cost framework depend strongly on assumptions about the efficiency of intra-corporate control. Internal organization allows for the maintenance of stable incentives, for effective controls and sanctions, and for goal complementarity and conflict resolution through joint ownership of resources. Furthermore, for certain types of uncertainty, internal organization will serve as an effective mechanism to control and reduce risk[9]. However, the full exploitation of integration advantages is only feasible as long as market and technological conditions are stable enough to secure full amortization of highly transaction-specific investments. Furthermore, an integrated firm will offer advantages only as long as its accumulated internal incentive and control system remains responsive to ongoing external changes.

Integration advantages, which typically apply for rather stable economic conditions, must be seen in conjunction with limits to integration; the efficiency of intra-corporate control is dependent upon a certain degree of stability and predictability. Williamson sometimes tends to go too far in exposing the merits of internal organization[10]. He admits that there are limits to firm size but he does not analyze these limits consequently enough within his own axiomatic system. These *limits of internal organization* must be interpreted in terms of:

– *diminishing returns from entrepreneurship* related to the limitations of large firms to cope with certain types of uncertainties, and to maintain a high enough level of entrepreneurial activity;
– furthermore, transaction cost savings of internal organization are impaired by *increasing costs of management and coordination* within firms.

Limitations to firm size based on the first explanation, i.e. on *diminishing returns from entrepreneurship*, were originally formulated by Knight (1965):

The question of diminishing returns from entrepreneurship is really a matter of the amount of uncertainty present. To imagine that a man could adequately manage a business enterprise of indefinite size and complexity is to imagine a situation in which effective uncertainty is entirely absent (Knight 1965, 286f).

Williamson (1985, 133) re-interprets these diminishing returns from entrepreneurship within his own analytical framework, as being primarily explained by bounded rationality: "As uncertainty increases, problems of organization become

---

9 See Williamson (1985, 72ff) and Picot, Dietl (1990, 181).
10 At least this is the case for his major publications (Williamson 1975, 1985). In his latest contributions (see Williamson 1990), he has further explored the economic advantages of "hybrid modes" over integration.

increasingly complex and bounds on cognitive competence are reached." However, he believes that these diminishing returns from entrepreneurship are just a matter of organizational design and that there are effective ways of maintaining a high level of entrepreneurship even in very large organizations[11]. Similarly, he argues that internal organization will help to reduce uncertainty, while he tends to neglect additional *uncertainties created* through the internalization of activities. This is exemplified in his description of the effects of the merger of two companies which operate in an uncertain environment:

> Joining the two does not increase the aggregate uncertainty. Since the gaming moves and replies of rivalry have been removed, uncertainty has arguably been reduced. Moreover, ... decisions need not be forced to the top but can always be assigned to the level at which the issues are most appropriately resolved. ... The resulting combined firm can therefore do everything that the two autonomous firms could do previously *and more* (Williamson 1985, 133).

This view appears to neglect the effect that market signals have on guiding and disciplining internal management decisions. Williamson assumes that the merger of two firms will reduce the extent of exernal gaming, while he does not consider that external gaming is often only *substituted by internal gaming*. Internal gaming allowed for by the reduced control and discipline of markets will often result in uncertainty being at least as high, or even higher than in the pre-merger situation.

The extent of internal gaming may be effectively controlled, but will cause the costs of internal management and coordination to rise. Even though decisions can "be assigned to the level at which the issues are most appropriately resolved", internal gaming will often result in situations in which top management will repeatedly have to play a referees role. Integration will then *not* lead to more delegation, nor to a greater degree of decentralization. By contrast, if uncertainty is high, and if middle managers receive less precise signals from the market-place, top management will often become more involved in decisions for which there are opposing constituencies within the firm. Costs of internal management and coordination will rise considerably and capabilities of top management to oversee and control a wide array of activities will soon become exhausted.

---

11 These new methods of organizational design which can be called "intrapreneuring" (Pinchot 1985) or "adhocracy" (Mintzberg 1983), have received strong attention within the management literature. Diminishing returns to entrepreneurship can be overcome through an appropriate formation of strategic business units, committees, matrix organizations, and through the revision of internal incentive and reward structures. According to our view, these managerial devices can stretch the limits of a firm's appropriate size. They cannot, however, extend limits beyond a certain scale level, and they will often lead to their own inherent problems of coordination and efficiency.

The interplay between diminishing returns to entrepreneurship and increasing costs of management and coordination within integrated firms will be aggravated inasmuch as firm-specific assets are characterized by *long exit* lags. Different agents within an institution will have invested into different types of capital goods, knowledge and skills. Innovations will lead to the expropriation of quasi-rents for particular groups, and this leads to increasing intra-firm rivalry, greater involvement of top-management in conflict resolution, which results in sharply rising costs of internal management and coordination. A greater percentage of managerial resources and attention will be shifted away from the marketplace, and will be tied up in the internal conflict-resolution process. Changes in the environment will be filtered, and responsive organizational adaptations will become restrained by past investments in the firm-specific knowledge base.

Investments in firm-specific and agent-specific knowledge bases with long exit lags will also aggravate serial reproduction losses and incentive anomalies. Bounded rationality and highly-specific knowledge leads to limited control spans of managers at every single hierarchical level. Increasing firm size will necessarily lead to the addition of new hierarchical stages which perturbates the effective transmission of knowledge across vertical levels. Even though information may be modified only to a minor extent at every single level, the cumulative *reproduction loss* will become considerable if many hierarchial levels have to be bridged, and if the degree of uncertainty is high[12]. Williamson (1985, 135) appears to be overly optimistic with respect to this effect and argues that "the serial reproduction loss solution does not apply if ... selective intervention is admitted". This selective intervention, however, cannot be implemented without additional management costs.

The risk of expropriation of quasi-rents for agent-specific assets, and the difficulty of calibrating competing knowledge pools lead to considerable *incentive anomalies*. Williamson (1985) himself admits that such effects related to incentive anomalies may be very powerful in explaining limits to firm size. He shows that markets provide *strong incentives*, while the integration of economic activities within firms will often result in a *weakening and impairment of incentives*:

The transfer of transactions out of the market into the firm is regularly attended by an impairment of incentives. It is especially severe in circumstances where innovation (and rewards for innovation) are important (Williamson 1985, 161).

---

12 This *serial reproduction loss* was introduced into the organization literature by Bartlett (1932, 175). While Williamson (1967) had emphasized this effect in an earlier paper on optimal firm size, he later tended to believe more in the effectiveness of new management methods to take control of this detrimental effect.

A rapid pace of technological change and strong market perturbations thus reverse the differential evaluation of institutional structures with which organizational theorists have become familiarized within the simplified, "bipolar" market and hierarchy paradigm. Williamson (1985, 162) admits that both markets and hierarchies "have distinctive strengths and weaknesses", while there are situations in which *neither* of the two forms provides the right institutional framework for organizing transactions. While markets provide strong incentive features, they often have weak governance features. Conversely, hierarchies are strong with respect to gover nance features but are characterized by weak incentive features.

New, *hybrid modes* of governance and organization will have to be designed frequently, with a combination of strong governance features and strong incentive features. Williamson (1985, 144) suggests that the urgency with which such hybrid modes must be sought is strongly related to the degree of innovation. Why this is the case, and which types of hybrid organization are most conducive to technical change, however, cannot be answered from within a "bipolar market and hierarchy framework". In order to become more specific and explanatory, we have to explicitly consider the time-profile of investment and we have to be more precise about the reasons leading to uncertainty. This will be outlined in the following two sections.

4.3 Extensions of Neo-institutional Economics to Hybrid Modes of Organization

The market and hierarchy paradigm outlined in section 4.2 provides a rich framework for analyzing the relative advantage of alternative modes of coordination, but has so far been rather sketchy with respect to hybrid modes. A few authors have tried to extend the market and hierarchy paradigm in this direction. Alchian (1984) has provided a general outline for analyzing different forms of coalitions. Ouchi (1980) has focused on intermediate forms such as clans, has interpreted linkages between Japanese firms as clan-type organizations, and has recently proposed new collaborative solutions to the management of complex R&D projects (Ouchi and Bolton 1987). Teece (1986, 1987, 1991) and Pisano, Russo and Teece (1988) have developed a rather coherent framework for analyzing collaborative forms of organization of the more stable and equity-based kind. In addition, a growing number of authors has developed descriptive models of interactions between firms which can be called "dynamic networks" or "strategic networks"[13].

---

13 The term "dynamic network" is used by both Miles and Snow (1984) and Picot and Dietl (1990). Jarillo (1988) uses the term "strategic network". A survey of these new approaches can be found in Ochsenbauer (1989).

We will distinguish between "hard" and "soft" models of cooperative activity between firms. *"Hard models"* are related to activities which are rather time-consuming and which require considerable investments (financial and real capital assets) for each participating partner. Interactions tend to be formalized and secured through legal contracts of the "quoad sortem" type and/or through clearly specified ownership contracts. On the other hand, *"soft models"* of dynamic interactions describe cases in which most transactions are market-mediated. Participating partners are free to choose other market participants, but are interlocked into close communication circles which offer transaction cost advantages over open, spot-type interactions. "Capital" committed by members of the network consists more of "cumulated social relations" and trust building. In addition, members of a network provide resources through "quoad usum" type of contractual arrangements, since simple trading of resources is made difficult due to evaluation problems. In this section 4.3, we will concentrate on "hard" models of cooperation, while we will describe the other, more "open" types of contractual arrangements in section 4.4.

Recently a number of neo-institutional economists have turned their attention towards the analysis of formalized modes of collaboration and strategic alliances. In the following, we will concentrate on a description of the work done by Teece and some of his co-authors[14]. They attempt to explain the *"postmodern features"* of industrial corporations (Horwitch 1989 and Dunning 1988), which develop extensive collateral relationships with other companies, and for which "the boundaries of the firm are extremely difficult to delineate, particularly when there are complex alliance structures in place" (Teece 1991, 8). Teece and his colleagues try to structure these complex alliances from within the market and hierarchy paradigm, but admit that additional explanatory factors are needed. These become particularly important whenever innovations are involved, and will then have a significant impact on transaction cost advantages of alternative modes of coordination. In particular, certain configurations of innovation characteristics will explain limits to internal organization which will consequently induce a search for new hybrid modes[15]. This is illustrated in *Fig. 4.6.*

These *characteristics of innovation* which lead both to shortcomings of market transactions, and to limits of internalizing transactions within a single firm include:

---

14 A number of interesting studies have been published by David J. Teece, David C. Mowery, Gary P. Pisano, and Michael Gerlach, who were involved in joint research at the University of California, Berkeley. More recently, Oliver E. Williamson, the protagonist of transaction cost economics, has teamed up with this group in Berkeley.

15 Teece and his colleagues thus offer further explanations for the impact of innovation on the selection of new hybrid forms of organization, which Williamson (1985, 144) had only vaguely mentioned.

- the degree of *appropriability*;
- the extent to which a *dominant design* has been manifested; and
- the extent to which an innovation requires the use of different *complementary assets*.

The influence of all three characteristics of innovation will be further affected by entry and exit lags. In the following, we will explore the influence of these innovation characteristics on the likely success of new technologies, on the rewards to innovators, and on the mode of governance and organization that will preferably be chosen.

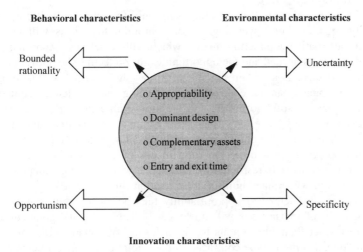

Fig. 4.6:   Innovation Characteristics and the Market and Hierarchy Paradigm

4.3.1   Appropriability Regimes

Appropriability regimes can be defined for a technology or an industry; they describe the legal and institutional framework through which individual agents can clearly specify, negotiate, monitor and implement ownership rights to particular segments of the knowledge base. Appropriability regimes will be defined as *weak*, whenever the knowledge base is difficult to protect, because information can easily be codified and transmitted, and because legal protection mechanisms are ineffective. Appropriability regimes will be called *strong* whenever information is tacit, non-codified and costly to transmit, and if legal mechanisms are effective in protecting the relevant knowledge base.

Appropriabilty regimes are typically weak for early phases of the innovation process and for industries in which basic research plays a strong role (Ouchi and

Bolton 1987). The *externality problem* related to knowledge production and R&D has been emphasized by Arrow (1962), Coase (1974) and Nelson (1959, 1962): private companies have to invest considerable amounts of R&D, while there is an inevitable "leak" of results to other firms. Market contracting between innovating firms will require them to disclose part of the relevant knowledge. Only part of this spill-over effect can be controlled or legally protected. Empirical research indicates that appropriability characteristics vary considerably across industries (Levin et al. 1984). Depending on the industry and the type of innovation involved, we have to differentiate between situations for which the degree of appropriability is very low (typically for basic R&D), low, medium, or high (as illustrated in *Fig. 4.7*).

Market transactions will work effectively only for sufficiently strong appropriability regimes. For lower degrees of appropriability, firms will prefer to switch to alternative contracting modes, which will be selected according to the types of resources needed and the opportunities for protecting the relevant knowledge base. If there is a certain amount of knowledge externality, where appropriability problems can be controlled by reducing one's potential contacts to "reliable agents", "soft" forms of collaboration within networks may suffice. Firms exchange knowledge with other firms within a network in a "quoad usum" type of arrangement. They do not have to rely on sales, rental or equity ownership contracts, but grant each other the right to use part of their knowledge base. Access to the network is restricted to those firms which provide complementary knowledge, and which have built up trust relationships.

As soon as the degree of appropriability falls below a certain critical level, network types of transactions will no longer be sufficient, and companies will prefer to restrict their interactions to "hard forms" of collaboration, preferably through "quoad sortem" type contracts, through joint equity investments by participating agents, and through arrangements with a high degree of exclusiveness. Even those kinds of arrangements may become uncontrollable if the degree of appropriability falls below a minimum level; companies will then only pursue innovation activities through a fully integrated solution (pure in-house development in one firm or a merger of two firms)[16].

The impact of low appropriability is further aggravated if there are long time horizons involved. If both *entry time* (time to develop a new technology) and *exit time* (time to amortize and use the services of a new technology) are considerable,

---

16 Ouchi and Bolton (1987) differentiate between *private property* (equivalent to "strong appropriability regimes"), *leaky property*, and *public property* (equivalent to very "weak appropriability regimes"). They show that the selection of the institutional form is closely related to the underlying appropriability regime. In case descriptions of collaborative R&D projects, they show that the success of collaboration depends on the appropriate identification of interesting search fields *between* private and public konwledge.

firms have greater incentives to control activities through as much integrated and in-house oriented development as possible. Additional reasons, which will be explained in the following sections 4.3.2 and 4.3.3 are needed to explain that firms will still tend to rely on know-how of other partners which cannot be controlled in-house. If this is the case, and if entry and exit times are long, firms try to secure themselves by forming only equity-based joint partnerships.

Degree of appropriability			
High	Medium	Low	Very low
Strong appropriability regime		Weak appropriability regime	
Market solution	"Soft collaboration" (e.g. networks)	"Hard collaboration" (e.g. equity joint-ventures)	Internal solution
"Quid pro quo"	"Quoad usum"	"Quoad sortem"	"Quoad dominium"
Type of contractual arrangement			

Fig. 4.7:   Impact of the Degree of Appropriability on Organization

4.3.2   Formation of a Dominant Design

Major innovations typically are not introduced once and for all but evolve only gradually. Technical standards, design and performance characteristics are established only as a result of a rather extensive and time-consuming trial and error process. This process can be broken down into a pre-paradigmatic stage, during which a dominant design is gradually formed, and a paradigmatic stage for which an agreed upon standard has become established[17]. During the *pre-paradigmatic*

---

17 Historical examples for dominant designs are the Model T Ford, the VHS standard for videorecorders, or the Douglas DC 3 aircraft.

stage, "product designs are fluid, manufacturing processes are loosely and adaptively organized, and more generic types of capital goods are used for production. Competition among firms manifests itself in competition among designs which are markedly different from each other". In contrast, the *paradigmatic stage* features dominant design characteristics for products and technical standards, and competition increasingly shifts to price, leading to a growing emphasis on economies-of-scale. Capital equipment becomes highly dedicated since "reduced uncertainty over product design provides an opportunity to amortize specialized long-lived investments" (Teece 1987, 69)[18].

It is primarily the *pre-paradigmatic* stage which offers many opportunities for collaborative activity. As long as no single, dominant design has become established, the success of any single firm crucially depends on decisions taken by others. This interdependence can be interpreted as network externality (Katz and Shapiro 1986). In order to safeguard investments for innovations, for which a dominant design has not yet become established, firms will be inclined to seek other forms of coordination than can be provided by pure *market* signals. Price signals are almost useless because there are no homogenous products. Detailed and reliable information about new product qualitities and about technical standards cannot be appropriately transmitted through prices.

Market transactions, however, cannot be effectively substituted for by *integrated* modes of coordination during the pre-paradigmatic stage. Only a large firm with a considerable share of the market can attempt to define a dominant design "in-house". An example often used is IBM, which set the System 360 standard quite a long time ago, and which has been a major promoter of the MS-DOS standard for personal computers. But even a dominant firm risks "gambling a company away" if it fails to use its strengths in existing markets for gaining a similarly strong position in uncertain future product markets. There are many examples in which suppliers with large market shares have not succeeded in establishing their preferred design. Sony has not been able to establish the Betamax videotape standard; Philips and Grundig were unsuccessful with their Video 2000 standard.

During the pre-paradigmatic stage of formation of a dominant design, neither the market, nor the integrated solution will thus represent a reliable and dynamically efficient coordination mechanism. Integration within a firm and the attempt to push a standard forward through sheer market power can easily lead to "lock-in" situations where a company "bets on a wrong horse" (Cowan 1989, and Arthur 1988). Conversely, coordination through pure market transactions between many firms will not lead to appropriate results, since information

---

18 This description of the process of technological evolution is based on Abernathy and Utterback (1978), and Clark (1985).

traded is "too thin" and since network externalities will lead to coordination failures[19].

This argument, which is based on dominant design characteristics of an innovation, is strongly related to our considerations of entry and exit time described in chapter 3 and in section 4.1. As long as entry and exit lags for an innovation are rather short, firms "betting" on a particular design during the pre-paradigmatic stage can become quite successful and can count on amortizing their investment in due time. This is quite different if entry and exit lags are long (as illustrated in *Fig. 4.8*). Firms that invest in long R&D programs that are specific to a certain design, run a high risk of not capturing their expenditures if a different design turns out to become dominant.

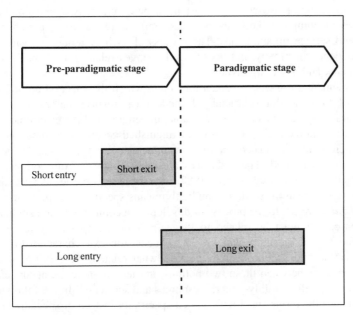

Fig. 4.8:   Dominant Design and Entry and Exit Lags

In such a situation, in which the correctness of choices will become evident only as a result of interactive behavior of several firms, even though choices have to be made today by independent agents, collaboration as an intermediate form of coordination will often turn out to be superior to both the market and the

---

19 An interpretation as a prisoners dilemma type structure is given in Gerybadze (1992, chapter 2).

integrated solution. Collaboration then serves as an externalized search procedure and as a reciprocal reinsurance to prevent the dangers of too long entry lags and uncertain amortization of investments.

4.3.3   Complementary Assets

Many innovations are of a *systemic* nature: in order to achieve a new task, a wide spectrum of resources has to be combined which often involves diverse owner-ship and very difficult coordination assignments. As an example, the introduction of a container freight system requires simultaneous innovations in shipbuilding, harbour facilities, road and rail transportation, as well as information systems. The introduction of new computer systems depends crucially on the simultaneous activities of computer hardware manufacturers, software firms, peripheral sup-pliers and service organizations. The success of such systemic innovations cru-cially depends on timely and coordinated changes related to all major systems components and assets involved[20].

Complementary assets or capabilities upon which the successful commercial-ization of an innovation is crucially dependent, can involve major components of an integrated system (such as the airframe, the engine and the electronics system in aircraft manufacturing), or can be distinguished according to functions: "Ser-vices such as marketing, competitive manufacturing and after-sales support are almost always needed. These services are often obtained from complementary assets that are specialized" (Teece 1987, 70). Teece uses the terms specialization resp. co-specialization, while he implicitly means specificity resp. co-specificity. *Specialization* refers to the process of developing a competence or a sophisticated asset base, and must be related to the *entry* process. *Specificity* refers to the dedicated use of an asset, and has an influence on exit characteristics. While specialization and specificity may be somewhat related, there is no systematic correspondance between these two notions; in the extreme case, agents can spe-cialize on providing highly-generic resources and services[21]. In the following, we will thus use the terms specificity and co-specificity instead of specialization and co-specialization.

Resource ownership for highly-specific assets is often concentrated by a few agents. Established institutional boundaries lead to organizational separation of resource ownership, be it in different business units within a company, or across

---

20 Teece (1986 and 1987) provides examples of unsuccessful innovations which have faltered chiefly because complementary assets had not been coordinated effectively.

21 As an example, modern flexible manufacturing systems are generic and multi-purpose in their application, while they demand an extremely high level of specialization on the side of firms which are involved in developing such new factory automation systems.

independent firms. These different units or firms have to form coalitions[22] which are strong and stable enough to give the right momentum to a major innovation[23]. Such a coalition and its "breakthrough" project will only become successful if a Pareto-superior solution can be designed, through which all members can gain simultaneously. The extent to which this is feasible depends on the types of assets involved and on asset distribution. Teece (1987, 71f) distinguishes between specific and cospecific assets:

Specific assets [own connotation added — A.G.] are those where there is unilateral dependence between the innovation and the complementary asset. *Co-specific assets* are those for which there is bilateral dependence. For instance, specific repair facilities were needed to support the introduction of the rotary engine by Mazda. These assets are co-specific because of the mutual dependence of the innovation on the repair facility. Containerization similarly required the deployment of some co-specific assets in ocean shipping and terminals. However, the dependence of trucking on containerized shipping was less than that of containerized shipping on trucking, as trucks can convert from containers to flatbeds at low cost.

If an asset is specific and unilaterally dependent on an innovation, the asset owner runs a high risk of expropriation of quasi-rents if the innovation turns out to be the wrong choice[24]. If the innovation is unilaterally dependent on a particular asset, its owner will obtain a strong negotiating position. The success of the innovation depends on his provision of services. By charging inappropriately high prices or by delaying his services, he can force the innovation to collapse, and this will lead to the expropriation of quasirents for owners of other specialized assets. There are many examples in which owners of monopolized assets receive the greatest share of revenues from an innovation (e.g. the providers of precious metals for catalytic converters), or where they can even "block" an innovation.

In Fig. 4.9, the degree of dependence of an innovation (or a project) on a particular asset is measured along the horizontal axis. The degree of dependence of the asset on the innovation (or project) in question is measured along the vertical axis. Generic assets illustrated by the area close to the origin do not pose

---

22 We can distinguish between internal coalitions (within a firm) and external coalitions (between firms).

23 This is particularly difficult if the support of many organizations with diverse and often incompatible interests is involved. This seems to be the case with the attempted introduction of High-Definition-Television (HDTV), a new video transmission standard with enhanced image resolution and a new format. For the problem related to the introduction of HDTV, see also our case description in chapter 6.

24 See also our analysis of unilateral vs. bilateral dependence and complementarity in sections 2.4.2 and 3.2.2.

any coordination problems. Owners of resources on which the innovation is uni-laterally dependent, by contrast, will gain a strong negotiating position (illustrated by *zone A* in Fig. 4.9). Within *zone B*, on the other hand, a central coordinator of a project will gain a strong negotiating position vis-à-vis individual resource owners.

Sustainable modes of collaboration will only be achieved in situations with a high degree of cospecificity and bilateral resp. mutilateral dependence (as illus-trated by *zone C* in Fig. 4.9). Inter-related competences and the risk of expropri-ation of quasi-rents will be more balanced between agents. This leads to a certain degree of reciprocity where A depends on B as much as B depends on A. Both will have a strong incentive to maintain a relationship which will jointly push innovation on into the market, and within which they may more easily agree on a "fair" sharing of profits.

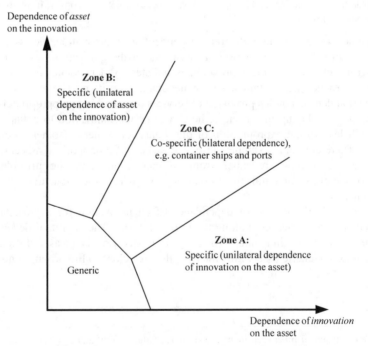

Fig. 4.9:   Complementary Assets: Generic, Specific and Co-specific

With this emphasis on the role of asset complementarity and resource depend-ency, Teece's arguments are very similar to the Austrian capital theoretical expla-nations of the value of complementary goods proposed by Menger (1871) and

Böhm-Bawerk (1921)[25]. Böhm-Bawerk (1921, 206ff) showed, that if none of the factors of a combination can be used without the cooperation of the other members, of which none is replaceable, "one single member has the full value of the group, and the other members are entirely valueless". Other, less extreme forms of resource dependency between agents are also dealt with in his explanation of the value of complementary resources. The cases distinguished by Böhm-Bawerk closely resemble Teece's nomenclature of specific and co-specific assets. Teece's explanation of innovation success is thus primarily a theory of distribution of rewards to owners of critical assets required for the innovation. The question whether a particular form of collaboration is efficient and sustainable, is then a matter of establishing an appropriate distribution and control mechanism, which holds the coalition together for a sufficiently long period.

Whether particular forms of cooperation can become efficient and sustainable, is certainly dependent on the technical characteristics of the innovation and on the types of complementarities between the assets involved (an argument that is emphasized by Teece). But it is at least just as dependent on the *time profile of investment*. If the introduction of an innovation in period $t = s + 1$ is dependent on the mobilization of resources R_A and R_B owned by independent firms A and B, both are willing to "team up" in period $t = s$. If either one of the two firms should decide to "go on its own" it would have to wait longer since both R_A and R_B have to mature over s periods, assuming that the know-how accumulated by each firm cannot easily be transferred to the other[26]. In this case, the assets that are owned by independent firms, and which are necessary for innovation are not transferable because of *a long entry time* (as illustrated by the length of the squares on the left hand side in *Fig. 4.10*).

Long entry time can, however, involve both a unilateral and a bilateral dependence between firms. If firm A controls a resource R_A, which can easily be divested or utilized elsewhere, its exit time is rather short, while firm B may need to hold on to a resource with a long exit time. This is illustrated by *case 1* in the upper part of Fig. 4.10, and may be compared with the relationship between the container ship owner (long exit time) and the truck owner (short exit time) mentioned earlier. In such a case, the dependence between both firms is asymmetric, and it will be rather difficult to include them in a stable bilateral agreement.

The chances for sustainable cooperation are greater, if the required resources R_A and R_B are both characterized by similarly long entry and exit times (as

---

25 See our description in section 2.4.2. One difference between the explanation of both Austrian economists was that Böhm-Bawerk used fixed proportions of complementary capital goods, while Menger allowed for variable proportions. The *fixed proportions* approach of Böhm-Bawerk, although often criticized, is quite suitable for analyzing innovations, since there are often temporary limits for the substitution of highly-specific factors, at least for the early phases of the development of a new technology.

26 If knowledge is tacit and if there are strong appropriability regimes, it will be difficult to transfer know-how across firms.

illustrated by *case 2* in the lower part of Fig. 4.10). Both firms have a strong incentive to pool some activities in period $t = s$, since they can both be sure of bringing an innovation to the market in period $t = s + 1$, which they otherwise would not be able to. In addition to this inducement to enter the coalition, they both have a strong incentive to maintain the relationship, since both would get their quasirents expropriated due to long exit times.

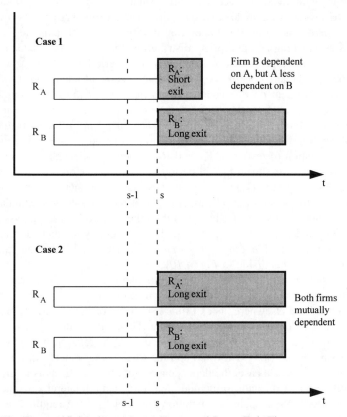

Fig. 4.10: Co-specificity due to Long Entry and Long Exit Time

4.3.4   Organizational Choices

The three characteristics of innovation, namely appropriability, design dominance and asset complementarity are of crucial importance for explaining which modes of governance and organization will be chosen. In particular, this will depend on the *interaction* between these characteristics, and on the comparative *time profile* of complementary resources. Pisano, Russo and Teece (1988, 30ff) distinguish between three distinct modes of coordination: (1) full equity integration modes, (2) equity partnerships, and (3) non-equity partnerships. The first is related to our "integrated solution" explained in chapter 1, while (2) and (3) are two alternative "cooperative solutions". Two other "market solutions", which will be explored in section 4.4, may be added: dynamic networks between suppliers and customers, and the extreme form of spot-markets.

A precondition for choosing one of the three forms of governance and organization is a minimal degree of asset complementarity. Agents choose to pool activities because their assets are complementary to each other; however, they may still be rather indifferent with respect to the particular mode of governance and organization to be chosen. Their decision will be influenced by *entry conditions*:

Owning rather than renting the complementary assets has clear advantages when they are in fixed supply. It is critical, of course, that ownership be obtained before the requirements of the innovation become publicly known, otherwise the price of the assets in question will rise (Pisano, Russo and Teece 1988, 30).

Pisano, Russo and Teece distinguish between critical and less critical assets, the first of which are in fixed supply primarily due to long entry times[27]. If long entry times are involved, firms try to control assets in-house which, however, contradicts their desire to exploit benefits of specialization:

Because there may not be time to acquire or to build the complementary assets that ideally it would like to control, an innovator needs to rank complementary assets. The need for ownership is higher for more critical complementary assets. . . . If the innovator is already a large enterprise with many of the relevant complementary assets under its control, integration is not likely to be the issue that it might otherwise be. However, in industries experiencing rapid technological change, it is unlikely that a single company has the full range of expertise needed to bring advanced products to market in a timely and cost effective fashion (Pisano, Russo and Teece 1988, 30).

For long entry times and a large array of dedicated complementary assets, even the largest firms will thus find it difficult to opt for an integrated solution. Their readiness to relax their requirements for tight in-house control will depend on *appropriability conditions*. Complementary assets combined with a weak appropriability regime will lead to only a limited willingness to choose anything other than an integrated solution. If partnerships with other firms are sought, they will often be based on joint equity and on formal agreements. If, on the other hand, complementary assets are combined with a strong appropriability regime, firms

---

27 In Böhm-Bawerk's (1921) explanation, the key question is to which extent resources are replaceable or irreplaceable. Highly-specific capital goods are primarily irreplaceable because they take a long time to mature.

will be more open to enter (formal or informal) collaborative arrangements, and may even rely on market sourcing, as long as their dependence on outside suppliers does not become critical.

The specific form through which control over complementary assets is achieved will also depend on *dominant design* characteristics. Complete integration will only be a reasonable strategy in the paradigmatic stage, or if the firm is large enough to influence the dominant design during the pre-paradigmatic stage. As long as a dominant design has *not* become established, and if the firm has only a negligible influence on the standard, collaboration with other firms will be a more appropriate strategy. The advantage of collaboration over the integrated solution will become particularly effective if complementary assets are characterized *by long entry and long exit lags*, and if the degree of change is high. Companies that want to pursue an innovation will not try to integrate fully, since it may turn out that the bundle of assets combined in-house will not be appropriate for dealing with successive generations of change. Since entry and exit lags are long, any company that relies on an integrated solution runs a high risk of becoming stuck with its own, highly-specific assets. On the other hand, relying on pure market forms of exchange will not suffice, since owners of strategic resources with long entry times will drive up prices, or will foreclose access to other users. The only answer will often be a long-term relationship between firms built on mutual trust, but which is malleable enough to allow for flexible reconfiguration of assets and coalitions to changing circumstances. The advantage of hybrid modes of governance and organization which Williamson (1985) conjectured for situations with rapid technological change, can thus be explained by the interplay of the three characteristics of innovation, together with a certain time profile of innovation-related investment.

4.4   The Network Model of Collaboration

Over the last few years it has become fashionable to reconsider a rather old concept of inter-firm relationships with a new set of concepts and analytical tools. Medieval guilds and the extensive trade relationships of the Hanse merchants in northern Europe were nothing more than networks built on trust and long-term interactions. The formation of the large modern corporation and its analysis within the economics and business administration literature may have distracted our view from this important aspect of inter-firm relations. On the one hand, the *economics* profession has concentrated on the simple market paradigm emphasizing many independent firms representing production functions for single-product activities, which are interacting anonymously on spot markets. On the other hand, the *business administration* literature has laid an emphasis on production and transaction cost advantages within large, hierarchical firms, which embrace a wide array of vertically integrated activities and multi-product functions.

A number of changes which have already been reflected in the preceding chapters, have led to an increasing reconsideration of new forms of *inter-firm relationships "beyond markets and hierarchies"*. There is no clear and generally agreed upon distinction between these alternative modes of governance and organization, and no precise indication as to where hierarchical relationships are given up, and where market exchange relationships are established, or vice versa. We would prefer to look at equity-based collaboration between a selected group of firms (described within the Teece framework in section 4.3) as a relationship "somewhere close to the hierarchical spectrum". This type of "closed" cooperation is to a large extent based on "quoad sortem" type contracts, and must sooner or later be strengthened through equity ownership contracts.

More "open" types of collaboration, for which "quoad usum" types of agreements are relatively important, can be represented as networks. The concept of a *network* has to be regarded as a mode of governance and organization being closer to the market mode of exchange, but for which participating agents have to rely heavily on dense communication and trust; the network mode of coordination is thus distinctly different from the extreme form of spot markets[28].

A number of empirical studies have shown that the competitiveness of firms and of whole industries depends increasingly on the extent to which dynamic networks of agents can be mobilized. Lorenzoni (1982) has shown in an interesting case study on the textile industry in northern Italy, how 700 firms "disintegrated" into 9,500 suppliers between 1951 and 1976, while their international competitiveness and innovativeness increased considerably. Håkansson (1987), Laage-Hellmann (1989) and several Swedish authors have exemplified, to which extent successful Swedish firms rely on sophisticated networks of supply-relationships in their home country. Similarly, the innovativeness and success of Japanese manufacturers is attributed to a large extent to complex customer-supplier relationships across several fields of expertise (Imai, Nonaka and Takeuchi 1985, Imai and Baba 1991, Kodama 1986, and Twaalfhoven and

---

28 *Spot markets* are fictions which are hardly ever fulfilled in real life. They require large numbers of (replaceable) agents with anonymous interactions. The information traded is primarily price information. There are few repetitive, binary transactions between the same agents. By contrast, *network* transactions are characterized by few agents each representing specialized activities. These agents need to communicate complicated product and process specifications; price is only one element which is non-separable from the rest of the communication spectrum. Frequent transactions between the same agents will become established since they allow for transaction cost savings.

Hattori 1982). Case studies in other countries tend to confirm this type of explanation[29].

Most of these studies, however, tend to be descriptive or rather arbitrary in their selection of explanatory factors. There are few really convincing economic explanations for the superiority and efficiency of the network form of organization. Jarillo (1988) seems to have gone furthest in his configuration of "building blocks in a theory of strategic networks":

Networks are seen as complex arrays of relationships between firms. Firms establish those relationships through interactions with each other. These interactions imply investments to build the relationships which gives consistency to the network. Competing is more a matter of positioning one's firm in the network than attacking the environment. The care of the relationships becomes a priority for management (Jarillo 1988, 22)[30].

An important step forward relative to the extensive network literature which is strongly built on a description of social relationships, is Jarillo's interpretation of *relationships as investment:* "These relationships have all the characteristics of investments, since there is always a certain 'asset specificity' to the know-how of, say, dealing with a given supplier instead of a new one" (Jarillo 1988, 34). This interpretation of relationships as investments allows one to develop a rigorous and more consistent economic framework for the analysis of the relative advantage, efficiency and sustainability of networks.

A *strategic network* is a certain form of governance and organization of complex projects for which participating agents:

- need to pursue a rather *long-term* perspective;
- need to rely on *goal congruence*;
- must be willing to agree on relatively unstructured *tasks* in a rather flexible way;
- must be ready to deal with each other through *"quoad usum" type contracts*, which are often just loosely specified;
- in such situations, *trust relationships* must prevent that one agent mis-uses loosely specified contracts and tasks in his favor.

Strategic networks are suitable mechanisms for governing unstructured and risky projects "beyond hierarchies", which typically cannot cope well with unstructured tasks and unspecified contracts, but also "beyond spot markets", which are

---

29 A description of the strong role of innovative relationships between customers and suppliers for the avionics industry in Britain, France and West Germany can be found in Gerybadze (1987). Baur (1990) has analyzed the interface between large automotive firms and their suppliers in Germany. Theoretical reasons for new types of customer-supplier networks have been analyzed by Siebert (1990).
30 Based on an interpretation of networks as cumulated investments in social and economic relations originally proposed by Johanson and Mattson (1989).

not the appropriate mechanisms for maintaining durable agreements and trust relationships.

Jarillo's explanation of strategic networks is directed towards the fusion of Porter's (1985) value chain concept with Williamson's (1985) transaction cost analysis. The *value chain concept* decomposes activities of business firms (product segments and functions), and tries to identify strategic differentiation for certain market participants[31]. *Transaction cost economics* provides appropriate tools for integrating highly-differentiated activities of numerous market participants, and for designing appropriate institutions[32]. Both concepts combined allow for a similar process of organizational design for multilateral investment, as Kosiol (1962) has suggested for task analysis and task synthesis within a single firm[33].

The concept of the value chain (Porter 1985) is very useful in this effort to break up the firm. Distinguishing different activities within the firm that are, to some extent, independent although inter-related, is important because it reflects reality much better than thinking of the firm as a one-dimensional production function or a 'typical integrated manufacturing firm'. Viewing firms as 'value chains', i.e. collections of activities that add value between suppliers and customers, makes it possible to apply Williamson's concepts with the necessary rigor, for he refers transactions costs to specific 'activities' easily assimilable to 'functions' (or subcomponents of them) of the value chain. These two theoretical developments fit admirably well with each other, for the concept of value chain does not but decompose the firm in distinct 'activities', while the 'transaction costs' approach makes of the transaction (the specific kind of repeated activity) the unit of analysis (Jarillo 1988, 35).

This method of organizational design is closely related to our proposed new concepts which have been outlined in chapter 2, and which will be further developed into an integrative framework of cooperation design in chapter 5. The basic criteria for the choice of institutional structures are the costs of operating institutions (Coase 1937), which are primarily explained by comparative transaction costs. According to Jarillo (1988) and Farmer and MacMillan (1976, 1979), decision-makers in a network are in a repetitive choice situation in which they compare IC, the costs of an internal solution (in-house contracting) with EC,

---

31 The value chain concept, which has become extended and popularized by Porter (1985, 1990), was already described in section 2.4.1, where we have interpreted it as a reformulation of older concepts developed by process oriented theories of organization.

32 While Porter is still interested in the *business firm* as the unit of analysis, Williamson concentrates on the *transaction* as basic unit of analysis. Teece's extension and our own new analytical framework is concentrated on the *project* or the *chain of activity* as unit of analysis. From this last perspective, organizational design and optimization can proceed in a most flexible and unconstrained way.

33 See our analysis in section 2.4.1. An interesting approach which combines the analytical and integrating functions of organizational design can be found in Galbraith (1977, 1983).

the costs of a network-mediated market solution (subcontracting to network participants). The *integrated solution* will be preferred whenever:

$$EC = EP + TC > IC.$$

EC	External Cost
EP	Cost of External Production
TC	Transaction Cost
IC	Internal Cost

If, by contrast, a certain project involves too many complex tasks which require highly-specific knowledge, and which have to be respecified frequently, it will be very unlikely that an integrated solution will offer sustainable cost advantages over the subcontracting solution, which can involve both pure market contracting and networking.

Strategic networks will offer distinctive cost advantages in comparison with both the integrated solution and the market solution, if complex tasks have to be performed by independent agents who can mobilize highly-specific knowledge bases. The costs of transfering knowledge and of agreeing on contracts can be kept at a low level within a network. There are three reasons why external costs (EC) can be reduced relative to internal costs (IC), if agents collaborate within a network. *First, transaction costs (TC)* can be reduced by contracting only with a small group of well-known and trust-worthy market participants. Similarly, transaction costs may be reduced by channeling all communication through a hub-firm which may be a general contractor or a systems integrator[34].

Second, a functioning network allows for the effective reduction of *production costs (EP)* through specialization effects:

It allows a firm to specialize in those activities of the value chain that are essential to its competitive advantage, reaping all the benefits of specialization, focus and possibly, size. The other activities are then farmed out to members of the network that carry them out more efficiently than the 'hub firm' would, since they are specialized in them (Jarillo 1988, 35).

Third, a network provides transparancy and a regular and objective monitoring of changes in the external and internal cost structure. This leads to discipline and to an appropriate incentive alignment for the participating members of all internal and external sub-coalitions within a network.

A very important benefit of a networking arrangement over an integrated solution is, according to Farmer and MacMillan, that efficiency is fostered because the 'market test

---

34 A network *with* a hub can be regarded as a more hierarchically organized network than one without a hub.

is still applicable. No matter how close the relationship between buyers and sellers, no matter how long it has endured, if better trading terms (considering quality, quantity, timing and price) can be obtained elsewhere, there is no permanent tie to stop either party making alternative arrangements' (1979, 283). Thus networking introduces a cost discipline that may be absent in an integrated firm with its captive internal markets (Jarillo 1988, 35).

These three arguments, namely specialization advantages of several independent firms, transaction cost savings through a specialized trading and communication structure, together with the incentive alignment and discipline established, can explain why strategic networks can assure sustainable cost savings over all other modes of governance and organization.

This sustainable comparative advantage of strategic networks can also be interpreted within our capital theoretical model. If there are several firms which have invested into complementary capital goods or knowledge with long entry and exit times, the incentives for all participants to form a network are rather high. Each participant can gain by relying on long lead times achieved by others. In period t_1, company A can build on the specialization advantages of firms B, C, and D, which would be too time-consuming for A to replicate (see *Fig. 4.11*). On the other hand, companies A, B, C, and D are not prepared to trade their capabilities over spot markets because of long exit times. They all prefer to interact within the close circle A, B, C, D, where they can rely on repetitive transactions, and where the risk of an expropriation of quasi-rents is comparatively low.

These trust-based relationships and implicit agreements that firm A will "go along" with firms B, C, and D, however, will only be maintained as long as each firm remains reasonably price-competitive and innovative. If firm D misses switching to an alternative new technology which will be captured by firm E, A is still flexible enough in period t_2 to switch to E as an alternative supplier. The dynamic network thus keeps participating firms under permanant "creative pressure" to remain price-competitive and innovative.

Long entry and exit times together with rapid change were also used as explanatory factors for more equity-based and tightly controlled cooperative arrangements between two firms (as outlined in section 4.3). What can explain the comparative advantage of dynamic networks over "harder" and more codified forms of collaboration? The answer is dependent on the type and characteristics of assets involved. If there is a rather small number of complementary investment goods, each of which requires high entry and exit costs, together with long entry and exit lags, more codified forms of cooperation between firms appear to be the best solution. If investments have to be "truncated" in capital equipment, participating firms will have to rely on contractual arrangements emphasizing "quoad sortem" type contracts for some assets, and equity ownership for others.

If, on the other hand, there are many diverse complementary tasks, for which highly-specific knowledge bases are characterized by long lead times as well as

long exit times, while entry and exit costs are comparatively low, dynamic networks are more suitable forms of coordination. "Capital invested" is not of a
"hardware" type but is more related to the time and endurance needed to build
up social relationships and trust. Participating agents contribute knowledge and
real assets through "quoad usum" type of arrangements. Networks within a certain distributed base of core competencies or at a regional level can be highly-ef-
ficient and stable over long periods of time. They are a strong factor in explaining
comparative advantages of firms within an industry, a region, or at the national
level[35].

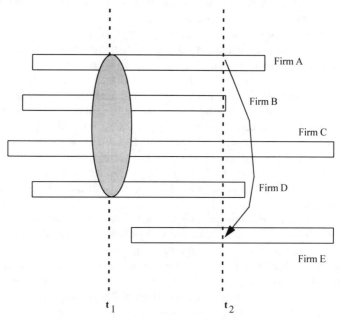

Fig. 4.11: Long Entry and Exit Times of Firms Within a Dynamic Network

---

35 More recent studies of the international competitiveness of industries or nations emphasize
   this strong influence of efficient networks. See Ohmae (1990), Porter (1990), Teece (1991),
   and Prahalad and Hamel (1991).

Part III: Project Structuring and Cooperation Design

5   A Model for Structuring Cooperative Investment Projects

5.1   Outline of the Model

In this chapter, we want to introduce a general method for structuring complex investment projects. This method will later be applied to study specific empirical problems of investment (chapter 6) and finance (chapter 7). Our method is built upon the capital theoretical and neo-institutional concepts introduced in chapters 2 to 4; these concepts are integrated into a coherent structuring framework which is generic and flexible enough to allow for an "open design" of complex, collaborative projects.

Whereas most existing concepts of organization theory and neo-institutional economics still view either the business firm or a single transaction as the basic unit of analysis, our method is based on the *project as unit of analysis,* and as the starting-point for any structuring process. The older concepts were used to analyze and systematize all tasks and functions within a particular firm with predetermined strategies, business objectives and tasks. Our process redesign and project structuring framework outlined in this chapter leaves greater flexibility with respect to agent participation, goal formation, task selection, and organizational structure. The investigation of the investment process is started in a very early, conceptual phase. We do not assume a given institutional structure, for example, a firm A, with a predetermined objective function[1]. Instead, we try to structure an investment project, and the way it is organized and financed, on the basis of goals and capabilities that can be independently pursued and controlled by diverse groups of agents.

Each of these agents, which are interested in particular types of investment projects, can explore and find out that there are other agents with similar goals, who may possess complementary capabilities. Agents with related goals can decide to compete with each other, or they can form coalitions, depending on the way resources and capabilities are distributed. If agents prefer to enter a coalition,

---

1   The managerial and the behavioral theories of the firm, as well as modern theory of finance view the firm as instrumentality of individual agents, and not as an autonomous entity with a predetermined objective function. According to Cyert and March (1963) and March (1989), firms persist in a state of "quasi-resolution of conflict", which is stabilized through a nexus of treaties among participants. While Cyert and March's analysis was directed at "quasi-resolution of conflict" *within* an integrated business firm, our model tries to extend this view towards collaborative modes of governance and organization.

they can again choose between an internal (integration within a single firm) or an external coalition (cooperation). The appropriate organizational structure is derived as a result of goal specification, process redesign and task analysis, and is based on the analysis of the resource ownership pattern. Institutional structures are not assumed to be given, but will be selected according to their relative economic advantage, and their comparative performance in bringing interests and capabilities of different groups of asset owners into alignment.

Our proposed method can be used to analyze a wide array of cooperative institutional arrangements. While most existing studies on networks and collaborative projects remain rather descriptive, a few authors have attempted to develop more general theoretical concepts. New theories and new process redesign concepts are directed at figuring out general relationships between the following "building blocs": (1) agents, (2) goals, (3) processes and tasks, (4) resources, (5) resource ownership, (6) capabilities, (7) contract modes, and (8) discrete structural alternatives. Each "building bloc" can be described by a finite set of elements. A project is seen as a particular configuration or "ensemble" of these generic "building-blocs". While some researchers presently work along similar lines, there has so far been no existing approach published in the literature, that has succeeded in developing an *integrated project structuring framework*.

The application of the model outlined in this chapter can be interpreted as a problem-solving process over time. One typically starts with the identification of a problem, and goes on with the consideration of alternative problem solutions. Identified problems can be related to transportation bottlenecks, environmental hazards, insufficient company growth, or unemployment. In order to overcome perceived problems, and to achieve an appropriate problem solution, agents must pursue goals. As an example, a firm that wants to overcome growth or employment problems may pursue the goal of expanding its activities to foreign markets. Similarly, transportation problems can imply the goal of modernizing or extending the rail network within a particular country. To improve environmental quality, agents may pursue the goal of cleaning a river, such as the Elbe or the Rhine, within a predetermined time frame[2].

Perceived problems and related goals can be attributed to particular agents or groups of agents. Certainly, large and complex problems will often involve very large groups and diverse constituencies, while small and non-complex problems can be solved by small groups. Any effective problem-solution, no matter how large and complex the project to be achieved, however, will require clear identi-

---

2   This will typically imply attaining certain standards of water quality (oxygen content to be increased, toxic metal content to be reduced) within a five- or ten-year time period. The Rhine has been a target of German environmental policy during the 1980s. Improving water quality of the Elbe has gained top priority for this decade.

fication of the group of agents involved, and to keep that group within a contain-able size-range[3].

For any goal precisely enough specified, we will typically be able to identify a group of agents who have a similar or related interest. For these agents we will then go on to investigate in detail what might be the appropriate form for their interaction: they may decide to coordinate their activities within a fully-inte-grated, hierarchical firm. For other purposes, agents may prefer to interact through cooperative modes of governance and organization, be it through joint ownership contracts, or merely through non-ownership joint projects. For other purposes, still, it may be economically superior to interact through market-medi-ated sales and service contracts. Given this last market mode of coordination, participating agents can specialize on complementary activities; but they can also decide to pursue duplicated activities, and may end up in competition with each other[4]. By just looking at the goals which two or more agents have in common, we cannot exactly say which type of interaction or institutional form they will eventually choose[5]. However, we can use the information on the congruence of goals as a starting-point for analyzing processes and tasks, and to pre-select alternative ways to achieve their goals.

The logical sequence of our proposed project structuring and process redesign framework is outlined in *Fig. 5.1*. Step 1 consists of a pre-selection of agents with similar goals (matrix 5.1a), who may consider formation of a coalition. In step 2, process alternatives are related to particular goals (matrix 5.1b), and agree-ment on a particular process has to be achieved. In step 3, relevant processes are described as sequences of tasks or activities (matrix 5.1c). The selection of a particular sequence of activities leads to the identification and deployment of specific resources (step 4, illustrated in matrix 5.1d). Finally during step 5 (illus-trated in matrix 5.1e), the analysis of the resource distribution pattern and of the capabilities of individual agents will influence the types of contracts and the institutional arrangements to be chosen.

During the most important first step within this project structuring frame-work illustrated in Fig. 5.1, we will use the available *information on agents*

---

3   We will show in chapter 8, that even large and complex problems may be decomposed such that effective organization and management can become feasible.

4   This last form of competition, in which each firm "plays strategically against the market" is described in Porter's (1980) original *competitive strategy framework*. This framework has been criticized by Håkansson (1987) and Jarillo (1988). In Porter's (1990) most recent publications, more open strategy models, embracing both competitive as well as collabora-tive behavior of firms, are also considered.

5   As has been outlined in section 2.3, the choice of the appropriate institutional form must be based on a detailed investigation of tasks, on resource specification, and on the analysis of the resource ownership pattern.

and goals in order to pre-select a specific goal and a related sub group of agents. In *matrix 5.1a*, goals are represented as rows, while agents are represented as columns. For numerical purposes, agents that pursue a particular goal, can be marked by "1" in the respective row, while agents that do not pursue this goal are marked by "0". The sub-group of agents represented by a "1" in the same row, i.e. the agents that pursue the same objective will then be candidates to form a coalition. In order to decide whether a coalition will really become viable, and which particular form of coordination should be chosen, we must know more about the specific processes, tasks and resources needed to attain the desired goal.

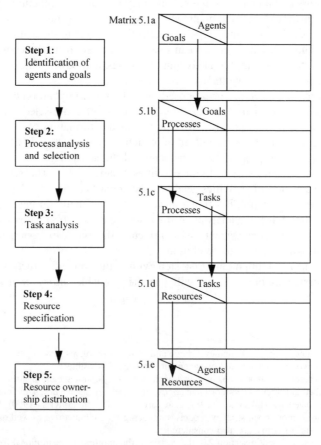

Fig. 5.1:   The Generic Sequence for Structuring Cooperative Investment
            Projects

Any goal represented by a row in Fig. 5.1a can be related to a finite number of processes. The *relationship between goals and processes* is described by *matrix 5.1b*. If elements in this matrix are either zero or one, we can easily select the process options which can be pursued in order to achieve one particular goal: only processes marked by "1" in the respective row will be considered further. In addition, if the strengh of the relationship between goals and processes is measured by a positive number between zero and one, we are able to rank alternative processes. As a result, several process options can be dismissed instantly; others will be considered further, and can be ranked according to their degree of goal-fulfillment. As a result, we may derive a short-list of one or only few dominant processes[6]. For this shortlist of dominant processes, we then need to pursue a detailed task analysis, an identification of project steps or activities, their time sequence, and their specific pattern of interrelatedness[7]. The results of this *task analysis* can be described by a matrix, as illustrated in *matrix 5.1c*; for practical and for illustrative purposes, they may also be represented by flow-charts. Based on the information provided through detailled task analysis, we are able to identify which types of resources (skilled labor, capital equipment, technical know-how, buildings, finance, etc.) have to be mobilized at which point in time (see *matrix 5.1d*).

It is primarily the question of *resource availability and resource ownership* which leads one to consider organizational questions. Resources are often proprietary, scarce, difficult to access, and often of a durable kind. If there are many different and highly-specific resources needed to run a certain process, it will be unlikely that single agents can be in control of all of them. As a result, different agents, who pursue related goals and processes for which complementary resources are needed, will seek certain forms of coalitions. The type of coalition to be formed, the benefits and costs derived from it by each participating agent, as well as the stability of the coalition will depend crucially on the *relationship between agents and resources* (see *matrix 5.1e*). Situations in which agents pursue similar goals, for which they all control part of the resource base in a complementary way, are ideal for cooperation. Duplicated ownership, by contrast, will result in a more competitive situation.

In order to analyze which type of organizational solution may be the most suitable coordination mechanism, it is important to consider the specific characteristics of the resources needed. It will be required to ask the following questions, which determine the entry and exit conditions specific for particular investment projects:

---

6   According to our analysis in sections 2.2 and 2.3, there will typically be only two or three dominant processes, which can be selected very early, if goals are specified well enough.

7   This task analysis can be pursued with the help of personal-computer-based project management tools.

- To which extent are resources *proprietary*?
- Can *entry* be prohibited or delayed by long entry times?
- To which extent are resources *replaceable* or substitutable?
- Are the required resources task-specific or coalition-*specific*?
- To which extent are resources durable, and characterized by high *exit* costs and/or long exit times?
- Are resource-owners endangered by early obsolescence and *expropriation of quasi-rents*?

Once the tasks and resources as well as their specific characteristics and owner-ship patterns have been identified, one can apply the theoretical framework out-lined in chapters 2 to 4. In these preceding chapters, we have analyzed the capital theoretical and neo-institutional concepts relevant for guiding decisions on appro-priate institutional design. The formation of institutional structure was described as an endogenous result of process redesign. The theoretical concepts proposed serve as a basis for analysis and evolution of a wide spectrum of alternative organizational solutions, including different forms of joint-ventures between firms, temporary strategic alliances, industry and trade associations, and dynamic networks on a horizontal, vertical as well as regional level.

Choices between different institutional arrangements are not arbitrary. For each ensemble of agents, goals, processes and resources, there will only be one or few organizational alternatives, through which an investment project can be main-tained efficiently. To select appropriate institutional structures and to support business decision-making processes, we can apply our proposed project structur-ing and process redesign methodology. This structured approach can be applied to many different types of investment decisions, and is particularly suited for projects, which are characterized by a complex task-structure, and for which we have to involve two or more independent agents. The proposed model for struc-turing complex projects is described in detail in the following sections.

5.2   Specification of Goals and Tasks of Independent Agents

We shall consider a group of independent agents A_k, $k = 1, \ldots, K$, who can be either individuals or firms. Agents are assumed to pursue a finite number of distinct goals G_g, $g = 1, \ldots, L$. These goals can involve rather broadly defined financial and economic objectives such as attempted growth or return on invest-ment targets. As an example, a group of investors may pursue the objective of realizing a return on investment of 20% in the retail business. Goals may also be defined more specifically: some investors may attempt to gain a 10% market share within a particular segment of the Japanese machine-tool mar-ket within three years. Specific goals can be directly or indirectly related to the search for new technologies and their application[8]. Finally, objectives can be formulated for a wider scope with a larger group of beneficiaries, such as the goal to improve air quality, to modernize the transportation system, or to generate employment opportunities within a region.

Whatever the goals pursued may be, agents will always be split into two fractions, the group of supporters and the group of non-supporters. If the goal involves gaining a 10% market share of the Japanese machine-tool market, the *group of supporters* will be rather small, and will typically only include a few firms with an active interest in machine-tools and in the Japanese market. Most other agents will be *indifferent* because they are interested neither in machine-tools nor in the Japanese market. In addition, some agents will openly resist the goal pursued (direct competitors or other adversely affected groups). For other objectives with a wider scope such as the goal for an amelioration of air quality, or for the improvement of the transportation system, there will be a much larger group of potential supporters, while at the same time there may be many agents who are indifferent or even against the attempted change. To pursue objectives, agents must be ready to coordinate their aspirations, particularly if there is a high degree of interdependence between activities and resources. The group of supporters has to be narrowed down, and it may be helpful to collectively organize its members. Opponents can then be neutralized, compensated, co-opted or integrated through some institutional or financial arrangement. To pursue goals effectively, the group of agents positively affected has to become clearly separated from the group of agents who are unaffected or indifferent.

For reasons of simplicity, we will consider only binary choices: some agents are identified as supporters of a goal[9], while all others who do not support this goal are considered as indifferent and non-interested. In accordance with matrix 5.1a outlined above, we have mapped *agents* along the horizontal axis in *Fig. 5.2*, and *goals* along the vertical axis. If goal G_g is *supported* by agent A_k, this will be indicated by a *"one"* in row l and column k. If agent A_k is *non-interested* in goal G_g, the respective value is zero. Based on this mapping of agents and goals, we are able to effectively narrow down the group of agents who have to

---

8 New technologies may be needed to attain commercial objectives such as a 10% share of the Japanese machine-tool market (indirect relationship between technologies and goals); in other cases, agents pursue the development of a new technology as a primary objective (direct correspondence between a goal and a technology).

9 Our model would become very complicated if we were to consider agents with different levels of interest and with different reasons for indifference and opposition. Our primary motive is to preselect the group of supporters for a goal, whatever their interest and level of aspiration may be. At later stages of the process, when a fairly small group of agents has been identified, it may be helpful to differentiate in more detail and also in a more qualitative way.

coordinate their aspirations and who may be required to form a coalition. Coalitions would not make sense if only one element in any row were positive while all other elements were zero, and if two separate goals can be pursued without dependence on the same resources. Complete separability of goals[10] would allow each of the agents to pursue its own interest, and no agent would have to take care of other agents' interests. If, by contrast, there is more than one supporter for an objective G_g, or if two separate goals are dependent on jointly-used resources, coordination between agents will be required.

In Fig. 5.2, the sub-group of agents $\{A_1, A_2, \ldots, A_k\}$ may consider formation of a coalition. While for goals G_1 and G_2, there is only one agent interested, goal G_g is supported by the sub-group of agents $\{A_1, A_2, \ldots, A_k\}$, who may find it useful to coordinate their activities in a more organized way[11].

Goals	Agents							
	A_1	A_2	A_3	$\cdots$	A_k	A_{k+1}	$\cdots$	A_K
G_1	1	0	0	$\ldots$	0	0	$\ldots$	0
G_2	0	1	0	$\ldots$	0	0	$\ldots$	0
$\vdots$								
G_g	1	1	1		1	0	$\ldots$	0
$\vdots$								
G_L	0	0	0	$\ldots$	1	1	$\ldots$	1

Fig. 5.2:   The Relationship between Agents and their Goals

---

10 Complete separability of goals requires that two agents pursue different goals, which are not dependent on jointly-used resources. Agents may be induced to form coalitions for securing access to jointly-used resources, even if they do not pursue the same goals. This is often the case in political decision-making ("log-rolling"). At this stage, we will omit resource-dependency as an inducement for coalition-formation, and will concentrate on the question whether agents pursue congruent goals or not.

11 At this point we cannot say if a coalition will be feasible and sustainable, nor is it possible to conclude what form of coalition or governance mode (integration, cooperation or market exchange) will be most appropriate. This can only be answered when we know more about the task structure and about the distribution of resource ownership. See sections 5.4 and 5.5.

In order to ascertain whether independent agents can be convinced about forming a coalition and whether they can agree on an appropriate solution for joint activity, we need to understand more about the processes and tasks required to attain the goals. Agents may easily agree on a joint target, but they may favor different approaches to reach this target. As an example, an improved *transportation* system can be achieved through individualized transport modes (e. g. automobiles) favored by some groups of agents; other agents will prefer processes emphasizing mass transportation modes (such as rail transportation). In order to improve *broadcasting* systems, satellite and cable transmission represent alternative processes. As will be shown in chapter 6, different constituencies and interest groups opt for each of these alternative process solutions. While agents may pursue similar goals, their preferences as to how these goals should be achieved are quite different and will often be in conflict. If they can come to no agreement, two groups with differing preferences for particular process alternatives may end up in entrenched competition with each other.

A very important requirement for the formation and sustainability of cooperation agreements is that coalition members agree on *one process* to be pursued in order to reach the joint goal G_g. In *Fig. 5.3*, we have illustrated the procedure which is required for process analysis and process selection (in accordance with step 2 in Fig. 5.1). To achieve a particular goal G_g, three processes P_{1g}, P_{2g} and P_{3g} are available. All three processes can be characterized by a sequence of tasks or activities, as illustrated by the graphs in the lower section in Fig. 5.3. Not all agents that are interested in goals G_g will also prefer to apply the same process. As a result of process analysis and process selection, however, we may identify a sub-group of agents who are willing to form a coalition in order to jointly pursue one single process P_{1g}. The shaded area in the lower section in Fig. 5.3 illustrates the sequence of activities preferred by this particular sub-group of agents. Agreement on one particular process or a sequence of activities may also be called a common *standard*[12].

Based on the described mapping of goals of different agents and of corresponding process alternatives, we can narrow down the group of agents who are likely to form a coalition. Coalitions will only be sought by agents who are characterized by a having a minimum degree of *joint interest*. This includes common interests with respect to goals pursued by the members of the coalition (as illustrated by positive row elements in Fig. 5.2). Furthermore, agents must express a common interest regarding the selection of a specific process through which their joint goals are to be achieved.

---

12 Particularly during the early phases of technological evolution, two or more processes compete against each other, and it is hard to anticipate which one will eventually evolve as the dominant design. Two or more coalitions are formed and each tries to convince the other's members to convert. See Arthur (1988) and Cowan (1989).

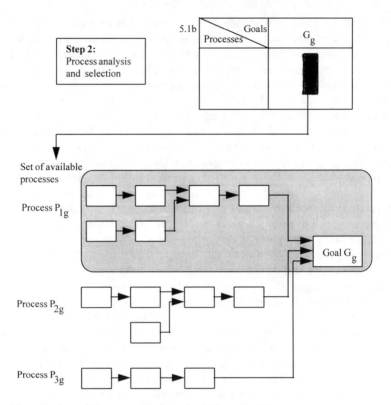

Fig. 5.3:   Goals and Processes Preferred within a Coalition

Given a specific goal G_g, a selection of a process through which this goal can best be reached, and the subset of agents with a preference for G_g and a specific process P_{1g}, we can start with a detailed *task analysis*[13]. Tasks are defined as interrelated process steps or activities which can be ordered according to their time sequence, or in a logical sequence. Tasks and activities[14] can represent:

– *components* or modules for assembled products (e.g. the decomposition of automobile manufacturing into major parts such as the body, the engine, the drivetrain and suspension system, as well as electronic subsystems);

---

13 The methodology of task analysis has been developed within the tradition of process-oriented German organization literature, particularly by Nordsieck (1934) and Kosiol (1962) as described in section 2.4.

14 In accordance with the nomenclature introduced in chapter 2, the terms "task" and "activity" will be used synonymously.

– *process steps*, particularly in the case of continuous flow processes (e.g. the typical process sequence for petrochemicals);
– *as well as functions* (R&D, procurement, manufacturing, out-bound logistics and sales).

As a result of process analysis and process selection (step 2 in matrix 5.1b), we are able to proceed with steps 3 and 4, namely with task analysis and resource specification. This is illustrated in the upper section in Fig. 5.4, where the two small matrices correspond to Figs. 5.1c and 5.1d respectively. For a more detailed analysis of tasks and resources, we have enlarged the original matrix 5.1d in the lower section of Fig. 5.4. The rows in this matrix contain tasks T_1, T_2, . . ., T_5, which are needed to perform the selected process and to achieve the desired goal.

For any single task, it is necessary to combine specific resources in an ordered sequence; the resources needed to perform each particular tasks are listed along the vertical axis in the enlarged matrix in Fig. 5.4. To assemble a car, as an example, an automotive manufacturer has to control a diverse array of specialized parts, machinery, labor, as well as resources needed for in-bound and out-bound logistics. In order to operate a satellite broadcasting system, an organization has to be in control of a satellite, the corresponding earth stations, transmission systems, and a number of related resources. Not all resources required must simultaneously be owned and controlled by one single firm. For each single task, we can specify the resources that will be needed such as:

– *labor* and human skills (nominated by L in Fig. 5.4);
– *technologies* and specific knowledge (T);
– *capital equipment*, machinery and buildings (C);
– *natural resources* (N);
– *financial resources* (F);
– as well as *legal and regulatory* resources (R)[15].

Elements of the matrix in Fig. 5.4 may contain numbers or qualitive indicators. They may be represented by a binary code (0,1), with the *"one"* meaning that a specific resource is needed for task T_m. The correspondance between resources and tasks can also be described by an input/output table: its elements could then be described as coefficients indicating the quantity of a resource needed to perform a certain activity level. In addition to such purely quantitive relationships,

---

15 *Legal* and *regulatory resources* are very important for explaining the feasibility and the adoption of new processes and technologies (e.g. in pharmaceuticals, genetic engineering, transportation and in telecommunication), and must therefore often be considered as a "critical asset". As a result, public agents who are in control of such critical assets must be involved in the joint decision-making process. See also our analysis of public-private partnerships in chapter 8.

Fig. 5.4 could also be used as a basis for an extended description of the time sequence or of qualitative process characteristics.

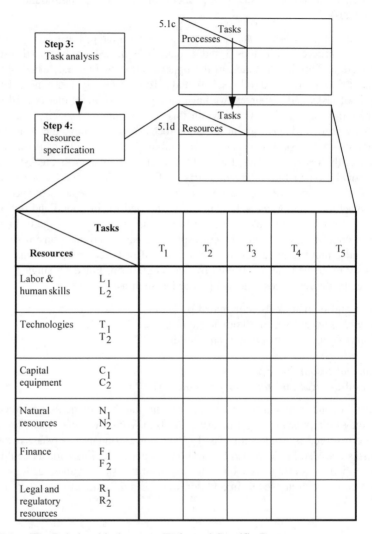

Fig. 5.4:   The Relationship between Tasks and Specific Resources

Given these resource requirements to be derived from task analysis, we will also have to distinguish between *critical and less critical resources;* otherwise we would have to encounter too complex choice situations. For many tasks we would have to mobilize hundreds or even thousands of distinct varieties of resources. An automotive manufacturer has to control several thousand different parts and components, only a certain fraction of which will gain a critical dimension for him. While the term "critical resource" is often used in business and strategic planning applications, its theoretical content has rarely been precisely defined. It is our intent to show that the "critical character of resources" is determined by entry and exit conditions which have already been analyzed in chapters 3 and 4. *Entry conditions* are characterized:

– by the extent to which resources are *proprietary;*
– by *entry* times and entry cost;
– and by the extent to which resources are *replaceable* or substitutable.

Exit conditions, on the other hand, are characterized:

– by the degree of *specificity* of resources;
– by *exit time and exit cost;*
– and by the extent of potential *expropriation of quasi-rents* for resource owners.

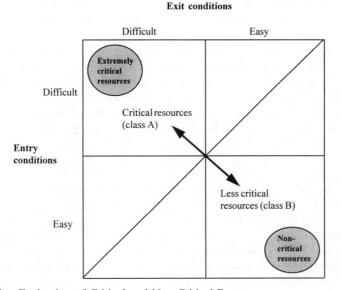

Fig. 5.5:   Evaluation of Critical and Non-Critical Resources

Based on these characteristics of entry and exit conditions, we can evaluate all resources required to perform a particular task (see *Fig. 5.5*). Some resources can hardly be made accessible, or entry is very expensive and time-consuming (as illustrated in the upper section of Fig. 5.5). Other resources may be rather easy to access, and may be mapped in the lower section in Fig. 5.5. In a related way, resources can be grouped in two classes characterized by different exit conditions, which are represented by the left side (for difficult exit), and by the right side (for easy exit) in Fig. 5.5. All resources mapped northwest of the diagonal line in Fig 5.5 will be classified as *critical resources*, or as resources of class A. All resources south-east of the diagonal line will accordingly be classified as *less critical* or as *non-critical resources*, or as resources of class B.

We can also further distinguish between different degrees of entry and exit conditions. *Extremely critical resources* will be located accordingly near the north-west corner in Fig. 5.5. These extremely critical resources display characteristics which correspond to Böhm-Bawerk's case of rigidly fixed proportions, which has been described in section 2.4: none of the factors of a combination can be used without the cooperation of the other combination member(s) (extremely difficult *exit* conditions), and none of the factors is replaceable (extremely difficult *entry* conditions). At the other end of the spectrum, we find resources with very easy entry and exit conditions, and which may be located near the south-east corner in Fig. 5.5. These non-critical resources which do not call for any type of coordination other than pure market contracting, correspond to Böhm-Bawerk's extreme case of full replaceability and undifferentiated value within and outside of a combination.

In the following, the concern will be with the coordination and organization of projects which require *critical* resources; we will focus our analysis primarily on the class A type of the resource spectrum. For many large and complex investment projects, the tasks to be performed will often require very sophisticated and highly-specific resources. At the same time, resource ownership will be dispersed and segregated, i.e. each economic agent will only command a tiny fraction of the whole resource spectrum. Highly-segregated resource flows have to be coordinated, and independent agents will often be required to form coalitions. The principal question is then, how agents can secure complete access to very specific and unevenly distributed resources, and how they can make sure that each resource can be mobilized at the right quality level, time and location. For extremely critical resources located at the far north-western end of the resource spectrum in Fig. 5.5, agents will be inclined to become organized within an integrated firm. Collaborative agreements will be most appropriate to secure coordination of those resources which are located above the diagonal line in Fig. 5.5, but which are not characterized by extreme values of entry and exit conditions. Resources located *below* the diagonal line, by contrast, can be coordinated by market-type transactions, be it through market networks (for resources located near the diagonal line), or through perfectly competitive spot markets, the extreme form of coordination applicable only for resources located close to the south-east corner of the resource spectrum in Fig. 5.5.

To analyze which particular institutional arrangement will be chosen to co-ordinate critical resources, we will have to specify the characteristics of resources as well as the resource ownership pattern in more detail. This will be done in section 5.3.

5.3 Distribution of Resources between Independent Agents

In Fig. 5.2 we have illustrated the relationship between agents and goals. We have focused on a specific goal G_g, which is pursued by agents A_1, A_2, ..., A_k. We will assume that these agents can all agree on the same process (P_{1g}) in order to achieve goal G_g. Fig. 5.4 lists all resources required to run process P_{1g} efficiently. The more the required resources are characterized by restrictive entry and exit conditions as specified in the preceding section, and the greater the requirement to benefit from past investments in highly-specific capabilities and skills, the greater the probability that each agent will own or control only a very narrow range of the required resource spectrum. Depending on the extent to which highly-specific, non-transferable assets are owned by others, agents are more or less strongly induced to participate in collaborative agreements. Whether cooperation can become a cost-minimizing, sustainable solution, will depend on the distribution of resource ownership and on the type of interdependence between agents A_1, A_2, ..., A_k.

In accordance with step 5, illustrated in matrix 5.1e, we can proceed with an *analysis of the resource ownership distribution*. *Fig. 5.6* provides information on resource ownership and on the relative strengths of independent agents. Again, we can simplify the resource distribution pattern by allowing only binary choices. An agent can either possess the resource in the appropriate form (marked by "one"), or he will not possess it (marked by "zero")[16]. For illustrative purposes, the shaded areas in Fig. 5.6a to 5.6c symbolize resource capabilities, while blank areas indicate that agents do not possess the resource in question. We will differentiate between three stylized *resource distribution patterns* which can be described by the following characteristics:

– the type and degree of *complementarity* between resources;

---

16 We could also modify this assumption by allowing for a more differentiated evaluation of strengths and weaknesses. Such a more differentiated evaluation could be achieved by attributing a positive number in the interval [0,1] for each individual agent in the respective row. Our structured approach allows for a two-step procedure. During the *first step*, resource holders are identified by binary classifications, indicating whether an agent controls the resource in question. In a *second step*, strengths and weaknesses may be identified through a more detailed evaluation of resource capabilities for each individual agent.

– the extent to which a coalition controls the whole spectrum of resources needed (*completeness*);
– and the *distribution of property rights* among members of a potential coalition.

The resource distribution pattern to be described by these three characteristics will influence to which extent agents will be willing to form coalitions, which particular contractual arrangements are most likely to be chosen, and to what extent a particular coalition will be stable and sustainable. To illustrate this, we will first look at different combinations of the first two characteristics, namely the degree of complementarity and the extent of completeness. We will distinguish between three different cases:

– *Case 1* (*completeness and complementarity*): resources of different agents within the potential coalition are exhaustive *and* mutually exclusive;
– *Case 2* (*complementarity, no completeness*): resources owned within the potential coalition are mutually exclusive, but not exhaustive;
– *Case 3* (*completeness, no complementarity*): exhaustive resource ownership within the group is complicated due to competing, partially duplicated ownership (resources owned by member agents are not mutually exclusive).

In *Case 1*, which can be illustrated by the matrix in *Fig. 5.6a*, members of the potential coalition $(A_1, \ldots, A_k)$ possess the full range of resources and skills required to attain the joint goal G_g. Furthermore, resource ownership is highly complementary, since each agent possesses resources which the other agents need (mutual exclusiveness). In such a situation, there are strong incentives to enter the coalition and to keep it sustainable for a certain time period. All agents within the coalition are reciprocally dependent on each other. As a group they control the whole spectrum of resources needed, and their team is self-sufficient. This will stabilize the coalition and will allow for a structure of mutual benefit.

In Case 2, which is illustrated in *Fig. 5.6b*, members of the potential coalition possess some complementary resources, but are also critically dependent on resources and skills owned by non-coalition members (non-exhaustiveness). The coalition $\{A1, \ldots, Ak\}$ can only be stabilized, if the in-flow of resources owned by others can be secured and consistently maintained. However, there is a risk that agents $A_{k+1}, \ldots, A_K$ distract key resources for other purposes, or that they charge unfavorable prices. The success and sustainability of the coalition $\{A_1, \ldots, A_k\}$ is highly dependent on these external conditions[17].

---

17 An extreme situation would involve members $A_{k+1}, \ldots, A_K$ in a competing coalition (coalition 2), pursuing a competing process that can be fully maintained on the basis of resources owned within this second coalition. Coalition 1 would be asymmetrically dependent on coalition 2, which would result in the eventual dominance of the process favored by the last.

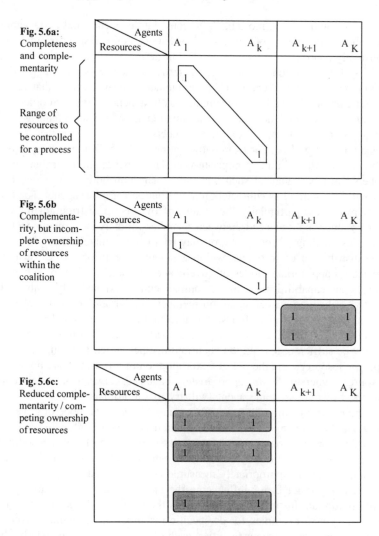

Fig. 5.6a: Completeness and complementarity

Range of resources to be controlled for a process

Fig. 5.6b Complementarity, but incomplete ownership of resources within the coalition

Fig. 5.6c: Reduced complementarity / competing ownership of resources

Fig. 5.6: Distribution of Resource Ownership in Coalition $A_1, \ldots, A_k$

Finally in *Case 3*, the potential coalition controls all necessary resources, but members $A_1, A_2, \ldots, A_k$ are characterized by the same resource endowments. All members may want to pursue the same goals and processes, but none of them needs the other to achieve his goal. There is no reason to share complementary resources, and there is a high probability that agents $A_1, A_2, \ldots, A_k$ will end up competing against each other.

Coalitions will thus be more likely to come into existence and to be stable and sustainable if the range of resources needed to attain a specific goal can be exhaustively controlled by its members[18]. Furthermore, resources provided by the members of the coalition should be characterized by a *high degree of complementarity* or mutual exclusiveness. This complementarity will imply that resources and strengths of all members are symmetrically dependent on each other; such a symmetric interdependence leads to a situation in which all agents gain from sharing resources with other coalition members.

Each member will benefit from participating in the coalition, but he must also be able to contribute in an appropriate way. The benefits and contributions from members must be balanced such that individual contributions provided by one agent will be regarded as equivalent to contributions of other agents. The ownership of resources, particularly the pattern of ownership distribution for critical resources must be balanced between members, otherwise some agents will become less willing to contribute, or may try to subordinate others.

The distribution of resources within a potential coalition will have a strong influence on appropriate modes of governance and organization to be chosen. If resources and capabilities are highly complementary, exhaustively controlled and mutually exclusive between coalition members, collaborative modes of governance and organization will offer sustainable solutions. Contractual arrangements of a loose kind ("quoad usum" type agreements as described in sections 2.5 and 3.3) may be sufficient to hold the coalition together, at least as long as the value of specific resources and the risks of expropriation of quasi-rents are not too high. If resource ownership is *not* appropriately balanced between potential coalition members, by contrast, some agents will try to subordinate others, either within an integrated firm or through some other, quasi-hierarchical mode of governance. Finally, another extreme mode of coordination is market contracting which will only be feasible if resource complementarities are not too high, if resources are not overly specific and tightly controlled by individual agents, and if individual contributions can be appropriately measured and monitored[19].

Another important factor influencing the choice of contractual arrangements and of appropriate institutional structures is the extent of *co-specificity* between resources. Typical examples for co-specific resources are containers, container-ships and specialized harbour facilities, each of which are often owned by differ-

---

18 Exhaustive control of all resources is a very rigid assumption. It may be relaxed by the weaker assumption that only those critical resources are controlled, on which the functioning of the coalition and the realization of its purpose crucially depends. Coalition members will attempt to own and control all these critical resources, while other complementary, though less critical resources may be purchased from external sources.

19 In section 5.4, we will provide a more detailed analysis of the conditions under which each of these three modes of governance and organization show their respective advantages and disadvantages.

ent agents[20]. For such cases of co-specificity, members of a coalition provide resources, the value of which will depend crucially on complementary resources owned by other members. It is a common hypothesis in the cooperation literature that collaboration can flourish best under conditions in which agents are symmetrically dependent on each other[21]. If one agent can leave the coalition more easily than the other, and if A_1 can force A_2 to do what he wants him to do, while A_2 cannot reciprocally put pressure on A_1, then this is not a suitable condition for sustainable collaboration.

This last situation is illustrated in *Fig. 5.7*. We have four agents $A_1, \ldots, A_4$, each possessing a complementary resource R_r, $r = 1, \ldots, 4$, needed for a process P_{1g}. Now assume there is an alternative process P_{2g} requiring resources $R_{r'}$, $r' = 4, \ldots, 7$. Agents $A_1, \ldots, A_3$ are locked into the coalition, while agent A_4 is free to use R_4 for both processes. We assume that agent A_4 can easily find other coalition members possessing the resources needed for process P_{2g}. Resources $R_1, \ldots, R_3$ are co-specific among each other, but asymmetrically dependent on R_4. The value of resources owned by agents A_1, A_2 and A_3 is crucially dependent on the existence and sustainability of the coalition applying the joint process P_{1g}. If process P_{1g} is *not* applied, the return on the investment cost is non-salvagable for agents A_1, A_2 and A_3. To prevent expropriation of quasi-rents through non-application of process P_{1g}, those agents have to enter into protective contractual arrangements[22]. Agent A_4 will be invited to participate in these contractual arrangements, since agents A_1, A_2 and A_3 are crucially dependent on him. Agent A_4 knows about their asymmetric dependence; he can always switch to process P_{2g}, while the other three agents are "locked into" the coalition applying process P_{1g}. Agent A_4 will thus be inclined to behave strategically, and will not act in the best interest of the coalition. Under the assumption of opportunistic behavior, unilateral specificity and asymmetric dependence will not result in a situation in which a stable and sustainable coalition can be maintained.

Cooperative modes of governance and organization are thus only feasible under very favorable circumstances that are characterized by symmetric dependence and *co-specificity* of assets owned by all coalition members. Exhaustive ownership of critical assets within a coalition and balanced co-specificity will result in symmetric interdependence and mutual benefit, while asymmetric dependence will result in strategic behavior by some members, which will lead to the instability of a coalition.

---

20 See Teece (1986, 1991) and our analysis in sections 3.2.2 and 4.3.3. Resources are defined as *unilaterally specific* or asymmetrically interdependent, if resource owner A_1 is dependent on resources owned by agent A_2, while A_2 is not dependent on A_1. The owners of *co-specific* resources, by contrast, are symmetrically dependent on each other.
21 See Axelrod (1984), Buckley and Casson (1988), Harrigan (1986, 1988) and Olson (1968).
22 See Alchian (1984, 36), Klein, Crawford and Alchian (1978), and our description in section 2.5.

The likelihood with which coalitions come into existence and the conditions under which they can be maintained at a stable level will thus depend on:

- the *congruence* of goals and processes pursued by agents;
- the *completeness* and exhaustiveness of resources owned by members of the coalition;
- the *complementarity* between resources owned by different members (mutual exclusiveness);
- on equivalent resources and ownership rights being *balanced* between participating members;
- and on complete *co-specficity* of assets owned by different members of the coalition.

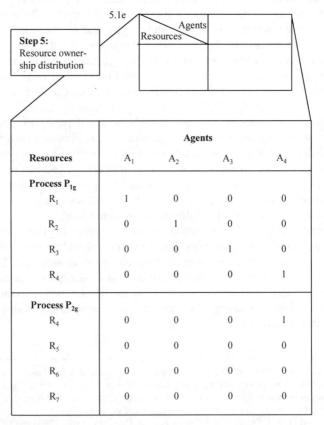

Resources	Agents			
	A_1	A_2	A_3	A_4
Process P_{1g}				
R_1	1	0	0	0
R_2	0	1	0	0
R_3	0	0	1	0
R_4	0	0	0	1
Process P_{2g}				
R_4	0	0	0	1
R_5	0	0	0	0
R_6	0	0	0	0
R_7	0	0	0	0

Fig. 5.7:   Co-Specificity of Resources and Asymmetric Dependence between Agents

If all these five restrictive conditions hold, coalitions will become stable and self-sustaining. Collaborative modes of governance and organization can be maintained even without any tight contractual arrangements, at least as long as the danger of expropriation of quasi-rents is not too high. All agents involved are willing to maintain their relationships since they can all benefit from each other. If any one of these restrictive conditions is *not* fulfilled, other modes of governance and organization must be sought. In the following section we will thus investigate which discrete institutional structures can best be fitted to a certain configuration of activities, and to the prevalent resource distribution pattern.

5.4   The Formation of Appropriate Institutional Structures

After having completed the five steps of project specification outlined in the preceding sections, we can start with the design of appropriate institutional structures. Depending on the configuration or ensemble of agents, goals, processes, tasks and resources, only one or a few particular types of contractual arrangements will be appropriate to govern and organize a project. To select the appropriate contractual arrangement, we have to rely on the following information:

- the identification of *agents and goals*;
- the *process analysis* and the process selection;
- a detailed *task analysis*;
- the *specification of resources*;
- and on the analysis of *resource capabilities* and of the *resource ownership* pattern.

This infomation allows us to determine if there is a group of agents that is characterized by both a *congruence of goals* pursued, and by a *congruence related to processes* preferred. Both characteristics represent necessary conditions for forming a coalition. If two or more agents can easily agree on goals and processes to be pursued in order to reach their goals, they can decide to form a more or less stable coalition. If these conditions are *not* fulfilled, agents should not try to form a coalition, and should instead rely on pure market contracting. If they can in fact agree on joint goals and on the same process(es) to be pursued within a coalition, the decision about the appropriate institutional arrangement is the next step in the project structuring sequence. The type of arrangement to be chosen will then depend on:

- the specific *characteristics of goals and processes* related to an investment project;
- the *characteristics of resources* needed for the most relevant tasks;
- and the *resource ownership pattern* of the agents who will be involved.

	Attributes		
1.Characteristics related to goals and processes			
- Congruence of goals	Low	Medium	High
- Congruence of processes	Low	Medium	High
- Frequency of repetitive tasks	Low	Medium	High
- Degree of resource complementarity	Low	Medium	High
- Degree of change related to goals	High	Medium	Low
- Degree of change related to processes	High	Medium	Low
2.Characteristics of resources			
- Appropriability regimes	Strong	Medium	Weak
- Entry cost/Entry time	Low	Medium	High
- Replaceability of resources	Easy	Medium	Difficult
- Degree of specificity	Low	Medium	High
- Exit cost/Exit time	Low	Medium	High
- Extent of expropriability	Low	Medium	High
3.Resource ownership pattern			
- Completeness of assets (Exhaustiveness)	No		Yes
- Complementarity (Mutual exclusiveness)	Low	Medium	High
- Resource potential of coalition	Weak	Medium	Strong
- Balance of resources between agents	Low	Medium	High

"Pure market profile"

Fig. 5.8:   Factors Influencing the Design of Institutional Arrangements

If goals and processes do not change frequently, an *integrated solution* will offer production and transaction cost advantages, particularly if the required resources are highly-specific and tightly controlled by individual agents or groups of agents. If the degree of change related to goals and processes is high by contrast, an integrated firm will *not* be able to secure production and transaction cost advantages based on the internalized exploitation of highly-specific, tightly controlled resources. Frequent changes in goals and processes require greater flexibility for the configuration of tasks, resources and agents, and an integrated firm will encounter diminishing returns from entrepreneurship (see section 4.2). *Cooperative modes* of governance and organization will become considerably superior to integration. As long as resources are co-specific and tightly controlled, cooperation must also be regarded as superior to market contracting. *Market contracting* will be preferred, on the other hand, as long as resources are not overly specific nor characterized by long entry and exit lags, if goals and processes change frequently, and if it is rather unlikely that independent agents can agree on goals and processes to be pursued jointly.

Fig. 5.8 summarizes the most important factors that influence the selection of the appropriate institutional arrangement. On the upper part of Fig. 5.8 we describe the general *characteristics of goals and processes* (section 1). These general characteristics include the congruence of goals and processes pursued by a group of agents, the frequency with which repetitive tasks have to be performed for which the same set of resources is called for, and the degree of change related to goals and processes. Information needed for evaluation can be gained through the identification of goals and agents, and through process analysis and process selection as outlined in section 5.2. In the middle and lower part of Fig. 5.8, we have outlined the *characteristics of resources* (section 2), and the *resource ownership pattern* (section 3). Information on these characteristics is derived from task analysis, from the specification of resources, and from the analysis of resource ownership and of the distribution of firm-specific resources (as described in sections 5.2 and 5.3). We will distinguish between three different *attributes* for each characteristic. As an example, the degree of asset complementarity can be low, medium or high. Depending on the configuration of these attributes, we can specifiy the appropriate contractual arrangements. This will be described in the following.

5.4.1   Superiority of Markets

We begin with the description of a situation in which goals, processes and tasks can be easily separated. Individual agents pursue goals and processes but do not need to interact closely with other agents. There will be a rather low congruence of goals and processes. Similar tasks will not be performed frequently, and owners of specialized resources do not have to interact in a repetitive way. Even if two agents happen to pursue the same goal, they do not need to know each other and do not need to agree on goals or processes, because there is a low degree of resource complementarity. The degree of change related to goals and processes may be rather high. All these attributes related to goals and processes conform to section 1 of the left column in *Fig. 5.8*. In an extreme form, interactions between agents could be described by the neoclassical model of anonymous spot contracting. Well-functioning markets would take care of the coordination of the economic activities for a very large number of traders. These markets may even function effectively if individuals change their goals frequently, and if processes of production and distribution change considerably.

However, the smooth functioning of markets will only be satisfied as long as resources required for maintaining production and distribution activities are characterized by relatively easy entry and exit conditions, which are summarized by the characteristics of resources being listed in section 2 of the left column in Fig. 5.8. For strong appropriability regimes, low entry costs and times, and for easily replaceable, non-specific resources, for which exit costs and times are low, and for which resource owners do not run the risk of expropriation of quasi-rents, markets will function as the appropriate coordination mechanism. As long as such *non-critical resource characteristics* hold, individual agents do not have to to take care of controlling an exhaustive spectrum of resources, or of agreeing on a complementary and balanced sharing of resources. All they need to be concerned about is controlling the narrow spectrum of resources needed to perform their individual role in the market. The catallaxy of the market will arrange for the compatability of individual plans, and for the smooth coordination of resource-flows[23].

If characteristics of goals, processes and resources diverge significantly from this *"pure market profile"* in Fig. 5.8, i.e. if production and distribution processes require highly-specific capital assets which are co-specialized, difficult to access and characterized by long duration, market interactions will become more "complicated". Frequent distortions in resource-flows will become more likely; spontaneous and anonymous market interactions between traders will no longer be sufficient. Individual agents need to maintain more intense relationships. In order to pursue individual goals and related processes they need to interact more closely with other agents. They need to agree on complementary goals and processes, and they have to participate in contractual agreements with owners of complementary resources. The formation of coalitions, be they through integrated or collaborative modes of governance and organization, will become inevitable.

5.4.2   Superiority of Integrated Solutions

Agents who pursue joint goals and related processes will form coalitions in order to coordinate the flow of complementary resource, and they will often prefer to coordinate activities in an integrated mode, with joint equity ownership of critical resources. Vertical *integration within a single firm* will offer production and transaction cost advantages, if the degree of asset complementarity is high, and if there is a high frequency of repetitive tasks, for which highly-specific resources are needed (Williamson 1985). But integration will not always be an efficient and sustainable solution, depending on the characteristics of resources, and on the patterns of change. Only if there is a rather *low degree of change* related to goals and processes, transaction cost savings can effectively be exploited within an integrated firm. Internalization advantages for moderate degrees of change will be particularly enhanced if weak appropriability regimes are pertinent (Ouchi and

---

23 See Hayek (1945, 1978) and Streit and Wegner (1988) for a description of catallaxy.

Bolton 1987), if high entry costs and long entry times are involved, if assets are highly-specific and difficult to replace, if exit costs and exit times are considerable, and if there is a considerable risk of expropriation of quasi-rents[24].

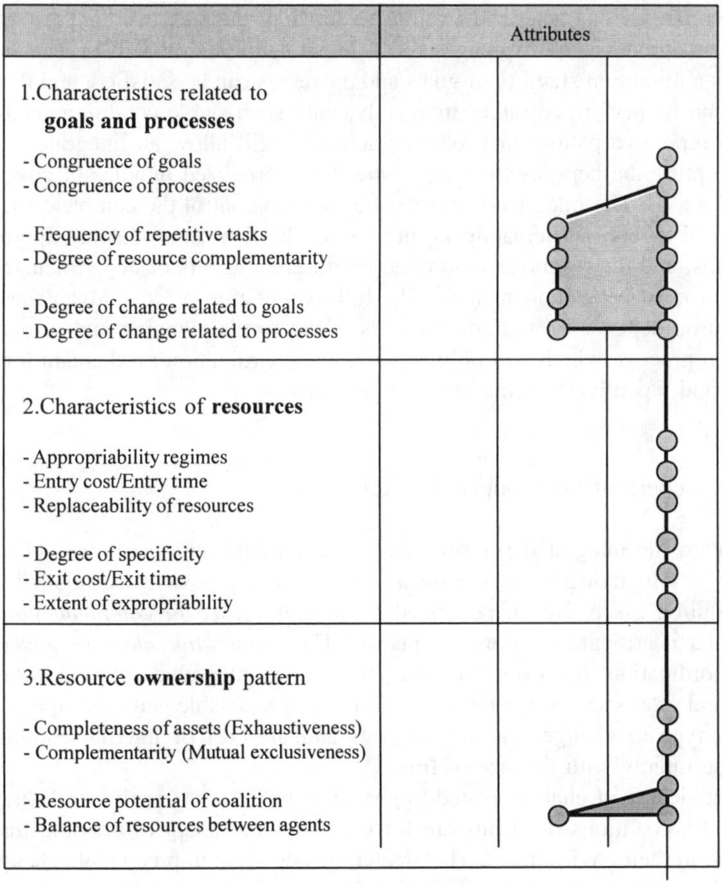

	Attributes		
1.Characteristics related to **goals and processes**			
- Congruence of goals			
- Congruence of processes			
- Frequency of repetitive tasks			
- Degree of resource complementarity			
- Degree of change related to goals			
- Degree of change related to processes			
2.Characteristics of **resources**			
- Appropriability regimes			
- Entry cost/Entry time			
- Replaceability of resources			
- Degree of specificity			
- Exit cost/Exit time			
- Extent of expropriability			
3.Resource **ownership** pattern			
- Completeness of assets (Exhaustiveness)			
- Complementarity (Mutual exclusiveness)			
- Resource potential of coalition			
- Balance of resources between agents			

Fig. 5.9:   Factors Influencing the Superiority of Integrated Solutions

---

24 An integrated firm will then be established as a set of contracts to prevent the expropriation of quasi-rents (see Alchian 1984, 36). Members of the firm are better off and more secure than if they were to interact through markets or collaborative arrangements. See also our analysis in sections 2.5, 3.3 and 4.2.

However, savings of both production and transaction costs within an integrated firm demand that goals and processes can be pursued in a fairly stable way. If, by contrast, goals and processes change frequently, internalized portfolios of capital goods, capabilities and skills may be prematurely devaluated, and potential cost savings from specific capital goods and internalized skill bases will easily become neutralized. This is illustrated in *Figure 5.9*, where the *"integration profile"* is characterized by low to medium degrees of change related to goals and processes. Advantages of an integrated solution will prevail only as long as a minimum stability of goals and processes can be satisfied, and if similar tasks can be performed rather frequently; only such stable conditions combined with a repetitive pattern of economic activities will allow an integrated firm to fully capture the benefits from higly-specific internalized bundles of co-specific capital goods. The integrated firm must be able to control the complete spectrum of critical assets; participating agents within the firm must display appropriate strengths, and the resources controlled by different agents or departments within the firm must be complementary. The full exploitation of cost advantages from integration depends on the effectiveness of the firm's planning and resource allocation process, which will only be a reliable coordination mechanism for fairly stable and repetitive patterns of economic activity.

5.4.3   Superiority of Cooperative Solutions

Similar to the integrated solution, collaboration between agents will be sought whenever a high degree of *congruence of goals and processes* is satisfied, and if the required assets are characterized by a *high degree of complementarity*, in particular if critical assets are co-specific. The *cooperative mode* of governance and coordination, however, will out-perform the integrated solution, whenever goals and processes change rapidly and in an unpredictable way, and if, as a result of this type of change, transaction costs and the cost of internal coordination increase rapidly with the size of firms[25].

If the degree of change related to goals and processes is high, as illustrated in *Fig. 5.10*, coalitions of agents are forced to flexibly adapt to ongoing transformations in their environment. The greater the degree of unpredictable change, the more diminishing returns from entrepreneurship and increasing costs of management and coordination will work against the economics of integration (see section 4.2). A certain level of pooling of activities may be useful due to economies-of-

---

25 This effect, often used as an argument for explaining the limits to firm size tends to be underestimated by some neo-institutional authors such as Williamson (1985). See our detailed description in chapter 4.

scale, and to high degrees of asset complementarity and resouce specificity. However, if integration is pursued too far, the flexibility and efficiency of organizations will often be at stake. Under such conditions collaborative arrangements will often turn out to be the superior solution.

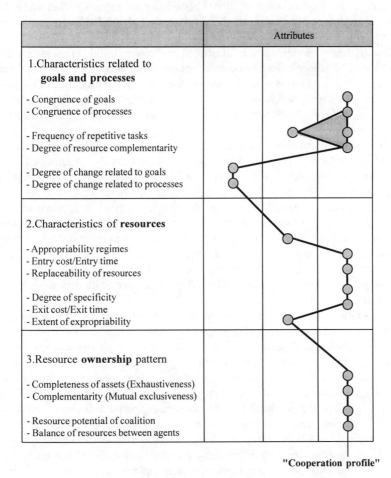

"Cooperation profile"

Fig. 5.10: Factors Influencing the Superiority of Collaborative Solutions

As illustrated by the *"cooperation profile"* in Fig. 5.10, hybrid modes of governance and organization are superior over integration for high degrees of change related to goals and processes, while the congruence of goals and processes, the frequency of repetitive tasks, and the degree of resource complementarity must be similarly high for both cooperation and integration. In contrast with the integrated solution, however, cooperation is only feasible for medium appropriability regimes, and if the extent of potential expropriation of quasi-rents is not too high. For cooperation to become sustainable, however, very *favorable characteristics of the resource ownership pattern*, such as complete-ness of assets and strong capabilities of partners with highly-complementary resource ownership must be fulfilled. Capabilities of partners within a collabor-ative arrangement must even be more favorably balanced than within an inte-grated firm.

The argument of *flexibility* is illustrated in *Table 5.1* and refers to our inter-pretation of collaboration agreements as options introduced in section 3.5. Agents $A_1, \ldots, A_6$ form a *coalition B* in order to jointly develop a process P_{1g}, for which each agent contributes complementary assets. Another *coalition C* of agents A_1, $\ldots, A_3$ and $A_7, \ldots, A_9$ is negotiated, but turns out to be inferior to coalition B, since members $A_7, \ldots, A_9$ do not possess the appropriate resources. Unfore-seeable technical changes may lead to a reconsideration of processes in the next period, and to a replacement of process P_{1g} by process P_{2g}. Agents $A_1, \ldots, A_3$ will suddenly discover that the other members of coalition B are no longer ap-propriate partners for them, and that they should now renegotiate with agents A_7, $\ldots, A_9$ to form coalition C. Had they decided to form an integrated firm with agents $A_4, \ldots, A_6$ in the previous period, their obligations as well as the switch-ing costs would be much higher, possibly forcing them to remain "locked in with the incompetent partners". As a result, the cooperative association appears to be the best solution whenever a very high degree of flexibility is required, even if high degrees of asset complementarity and resource specificity may work in favor of pooling.

Cooperation, however, will have disadvantages compared with the integrated solution for weak appropriability regimes, if entry and exit conditions are ex-tremely "tight", and if participating agents run a very high risk of expropriation of quasi-rents. For weak appropriability regimes and high risks of quasi-rent expropriation, cooperating partners will try to secure themselves through tight formal agreements, if possible through equity ownership contracts. If the danger of "leakage" and the potential loss for cooperating partners becomes too high, a switch to the integrated mode of coordination will appear to be inevitable.

As it has already been pointed out in section 5.3, collaboration agreements will only be sustainable for certain favorable patterns of distributed resource owner-ship. Partners must secure the full range of complementary assets, they should show an equal stature of capabilities, and resources owned by the different part-ners must be complementary and co-specific. Any diversion from this very pecu-liar resource ownership configuration favorable for collaboration will lead to conflicts, and to a potential breaking up of the coalition. Except for some very special circumstances under which all these necessary conditions hold simultaneously, cooperation agreements must be regarded as rather fragile solu-tions, being much less robust than full integration within a single firm, even though they represent much more flexible solutions.

Table 5.1: Relative Advantage of Flexible Collaborative Solutions

Agents / Resources	Coalition B						Coalition C					
	A_1	A_2	A_3	A_4	A_5	A_6	A_1	A_2	A_3	A_7	A_8	A_9
Process P_{1g}												
R_1	1	0	0	0	0	0	1	0	0	0	0	0
R_2	0	1	0	0	0	0	0	1	0	0	0	0
R_3	0	0	1	0	0	0	0	0	1	0	0	0
R_4	0	0	0	1	0	0	0	0	0	0	0	0
R_5	0	0	0	0	1	0	0	0	0	0	0	0
R_6	0	0	0	0	0	1	0	0	0	0	0	0
Process P_{2g}												
R_1	1	0	0	0	0	0	1	0	0	0	0	0
R_2	0	1	0	0	0	0	0	1	0	0	0	0
R_3	0	0	1	0	0	0	0	0	1	0	0	0
R_7	0	0	0	0	0	0	0	0	0	1	0	0
R_8	0	0	0	0	0	0	0	0	0	0	1	0
R_9	0	0	0	0	0	0	0	0	0	0	0	1

5.5 Distributed Ownership and Task-specific Contractual Arrangements

5.5.1 Decomposition of Tasks and Activities

The analytical framework outlined above allows tasks and activities to become decomposed and "moulded" into sophisticated institutional arrangements, which may be suitably adapted to the underlying task-requirements. Resources and capabilities needed for performing one task may be completely different from what is required for some other task, even if both tasks represent consecutive elements of one and the same production and distribution process. Industrial organization within advanced industrial society is thus increasingly decomposed even along the same production chain. As an example, large automotive firms increasingly specialize in some of the tasks required for the design, production and distribution of cars, while they leave other tasks to suppliers, development and design sub-contractors, or to independent dealers or service firms[26]. Bundling or unbundling strategies are pursued because manufacturers find out that each dollar invested in a particular activity leads to a greater return on investment than in another, related activity.

The reason for return differentials for separable, though related activities must be sought in different *capabilities* built up by firms over extended time periods. *Capabilities* were defined in sections 3.4 and 5.3 as accumulated ownership and control rights for bundles of critical resources. To acquire the capabilities required for successfully performing a particular line of business, a firm has to undergo *long gestation* periods (entry lags). Once capabilities are acquired, they can be utilized over relatively *long duration* periods (exit lags)[27], during which they offer competitive advantages, while they also restrain flexibility. Capabilities built up by a firm over extensive periods of time are often specific to only some particular tasks, whereas they do not offer much advantage for other, related tasks[28]. Because of long gestation lags, owners of specific resources can tempo-rarily exclude other firms and can thus exploit monopoly rents. Since specific resources are durable, their services can be mobilized at relatively low cost, and firms possessing these particular capabilities can earn considerable quasi-rents[29]. For both reasons, firms with task-specific capabilities are more efficient in per-forming certain activities; they will perform these particular tasks better, faster and cheaper than any competitor, and they are thus able to earn an above-average return on investment for this activity[30].

During an ongoing process of business evaluation, selection and decomposi-tion of activities, firms will screen all relevant tasks with respect to their specific resource requirements, and will make assessments of firm-specific strengths and weaknesses. They will focus on those tasks, for which accumulated capabilities and skills, together with entry and exit conditions, offer favorable conditions for

---

26 Strategies of decomposition, of bundling vs. unbundling of activities pursued by different automotive manufacturers are analyzed by Kern, Sabel and Herrigel (1989), by Baur (1990) and by Siebert (1990).

27 For entry and exit lags see our analysis in sections 3.1 and 4.1.

28 As an example, highly-specific capabilities in engine construction do not offer any advan-tage in automotive body construction.

29 For a differentiation between (entry-dependent) monopoly rents, and (exit dependent) quasi-rents see Klein, Crawford and Alchian (1978).

30 This capital theoretical and evolutionary foundation of the comparative advantage of busi-ness firms, which was introduced in section 3.4, was originally developed by Penrose (1959), but has since then not received much attention within the theory of the firm.

differentiation. They try to control all those tasks in an integrated mode, for which the complete range of critical resources can be mastered in-house.

Not all the tasks necessary for performing one process need to be fully controlled in-house. If processes are highly complex, and if some tasks require very sophisticated capabilities and skills, even very large firms are willing to delegate activities and to rely on collaborative arrangements with other firms. According to Richardson (1972), the cooperative mode will be chosen whenever firms try to bridge complementary activities for which the required capabilities are dissimilar.

Finally, *market transactions* are arranged for all those remaining tasks that are less critical to the process pursued by the firm. These tasks can be considered as less critical if they are easily replaceable without affecting the performance of the whole process. This would be the case for standardized parts or components for which there are typically several competing suppliers on the market. Also, some tasks simply do not require sophisticated capabilities with long entry and exit lags, and a firm will always be able to secure access to this activity in time, and at appropriate cost. Efficient boundaries will thus be established around all those critical tasks, for which a firm is able to exploit services from highly-sophisticated internal capabilities with long entry and exit lags, and which are difficult to transfer[31]. Collaborative arrangements will be maintained for all those tasks which are highly complementary, but for which a firm is not able to secure access to the required capabilities, as these are owned and controlled by other firms.

5.5.2 "Open" Cooperation for High-technology Related Tasks

Cooperation will be sought for tasks which offer sustainable comparative advantages to other firms but which a firm wants to secure for reasons of complementarity. Compared to the integrated solution, collaboration between independent partners will be superior and sustainable if goals and processes change rapidly and in an unpredictable way, if access to critical resources cannot be secured in due time, and if transaction costs and the costs of internal coordination increase rapidly with the size and complexity of the firm. Under these conditions, potential partners will not merge; but why should they really collaborate and enter into binding contractual arrangements instead of switching to a pure market mode of interaction? Compared to market exchange, cooperation will turn out to be

---

31 The term *"efficient boundaries of the firm"* is explained in Williamson (1985, 96ff), Teece (1991) and Imai and Baba (1991). In section 6.4, we will discribe the efficient boundaries of different types of firms within the satellite telecommunication industry.

superior if there is a high degree of specificity of investment, if contracts are difficult to negotiate and enforce, and if transaction costs associated with markets are comparatively high. Given these explanations, collaboration will only gain a stable balance as an intermediate mode of coordination between markets and integrated firms, if a high degree of asset specificity is combined with rapid change of goals and processes, and if contractual difficulties restrain the functioning of both markets as well as of integrated firms.

Can this explain why an increasing number of firms at a worldwide level is trying to pursue cooperative strategies in order to access new technologies? Do changes related to the development and application of new technology really display the characteristics outlined above which lead to a greater preference for, and to the sustainability of cooperative solutions? If this is the case, we could find a theoretical explanation for the argument often put forth in empirical investigations, namely that the process of technological change forces firms to participate in collaborative associations[32]. What is so different about technological innovation as compared to other activities which do not lead to a similar "mania" for cooperation? The answer appears to be that technological innovation is driven by task-specific skills and *knowledge-based capital*. Specific skills and knowledge have very peculiar characteristics which other resources (e.g. land, capital, natural resources) do not have to the same extent:

- the accumulation of knowledge often involves extremely *long gestation periods*, during which there is a very high risk of failure or mis-specification;
- specific knowledge is troubled by serious *appropriability problems* since the value of information can only be effectively assessed after its disclosure[33];
- specific knowledge is very *difficult to transfer* since it is often tacit and tied to people, to capital goods, or to the firm-specific context.

Consequently, if the key asset is highly-specific knowledge, it is very difficult to "buy-in" sensitive and strategic information due to the appropriability problem. Market contracting for very specific know-how will either be infeasible, or transaction costs will be prohibitively high. As a result, agents who are interested in the same process, and who try to gain access to complementary knowledge bases which they do not possess, will accept collaboration as the best solution.

Even if a firm would prefer to control strategic resources in-house, an integrated solution is often difficult to achieve if it is in urgent need of specific

---

32 See our analysis in chapter 1. In contrast to the explanations found in the literature, we view technological change as a process of capital accumulation with long gestation lags. Collaboration strategies are pursued to access technologies accumulated by other firms.

33 According to Arrow (1962), the value of information to a potential user can only be assessed after it has been disclosed to him. As soon as he has received the information, however, he is no longer willing to pay for it.

know-how. It may consider two strategies: (1) the build-up of own knowledge bases through internal R&D, or (2), the acquisition of another firm possessing the required skills and knowledge base. *The internal R&D* solution will be infeasible if gestation periods are very long relative to the expected period of know-how utilization. The firm will then inevitably have to rely on another partner who already possesses the know-how. Instead of cooperating, however, the firm may consider an *acquisition* of the other firm with the required knowledge base; this may turn out to be the appropriate strategy if goals and processes do not change too fast and if the rate of obsolescence of specific knowledge is not too high. If, by contrast, goals and processes change very rapidly, the acquiring firm runs the risk of buying into an almost obsolete knowledge base. Consequently, it wants to keep an option to easily switch to alternative technical solutions that are being offered by different partners. Cooperative associations will then turn out to be the only feasible solution, being superior to both market exchange and integration.

Most technology-related cooperative associations are in fact motivated by the desire of each partner to get access to specific knowledge bases appropriated by somebody else (Hagedoorn and Schakenraad 1989b). Since technological know-how in many high-technology related fields such as microelectronics, biotechnology and new materials is extremely sophisticated and specialized, any firm seeking the information required to perform a desired project, will find only very few partners, even on a world scale. For a specific new materials project, the appropriate partner may be an aerospace firm in the U.S., for another project requiring other materials characteristics, it will be most favorable to join forces with a chemical firm in Japan. These ties are often so diverse and project-specific, that it would be economically infeasible to integrate activities within a single firm. A pure market solution, on the other hand, would not lead to the appropriate developments, since the partners have to commit specific resources and will have difficulties in finding appropriate contractual arrangements. Cooperation agreements are more binding than market exchange, but less binding and therefore often less expensive and less risky than an integrated solution. Since technologies change so rapidly, partners want to keep an option open to switch to an alternative knowledge base if external market conditions, technologies and standards change suddenly and in an unforeseen way. As an example, firms in the information technology field form bilateral arrangements with partners "betting" on different software standards (Unix, OS/2, MS-DOS, etc.). As soon as one standard becomes dominant, the composition of alliances will be re-arranged and new forms of organizations will be considered.

Due to the problematic nature of specific knowledge and its intrinsic appropriability problems, it is very difficult to evaluate ex-ante, which particular part of the knowledge base owned by someone else will be contributing most to a joint project. The value and relevance of knowledge contributed by two or more partners can only be explored through the joint process of collaboration[34]. Co-operative associations thus perform the function of a *joint discovery procedure;* pure markets would be inappropriate to bring about the coordination needed between highly-specialized firms which are active in different parts of the world, and which are not yet involved in market interactions[35]. Nor would the acquisition of a firm or a merger be the right approach, since a reliable assessment of the value of the acquired firm can only be made ex-post, after transactions have taken place. It thus appears that the process of technological change caused by the intrinsic characteristics of sophisticated and highly-specific knowledge, opens up many new fields for which collaborative associations and strategic alliances offer the best institutional solution. Particularly for markets for which a rapid pace of technological advance, highly-specific, non-transferable knowledge bases as well as frequent changes in goals and processes are characteristic, cooperative associations may turn out to be a sustainable contractual arrangement. Collaborative projects may, under certain conditions, as outlined in section 5.4.3, help to economize on transaction and coordination cost, and will then allow for dynamic change with the lowest degree of friction and resource loss.

5.5.3   "Close" Internal Control of Critical Tasks and Resources

In spite of these advantages of new forms of cooperative associations outlined in the preceding sections, such flexible and open arrangements are often very difficult to manage, particularly if the number of agents is large, if goals and processes change frequently, and if unfavorable resource distribution patterns prevail. If this is the case, *dual modes of coordination* will arise: firms participate in a large number of flexible network relationships; at the same time, they try to overcome management problems of collaboration by maintaining close, in-house control of the most critical functions or sub-tasks.

The analysis of cooperation agreements, strategic networks and new reconfigurations of production and distribution chains must emphasize the complementarity and co-existence of different coordination modes. Open collaborative arrangements involving many independent partners must accordingly be seen in conjunction with the attempts of firms to *fully integrate critical tasks and resources.* Complex projects that appear "cooperative" at first sight may easily

---

34 Imai and Baba (1991) show that many technological alliances are mechanisms to open each partner's repository and to jointly explore which field of know-how may be most valuable to the joint project.

35 V. Hayek's (1978) description of the markets as a discovery pro cedure is thus appropriate for existing markets but does not appear to be applicable to "technology fissions" across markets for which totally new groups of interacting agents have to be formed.

become transformed and substituted by a more integrated mode of governance and organization. During the course of the project, some agents are able to accumulate capabilities and skills required to fully control some particular process tasks. These tasks may allow some agents to exercise control over other agents performing related tasks. Opportunism by economic agents, differentiated capabilities and skills, and information asymmetries will lead to persistent attempts by some economic agents to fully control a "core" of complex processes, without transmitting this insight to other agents, who may still believe in the cooperative character of the overall project.

Changes in the preferable pattern of co-existing modes of governance and organization will also be dependent on *project phases and functions*. While the collaborative mode may offer comparative advantages during early development phases, later phases of construction and implementation will often be characterized by a transition to a more integrated mode of governance and organization. Accordingly, R&D will often be pursued through cooperation between two or more independent firms, while manufacturing, sales and distribution often tend to be performed through a more integrated mode.

In spite of these persistent changes towards more comprehensive, integrated control of particular process-steps, functions and tasks, multilateral contractual arrangements may be a persisting pattern, even though one or a few participating agents may increasingly gain *control over some critical process steps*. The multilateral character of contract relationships assures an efficient allocation of complementary resources, while distribution is affected through asymmetrical control over critical tasks and resources. A few dominant firms are thus able to capture a relatively high share of return, and to exercise control over large production and distribution networks, which does not necessarily correspond to their share of resource ownership. They may in fact only own a small minority share of *all* resources required for a complex process, but receive their comparative strength through majority ownership and control of a few highly critical resources which are indispensible for some crucial process steps.

There are a number of distinct contractual arrangements, through which complex chains of production and distribution can be effectively managed and controlled by a single firm, which does not need to own a significant overall share of resources. *System integration*, prime contractorship, and open equipment manufacturing (OEM) contracts allow a systems firm to exercise control over a wide network of supplier firms, which may still own and control the greater share of resources. Similarly, franchise contracts often allow for the commanding role of the franchisor, while the largest share of resources is owned and contributed by the franchisees. The newly emerging patterns of organization and control of multinational enterprises are built on the use of these complex contractual arrangements, through which a central decision-making nexus can be expanded over a large array of activities and resources, not necessarily being under direct ownership of the core organization (Bartlett and Ghoshal 1989, and Dunning 1988).

A considerable share of cooperation agreements and strategic alliances may thus be explained by the use of sophisticated new contractual arrangements, which allow for the combination of centralized, *"quasi-integrated control"* and of distributed, multilateral ownership. To distinguish between "true" and "disguised" forms of cooperation, our structured approach described in the sections 5.1 to 5.4 may effectively be utilized. Complex projects, or large production and distribution chains can be broken down into tasks or activities. For each task, critical resources can be ranked according to their entry and exit conditions, and may be analyzed with respect to their ownership pattern. Concentrated ownership of the most critical resources for only one or a few tasks, which, however, have a crucial role for the whole project, will indicate that a firm is able to exercise a leadership role within a diverse network of collaborating agents. To explore such opportunities for central control within multilateral contractual arrangements, projects and agreements must be analyzed on a case by case basis. This will be done in the case descriptions in the following chapters.

6 Strategic Alliances and Restructuring in the Telecommunication Satellite Industry

6.1 Telecommunication Satellite Technology and its Evolution

Satellite technology has been developed since the late 1950s for transmitting signals (voice, data, images) between distant locations on earth by using orbital transponders. Application of this technology has offered access to strategic information, cheaper and faster transmission, and has allowed for a flexible extension of earthbound networks. As a result, satellite technology has evolved as the major growth area of space utilization, and has led to the formation of a major new industry.

The launch of Sputnik in 1957 proved the feasibility of using an orbital vehicle for transmitting radio signals; politically, this project resulted in a "shock" to Western countries and to the United States in particular, who became afraid of loosing their technological leadership position. The U.S. responded by transmitting President Eisenhower's Christmas message in 1958 through a tape recording on board a NASA satellite (Score project). NASA, which was restructured as a dedicated space agency, soon developed the projects Echo I and II, while the U.S. Department of Defense began to develop and operate a series of satellite projects. Throughout the 1960s, projects such as Telstar in 1962, Syncom in 1963 and Early Bird in 1965 led to a wide-spread acceptance of satellite technology, and to the greater perception of its commercial opportunities, examples of which were the TV transmission of the Olympic Games, and the setting up of transcontinental telephone lines[1].

The introduction and application of satellite communication systems represents a *systemic innovation* of considerable size and complexity[2]. To achieve the required smooth interaction of complementary assets, diverse groups of agents have to coordinate their activities through a variety of contractual arrangements. Since the early evolution of satellite systems, the typical coordination mechanisms have been *collaborative arrangements* "between markets and

---

1 A detailed summary of the early evolution of satellite technology can be found in Martin (1978).

2 For a description of systemic innovations, which consist of many interrelated sub-systems, and the success of which depends on the mobilization of diverse, co-specialized resources, see Freeman and Perez (1988), Kline and Rosenberg (1986), and Teece (1986).

hierarchies"[3]. Furthermore, cooperative agreements often involved both private and public agents, because the last were often in control of critical resources (technologies, infrastructure, regulation).

The preferred modes of governance and organization for satellite investment projects have changed quite significantly during the last 30 years. It is our intent to describe and explain the most pertinent changes, which have resulted in a *greater role of private investment* as a substitute for public investment, and in a *greater reliance on vertically-integrated control*. In spite of these long-term changes in the pattern of ownership and control, sustainable modes of collaboration still remain important for coordinating some elements and sub-systems of satellite-related investment projects[4].

The advent and early diffusion of satellite communication would have been unthinkable *without* a major organizational innovation, the formation of an institutional structure necessary to facilitate cross-border flows of information over long distances. In 1964, the Intelsat organization in 1964, a multilateral joint-venture owned by a large group of national telecommunication authorities, became established in Washington, D.C. This institution had a strong impact on the international commercialization and diffusion of satellite technology throughout the 1960s and 1970s. Several successive generations of Intelsat satellites have since then been purchased and operated by this multinational organization. The structure of this multilateral investment project was also used as a prototype model[5]

---

3   Neither of the two "corner solutions" were feasible as a coordination mechanism, at least during the early evolution of this industry. According to our analysis in section 5.4, *markets* were not appropriate due to the "difficult" character of resources involved (appropriability problems, difficult entry and exit, resources non-replaceable and of highly-specific nature, large risks of expropriation of quasi-rents). At the same time, *integration* within a firm was not feasible, since no single, large firm in the world was able to control the full spectrum of resources in-house, and because goals and processes had to be changed quite often. Each single satellite project had a unique task-structure, and the low frequency of repetitive tasks did not allow for the exploitation of transaction cost advantages within a large, vertically-integrated firm. During later phases of industry evolution, however, the pendulum has eventually swung somewhat more towards the integrated solution (see particularly our description in section 6.4).

4   *Critical activities* and resources, as defined in section 5.2, will increasingly be owned and controlled by large, integrated satellite systems firms, while *less critical* activities and resources will be sourced-in through market contracting or through collaboration agreements. Which particular activities within the satellite production and utilization chain can be regarded as "critical", and which resources may be considered as "non-critical", will be analyzed in more detail in section 6.4.

5   A detailed case study of the Intelsat organization would provide useful insights into the management of sustainable collaboration. The ownership and control structure of this institution is in accordance with the requirements for sustainable collaboration as outlined in chapter 5.

for other institutions to become established in satellite telecommunications. Similar organizations with other groups of shareholders and slightly different missions became active in promoting satellite developments and applications in other parts of the world. European activities were first initiated by the European Space Research Organization (ESRO); later on, the European Space Organization (ESA) developed and launched a number of European satellite projects. Similarly, new international organizations allowed for the diffusion of this technology to other application areas (Inmarsat for maritime applications, Eumetsat for metereological applications).

While multi-agent participation and cooperative modes of governance and organization have been pertinent features of international satellite investment projects, this should not lead to the (false) implication that cooperation and multilateral investment activity are truely superior modes of coordination. A differentiated assessment and evaluation appears inevitable. Accordingly, we will *first* argue that certain modes of governance and organization, which may have been inevitable during the *early* evolution of the industry, have become inappropriate during later development phases. *Second*, we will have to decompose processes, and differentiate between those satellite-related tasks which require integrated control, others which can easily be coordinated through markets, and finally those types of activities which call for cooperation. While the original mode of multilateral cooperation may still be suitable for some very large and complex projects, it may turn out to be disadvantageous for other satellite projects. *Third*, we have to distinguish between "true and hidden" modes of governance and organization: what may, at first sight, appear to belong to one generic form, may turn out to display characteristics of some other form if we analyze it in more depth[6].

In order to decompose international satellite business processes, and to derive the most suitable modes of governance and organization for separable sub-processes and tasks, we have to distinguish between:

- different user *objectives*, application areas, and related customer groups ("market mission");
- different business processes, *tasks* and *activities* ("process engineering");
- and different stages of *development* for projects, technologies, and the satellite business ("evolution").

Market missions and objectives are defined as value-creating activities directed at particular user groups and application areas. During the early evolution of

---

6   As an example, multilateral organizations and supplier networks may appear to be "cooperative organizations" even though they are often tightly controlled and managed "as if" transactions were organized within a single, integrated firm.

satellite technology, defense-related objectives were still dominant, and were characterized by the desire to get access to strategic information. Later on, early users of satellite communication were driven by the need for faster transmission of data, by the search for cheaper communication channels, and by the desire to extend network capacities. Satellite development allowed for the instantaneous fulfillment of all these objectives; in addition, it provided a process solution being characterized by much greater flexibility than alternative transmission modes, such as cable and earth-bound microwave networks.

Technology development was geared towards those user segments with the greatest *value-creating potential*. The diffusion of satellite technology was at its fastest in those *application areas*, in which potential users were able to formulate their needs, in which expected benefits of this new technology were relatively large, and where the costs of satellite communication were low relative to other available techniques. Accordingly, in terms of both the date of introduction and the attained adoption levels, application areas can be placed into the following order:

1. Military applications;
2. telephone transmission (primarily international);
3. broadcasting (TV, radio);
4. maritime information transmission;
5. business data services;
6. mobile communication services;
7. navigation;
8. meteorology; and
9. earth exploration (environmental/resource exploration).

In our following analysis, we will exclude defense-related satellite applications (1), as well as developments in the areas of meteorology (8), and earth exploration (9)[7]; we will concentrate on application areas 2 to 7 (telephone transmission, broadcasting, maritime information transmission, business data services, mobile communication services, and navigation), which will be summarized by the term *telecommunication satellite services*.

Within each of the major application areas, the particular *evolutionary path* (technological trajectories, type of satellite telecommunication services) is strongly influenced by organizational considerations. Projects get promoted and enhanced if a relatively small group of agents can agree on precise objectives and on a particular business process. If, furthermore, benefits can be easily appropriated by participating agents, while the coalition can find suitable agreements on

---

7   While defense-related applications are much less influenced by economic considerations, the
     area of earth exploration is still in its infancy, with not enough reliable data being available.

sharing risks, returns, and individual contributions, even very large and complex satellite projects can attain the required momentum. Such a *favorable* organizational and distributional pattern has been characteristic, for example, for intercontinental telephone transmission services operated by Intelsat.

If, on the other hand, the group of agents interested in a particular application of new satellite services is too large and inhomogeneous, and if this group is not able to agree on strategic objectives, processes and tasks, projects will be difficult to pursue from the beginning. Activities and decisions of individual agents will then be very hard to coordinate and control. Project risks may become insurmountable, potential benefits cannot easily be appropriated, and each member agent originally willing to contribute will eventually end up in despair. Such *"complicated projects"* are typically characterized by a high failure rate; in any event, it will be required to invest considerable resources as well as time, before a critical momentum can ever be attained. Such a constellation is typical for some projects in satellite broadcasting (area 3) which will be analyzed in section 6.3, and for new, global satellite navigation services (area 7).

The application of our method of structuring complex investment projects, which has been outlined in chapter 5, can be helpful for descriptive as well as for prescriptive purposes. In a more *descriptive* way, we can analyze satellite communication projects which have been pursued in the past; we can explain successes and failures based on our ex-post knowledge of how project-specific coordination problems have been approached. This is done in section 6.3, in which we compare three German respective European satellite projects.

In a more *prescriptive* way, we will analyze which mode of governance and organization should be applied in order to cope with the requirements of large, complex telecommunication satellite projects. We will describe some ongoing structural changes in the satellite communication industry, which seem to be in accordance with these prescriptive considerations (see section 6.4). Structural changes pursued at a worldwide level are then used as a guideline for the proposed restructuring process in the European telecommunication satellite industry, which will be described in section 6.5.

6.2   Decomposing Satellite-Related Business Processes and Industry Restructuring

The structuring and design of complex satellite investment projects will typically start with a precise definition of strategic objectives. These strategic *objectives* can cover the attempted improvement of the telephone system within a certain geographical area, for which satellite voice transmission offers the most flexible and cost-efficient solution. Another objective would be the improvement of the broadcasting system through state-of-the-art satellite communication technology (including digital transmission and high-definition image resolution). In the transportation sector, the application of satellite navigation services would comply with the objectives of improved safety and enhanced traffic capacity.

Any of these objectives such as the improvement of the telephone system in a certain geographical area will be pursued by independent agents who are often specialized on performing distinct, though inter-related activities and functions. Some agents act as potential customers for an improved telephone service, some others are specialized on the operation of such a service, some agents want to manufacture and sell the related hardware and equipment, and still others will perform the role of a regulator. To support and maintain an investment project directed at the improvement of the telephone system, all these groups of agents must agree on precisely defined objectives, as well as on processes and tasks to be pursued jointly. Decision-making and execution is complicated by the fact, that some agents pursue several, often competing projects at once. As an example, the improvement of telephone transmission via satellite is often in conflict with ongoing investment projects of operators and manufacturers for earthbound cable networks[8].

Another serious problem is caused by *long entry and exit time:* it may take several years for a new satellite project to become operational, and another eight to ten years until it is depreciated. During that time, strategic objectives and processes may change considerably due to ongoing technical change and the deregulation of services. Coalitions of agents that were originally in favor of a particular satellite project, will become unstable; the other extreme will involve a stable coalition being "locked into" a particular project, that has turned out to be an inappropriate and costly solution.

To prevent these risks while still being able to effectively pursue large, satellite-related investment projects, participating agents often seek complex contractual arrangements which typically lie "between markets and hierarchies". The most appropriate institutional arrangement, however, must be "designed" in a way which best suits the underlying business processes and the ownership distribution pattern for critical assets (see our analysis in chapter 5). Each satellite application area will require its own "custom-tailored" institutional framework. For *satellite broadcasting*, as an example, business processes can be decomposed into:

- the broadcasting satellite system (i.e. the manufacturing side);
- satellite launch and insurance services;
- broadcasting satellite operation services;
- TV or radio program transmission;
- as well as program reception (see our illustration in Fig. 6.1).

---

8   This conflict between a "satellite constituency" and a "cable constituency" will be described
      in more detail in section 6.5.

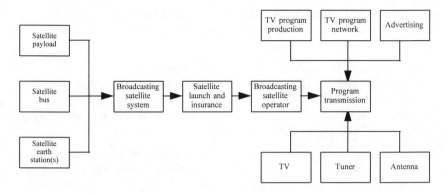

Fig. 6.1:   The Satellite Broadcasting Chain of Activities

Each business process can be further broken down into tasks, as is illustrated in Fig. 6.1. The *broadcasting satellite system* consists of the electronic payload (i.e. the signal transmission and data processing units), the satellite bus (i.e. the mechanical "carrier"), and of satellite earth stations. *TV program transmission* is crucially dependent on program production, on the work of network providers, and on advertising. On the *consumption side*, TV equipment, receiving antennas and tuners have to be made compatible for satellite technology. Most of these activities are performed by numerous independent and specialized agents. TV program production, network management, and advertising are performed by seperate institutions within the media and broadcasting sector. Most firms involved in program transmission do not actively get involved with the operation of bradcasting satellites. Satellite operators, on the other side, are most often organizationally separated from satellite hardware manufacturers. On the side of satellite hardware manufacturing, certain tasks such as the provision of the electronic payload and of satellite earth stations are often performed by specialized firms.

Another important dimension for business process analysis is the attempted *system integration level*. For some combinations of activities within the satellite broadcasting chain of activities outlined in Fig. 6.1, it will be economical to integrate, while for other activities, distributed ownership and control will be more appropriate. In any event, it is important to develop contractual arrangements between participating agents, in order to secure the smooth coordination between highly-specific resources and complementary activities. Cooperative arrangements can be extended to different levels of systems integration; they may be restricted to a particular range of activities, such as satellite systems manufacturing, or they may encompass the whole satellite broadcasting chain (including the full range of production and service provision). With respect to the development, design and manufacturing of satellite hardware, as illustrated on the left-hand side in Fig. 6.1, systems integration levels can be be broken down into:

- the component level (the lowest integration level);
- the sub-system level (major sub-systems or modules of a satellite);
- the integrated satellite system;
- furthermore, we can add an additional hierarchial level, the provision of fully-integrated "turn-key satellite systems"[9].

Our analysis is directed towards a better understanding of the coordination and work-sharing on the *supply side*. Is it better in terms of cost-efficiency and service quality to fully-integrate, and to control the whole spectrum of activities and resourcees required for a complex satellite system within *one* single large firm? Would the other alternative of relying on pure market coordination be feasible? Or are hybrid modes of governance and organization a superior solution for the supply structure within the telecommunication satellite industry? The answer to these questions must be sought through a detailed analysis of production and transaction costs, of entry and exit conditions, and of specific innovation characteristics, as has been outlined in chapters 4 and 5.

The empirical status of the international satellite industry is characterized by numerous, collaborative teaming arrangements. Firms develop new technologies and new communication concepts jointly. They form temporary alliances for coordinating the manufacturing and logistics of a multitude of components and subsystems required for a satellite system. And they raise new sources of funds from several independent financial institutions cooperating for any one particular project. The rationale for these hybrid modes of governance and organization is often sought in the "traditional explanations" which have been introduced in section 1.3. An increasingly large size of investment for international satellite projects, the tremendous risks involved, together with the required level of synergy between diverse skill areas are most often used as arguments for explaining collaboration in the satellite telecommunication area.

These "traditional" explanations, however, are not convincing arguments for explaining the superiority and sustainability of collaboration. The *size of investment* for a typical satellite project is in the range of 300 to 500 million dollars, which is nothing that could not be "shouldered" by large, multinational firms. Project *risks* are not much greater than for many other investment projects pursued by private firms. For some risks, there is a well-functioning insurance mar-

---

9   While the supplier of a "satellite system" simply sells the satellite as a product, the provider of a "turn-key satellite system" offers the full system of the required infrastructure, often together with the service "satellite functioning in orbit".

ket[10]. The role of asset complementarity and the related level of *synergy*, even though being important for satellite systems, is not significantly more complicated than for manufacturers of more mundane products such as automobiles[11].

Reasons for the paramount role of cooperation in the satellite business should, instead, be sought in the *time pattern of entry and exit*, and in political and institutional restraints. The knowledge acquisition process for a firm participating in satellite projects is very time-consuming. Most firms have accumulated highly-specific knowledge over more than 20 years. Suppliers of specialized components, materials and sub-systems are selected for a competitive satellite project only because they can offer such a long track-record. The gestation period (research, development, test and manufacturing) for a single satellite project is typically 4 to 8 years. The satellite has an average lifetime (in orbit) of 8 to 12 years. Suppliers of an integrated satellite system with several successive generations of satellites must be ready for long-term support over 20 years and more.

These knowledge requirements, the related entry conditions and the time profile of investment is different for firms at the systems integration, sub-system and components level. A *systems integrator* is required to master sophisticated systems engineering capabilities, and he has to offer the financial and managerial strengths to support a program until its very end. Typical firms capable of performing such complex tasks are large companies in electronics, aerospace, or in the engineering and construction sector.

A supplier of dedicated *components and sub-systems*, by contrast, must be able to build on a long track-record of reliable products, which, for reasons often only known to him, do effectively "work in space". Systems integration firms must rely on sourcing from a diverse network of such specialized suppliers. Appropriability regimes for specialized supply firms are often rather tight due to the long entry times, and the tacit character of the relevant knowledge. These conditions work in favor of market contracting for specialized components and sub-systems, provided the geographic scope of the market allows for a sufficiently large and specialized supplier structure (through "global sourcing").

The resulting "ideal" mode of governance and organization would be a *dual structure*, i.e. a combination of the full integration mode for large systems firms, and of the market mode of transactions for the supply of specialized components and parts. The appropriate structure would be a market network with one centrally coordinating hub firm, a structure with which we are familiar in the automotive industry as well as in the engineering and construction sector. The pro-

---

10 Firms can insure themselves against the launch risk, which is typically the most uncertain part of a satellite project. As a result, the satellite insurance business has become a significant element for the international satellite industry.

11 While a satellite system contains between 10^2 and 10^3 sophisticated components and modules, a car is assembled on the basis of 10^4—10^5 different components.

posed dual structure for the satellite telecommunication manufacturing sector will be analyzed in more detail in section 6.4.

There are barriers to the evolution of such an efficient industry structure, which can be explained by a critical numbers problem. Knowledge requirements for some critical parts and components may be such that a particular firm is able to exploit a strategic position. Systems integrators get an incentive to integrate backwards to prevent potential hold-ups in terms of product reliability, delivery time and pricing, even though they are less efficient in developing and manufacturing the required specialized parts. Or customers try to lure new suppliers to the respective field, and have to experience set-backs (delays, unexpected malfunctioning, etc.).

Such critical number problems are of particular concern if we consider the development and procurement of satellite projects at the national level. Most countries other than the very large nations (e. g. U.S.A.) are too small to sustain a specialized supplier infrastructure for satellites at the national level. In conflict to such size and efficiency considerations, many smaller countries pursue eager national satellite projects and try to develop an indigenous supplier base. Since these smaller countries are shareholders of international operating organizations (such as Intelsat or Inmarsat), they demand a "fair return" of procurement for their national firms. Most of these smaller countries, however, are not capable of supporting a large national systems firm; consequently, they expect to be involved in the sub-systems and components business. The result is a political spread of sub-system and component contracting over "too thin" a national supplier group. Inefficiencies and market failures are in this way induced by political requirements and expectations.

In consideration of such significant political diversions, the international satellite market must accordingly be grouped into two different segments: competitive projects, for which the customer is a private firm, have to be distinguished from political projects, where the customer is a public or semi-public institution. *Competitive projects* involve the procurement of satellite systems primarily based on price and performance characteristics. Suppliers are selected on the basis of open bidding at a global level. The resulting supplier system can be described by the dual structure, i. e. the full integration mode for reputable international systems firms, together with a relatively large network of supplier firms that are located in several countries.

Political satellite projects, by contrast, are often characterized by a quota system, by the political selection of suppliers, and by politically induced forms of collaboration. Political decision-makers in large countries are inclined to select a preferred national systems integrator; smaller nations or political authorities waive their right to insist on national systems integrators, but demand instead to participate in the supply of parts and sub-systems. Private firms are enticed into all sorts of collaborative arrangements with suppliers from different nations, simply because this appears to be politically opportune, and because this is often the only possible way for less advanced firms to compensate for lack of know-how and experience.

Most satellite investment programs, particularly those pursued at national and European level, still fall into the second category of political projects. They offer shelter for second-best suppliers and ill-designed cooperative arrangements. As a result of the greater commercialization of satellite projects, and due to the growing need to reduce public spending, however, competitive projects are becoming increasingly important. Pressure will be exercised sooner or later on the appropriate restructuring of the group of supplier firms, and on a more consistent and efficiency-oriented structuring of large satellite projects. To describe the working of competitive forces being intertwined with political and regulatory restraints, we will first analyze some completed satellite investment projects in section 6.3. We will then describe in section 6.4, for which reasons and in which sequence the dual structure outlined above will eventually become more clearly established.

6.3   Cooperative Associations for European Satellite Projects

As outlined in the preceeding section, most national and international satellite programs must still be considered as political projects for which certain forms of collaboration are primarily sought for *non-economic* reasons. These reasons will be outlined in section 6.3.1. Sections 6.3.2 to 6.3.4 contain case descriptions of three European satellite projects. Two of these projects, the German TV-Sat and the DFS Kopernikus projects, were pursued within a multi-party collaborative arrangement, for which strategic objectives were not precisely enough defined, and which were not sufficiently directed at customer needs. These two projects are contrasted with a broadcasting satellite project pursued at a European level, which also involved participation of several independent institutions, but which was primarily pursued as a private business venture (the Astra satellite consortium). We will argue, that a clear specification of objectives, and a stringent, though flexible selection of processes, technologies, and appropriate institutional structures is decisive for the success of a large and complex investment project.

6.3.1   Economic and Political Reasons for Collaboration

Political satellite projects differ from private projects with respect to the strategic objectives pursued, and with respect to the costs related to achieving these objectives. This difference between public and private projects is influenced by the extent of exclusiveness, by the number of participating agents, and by the consistency and strength of incentives (Olson 1968). *Private projects* are most often pursued by a small numbers of agents with clearly specified objectives, by well-defined missions, and by a clear attribution of tasks and responsibilities[12]. Performance characteristics and technical alternatives are chosen so that predetermined objectives can be achieved at the minimum cost and in due time.

Public satellite projects, by contrast, are often characterized by a more sketchy formulation of objectives, by a relatively large and inhomogeneous group of agents, and, not infrequently, by rather dubious missions and contractual arrangements[13]. Financial funds for a satellite project often get allocated under one political administration during a predetermined legislation period. The budget is made available for a certain fiscal period, and public decision-makers do not have to be concerned about a certain customer group and its requirements. During the design and development phase, political priorities may change, participating agents "come and go", and often priorities and objectives related to a particular satellite project will successively become adapted and diluted. Changing priorities and missions make it difficult to pursue a cost-minimizing strategy and an effective controlling of the time schedule; in addition, public decision-makers do not get "punished" as much for cost overruns and time delays as is the case for private decision-makers.

As a result, economic considerations are typically less important for the design and organization of a public satellite program than is the case for a private project. The incentive to look for a cost-minimizing and risk-reducing mode of governance and organization will be less expressed. Political preferences and institutional prerogatives become an end in itself. Collaboration between certain groups and international partnerships are praised as virtues, no matter which effects they have on the economic efficiency and sustainability of a project. Institutional structures with politically preferred modes of governance and organization are *fixed before* strategic objectives are specified, and before the appropriate processes and tasks are selected.

In spite of this low emphasis on economic considerations, economic reasons are often stressed as justification for decisions which were determined at political level. The virtues of cooperation and the advantage of a preselected mode of governance and organization are praised by referring to alleged cost advantages. Certain groups of firms and teaming arrangements are established

---

12 The private investor has a clear interest of investigating customer needs and of specifying performance characteristics beforehand. He will watch closely any deviation from these targets and specifications, because he has to bear the losses incurred thereby.

13 A typical example can be found in the different approaches pursued for the satellite programs Astra, TV-Sat and DFS Kopernikus. The private Astra consortium did *not* place the satellite into orbit *before* most customers had signalled and identified their technical requirements (related to the video standard). By contrast, the Deutsche Bundespost (German PTT) launched its satellite long *before* it finalized the contracts with major customer groups.

politically, and are then justified on the basis of economies-of-scale considerations, or on the basis of assumed economies-of-scope. However, political decision-makers are often poor in assessing true levels of economies-of-scale or
synergies. Teaming arrangements and project size levels chosen freely by private firms typically differ considerably from modes of governance and organization, which are preselected by purchasing authorities and public decision-
makers, who base their choices on guesses about the underlying cost structure.
In many cases, economic reasons will at best be used as rationalization for
pursuing other political objectives. These include objectives such as (1) prestige, (2) national autonomy and self sufficiency, (3) national security, as well
as (4) fairness and equal opportunity considerations. National satellite programs
often emphasize the prestige of "having one's own high-tech communication
system", and the capability of having the satellite built primarily by national
firms. European programs apply the same objectives for the ESA member countries as a group. Teams of firms are then selected not because they offer the
best design at a cost-competitive level, but because they allow for a predetermined and desired geographical distribution of purchasing contracts. Or else,
firms are allowed membership to a coalition in order to satisfy fairness principles. In the following, this is illustrated for three satellite programs, the West
German TV-Sat and DFS Kopernikus projects, and the Luxembourg based Astra
project.

6.3.2   The German TV-Sat Project

Decisions for the new generation of broadcasting satellites in West Germany were
not determined by customer needs, but primarily by political and technical considerations. Germany had been excluded from participating in those space-related
activities, which were regarded as crucial for defense purposes. Satellite and
rocket technology was considered accessible only through West Germany's participation in the European organizations ELDO, ESRO and ESA[14]. It was only
in the mid 1970s that political decision-makers and technical experts in West
Germany were able to formulate space-related development objectives that could
be narrowed down to a national focus. Civil broadcasting satellite technology was

---

14 Originally, the European Launch Development Organization (ELDO) was established to
   pursue European rocket development projects, while the European Space Research Organization (ESRO) became active in providing, among other things, basic development for
   satellites. In 1975, both organizations were merged into the European Space Agency
   (ESA).

considered compatible with Germany's "low-defense exposure", and as an activity with a *national* scope[15]. Primary objectives were:

- to develop an advanced broadcasting satellite system with *national coverage*;
- to "leapfrog" in *technology* by promoting new concepts that were foreseen for the next generation of broadcasting satellites;
- and to develop and organize *national capabilities* in R&D, manufacturing and satellite.

The lead was taken by the Federal Ministry of Research and Technology (BMFT), which commissioned a feasibility study directed at formulating technical specifications for an "advanced communication system" (zukunftsorientiertes Kommunikationssystem — ZKS). Three large national suppliers (MBB, Siemens, and AEG with its former subsidiary ANT) participated in the study. During the course of this study, an international standardization committee (the WARC conference) agreed in 1977, that each country would be allowed to transmit five broadcasting channels through a national satellite. This agreement had considerable implications for the selection of technology and for organizational choices. A small number of channels (the regulatory restraint) together with a narrow beam (due to the goal of national coverage) was expected to be best met through the use of a *high-power satellite system*. The alternative "technological trajectory", the development of a *medium or low power* satellite, being more appropriate for a wider and international coverage, and less restricted with respect to the number of channels, was not considered useful at that time.

The high-power alternative was selected not only because of its compliance with national objectives and regulatory restraints, but also because it was expected to offer a much greater *potential for technical advance:* high power transmission was anticipated to allow for greater quality of image transmission, and to be more compatible with future video standards (primarily for high-definition television — HDTV). Furthermore, it was expected that much smaller and

---

15 West Germany was expected — deliberately or implicitly — not to become involved in a major defense-related satellite project. Strategic objectives of national promoters of satellite projects were therefore only realizable for non-defense application areas. Broadcasting satellites were considered as those types of satellites with the lowest *"defense exposure"*. Other types of satellites, such as those for earth exploration, navigation and communication, were of a "dual use" character and were considered as characterized by a "high defense exposure". Another reason to promote a national broadcasting satellite project was the belief that such a satellite system could effectively be operated with *national coverage*. This rationale to promote a German broadcasting satellite system primarily with national coverage, would later lead to restrictions for its commercialization potential, particularly in comparison with the Astra project (see section 6.3.3) which was explicitly directed at the pan-European broadcasting market.

cheaper antennas could be developed for the reception of signals from high power satellites than would be needed for medium or low power satellites.

Decision-makers who favored the high-power, high-quality technical alternative were biased in two ways: *First*, their choices were based on the *actual* configuration of technical performance characteristics and regulatory restraints, while decision-makers were not responsive enough to expected future changes[16]. *Second*, decision-makers overemphasized technical performance characteristics while they did not consider the commercial aspects (i.e. customer requirements and cost considerations) enough. The second bias was caused by institutional segregation: decision-makers responsible for technical specification were organizationally separated from agents who later had to pay for the system. Finance for the system was provided by the tax-payer and through development funds allocated by the postal authorities. The "final customers", i.e. private TV subscribers or, indirectly, the channel operators, were not able to "translate" their requirements into system design and specification at that date. By contrast, technical experts in research institutions, in the ministries and in private firms became decisive in the selection of technical alternatives and development tasks.

Due to these biases and the related organizational separation between final customers and suppliers, technical performance criteria and standards were successively adapted in a way which made the total satellite system more expensive. Transmission power and quality standards were increased without taking the impact on the cost per channel, the parameter to be decisive for adoption, enough into consideration. Industrial participants willingly responded to changes in performance requirements because they were paid by cost-plus contracts[17].

The cost of the TV-Sat system turned out much higher than expected, and the completion of the system had to encounter a four year delay. Only part of this can be attributed to technical adaptations, or to the inappropriate coordination between purchasing agents, specification authorities and suppliers. A greater problem were the delays in intra-orbit transportation. While it was originally expected that the TV-Sat 1 satellite would be placed in orbit in 1983, it was not,

---

16 The relative technical advantage of high-power systems later became successively reduced due to the ongoing evolution of medium and low power satellites. Furthermore, changes in the regulatory environment was not taken into consideration. Some of these changes had already been foreseeable at the time the decisions were made.

17 In the case of a *cost-plus contract*, the developer gets his cost reimbursed plus a certain, predetermined margin (often five percent of total cost). The R&D contractor has no incentive to convince the purchasing agency *not* to proceed with a costly overspecification. In many empirical cases, contractors willingly accept re-development work, even though they often foresee that the system will become too expensive for being successfully sold later on the commercial market.

in fact, launched until 1987[18]. This four-year delay coincided with considerable changes in satellite technology, and in the regulatory as well as the competitive environment. During 1983 and 1987, the satellite telecommunication market became deregulated in North America. This led to a great surge in direct broadcasting satellites, primarily in the medium and low power range. Sequential learning and scale effects, as well as ongoing technical changes in frequency transmission and receiving technology led to cost reductions, quality improvements, and to considerable reductions of the size of antennas to be used for small and medium power satellites. As a result, the originally perceived advantages of high-power satellite systems became gradually reduced, one could almost say neutralized, during the second half of the 1980s.

In spite of these time delays and the corresponding preponderance of substitute technologies, decision-makers became even more dedicated to pushing their original concepts. The high-power configuration with a small number of channels was promoted as the only technical solution that would allow for the introduction of HDTV standards. As a response to Japanese challenges that were aimed at imposing their own HDTV standards unilaterally[19], European TV equipment manufacturers decided to promote their satellite transmission norm MAC as an intermediary step towards a future HDTV standard (HD-MAC) which was to be specified at a later date. The perceived advantage of this "two-step approach towards the television of the future" was seen in a more gradual and cheaper replacement of successive generations of TV equipment[20].

Perceived overall cost advantages that might lead to inducements to innovate for both producers and consumers were, however, underestimated for two reasons. *First*, promoters of the MAC standard underestimated the coordination requirements that would have to be fulfilled in order to even agree on one single European norm. While decision-makers in France and West Germany agreed on the D2-MAC standard, other norms were introduced in Britain (D-MAC) and in Scandinavia (C-MAC). *Second*, cost estimates were primarily based on one

---

18 The Ariane rocket which had been selected for launching, encountered technical difficulties. In addition, the Challenger accident in the U.S. resulted in a virtual monopoly of the Ariane consortium, and in a long waiting-list for clients, particularly for those without opportunity for exit, which was the case for projects which had received public funding in Europe.

19 Japanese firms, in conjunction with MITI, had begun pursuing experimental HDTV projects in the early 1980s. In 1985, Japan had already developed TV receivers and studio equipment, and Japanese firms announced their willingness to push their preferred standard on an international level.

20 The present generation of television sets (average price approximately 1600 DM) could be replaced by MAC-compatible ones (average price 3500 DM), and these would later be replaced by HD-MAC-compatible ones (today's price expectations 8000 DM). Future prices depend on systems introduction and learning-curve effects. The intermediate generation (MAC-compatible televisions) would be able to receive signals from HD-MAC satellites.

single element of the satellite broadcasting chain of activity, which was illustrated in Fig. 6.1. Decision-makers were considering only the expected costs of transmitting TV signals via satellite, based on the assumption that coordination with providers of complementary assets could be achieved at relatively low cost. Overall systems costs, necessary expenditures for *complementary assets* (channel costs, TV programming and transmission, consumer expenditures for satellite antennas and receivers), as well as coordination requirements for all these interdependent elements were not taken sufficiently into consideration. Due to the first problem of different video transmission norms, markets for television sets, satellite antennas and receivers became fragmented across Europe, and prices had to be higher than necessary. This again led to considerable increases of overall systems costs. Serious delays and coordination failures due to the second reason led to a low acceptance of the new system by consumers, consumer equipment dealers and installers. These problems of low acceptance levels of consumers, and of non-coordinated activities of suppliers of complementary assets, which were in sharp contrast to the optimistic scenarios originally promoted by supporters of the system, were further aggravated by the breakdown of the first satellite (TV-Sat 1), which was launched in 1987. Technical difficulties with the solar panel led to malfunctioning and to a total dismissal of the satellite after it had been launched into orbit[21]. This failure led to a serious setback, and evoked further "frustration" on the side of receiving equipment manufacturers, and TV program providers. Uncooperative or even adversary relationships between providers of complementary assets were later responsible for difficulties, which continued even after the second satellite (TV Sat 2) had successfully become operational in 1989: TV equipment was not readily available, appropriate satellite dishes and receivers had not been developed and marketed, and TV program providers (the large national television networks ARD and ZDF) were not willing to transmit programs with a wide national coverage

---

21 Failure of the TV Sat 1 satellite to unfold both solar panels and to generate enough electricity may be interpreted as "bad luck", but they may also be related to the organization of the project. The failure was caused by inconsistent quality assurance procedures during re-assembly, while the satellite was transferred between agents in Germany, France and Kourou (the location of the launch site). While such mistakes may happen in any satellite project, failures of such a kind can be considered as less likely for a systems integrator able to manufacture and launch a large series of satellites. In this last case, transaction-specific investments for quality assurance will be more economical than if a manufacturer is only able to build a few satellites per decade. The German satellite manufacturing industry has never achieved the appropriate scale level, and is forced to invest an above-average share of expenditures for quality assurance, or as an alternative, to accept lower levels of systems reliability.

according to the new MAC standard[22]. For all these reasons, there was no visible advantage for consumers to switch to the new system which later became paraphrased as "television for the blind". Acceptance levels thus turned out to be extremely low, and promoters of the systems had to "fight an uphill battle" to get at least part of their original expectations fulfilled.

6.3.3   The Astra Satellite Project

The Astra satellite project, which was conceptualized during the first half of the 1980s, was distinctly different from the TV-Sat project described above with respect to its strategic orientation, its flexibility and its structural openness. Other projects with a strong political orientation such as the TV-Sat project or the French TDF satellites, had to be pursued within existing institutional structures. Diverse objectives of large national consumer electronics firms, postal authorities and political decision-makers all had to be taken into consideration, which strongly restricted program flexibility and strategic direction. This "blending" of diverse interests led to political agreements on technical priorities which, at the time the decisions were made, were supported by interest groups in the research institutes and within the public administration, which were not able to secure consensus among other groups being of stronger influence for later phases of the project. By the time the projects had to be re-adapted to a changing environment, the groups of technically-oriented decision-makers were not willing to depart from the original "grand design"; consequently the projects did not get enough support from related interest groups and from providers of complementary resources, who were more interested in the commercial prospects.

The Astra satellite project, by contrast, was started as a private business venture with clear objectives of participating agents. It was directed at the exploitation of opportunities in European-wide satellite broadcasting opened up by new technologies, by structural changes in broadcasting markets, and also by the political and structural rigidity of existing institutions. Commercial and financial

---

22 Both ARD and ZDF decided *not* to use their reserved channels for their more popular *first* programs, but used them instead for their cultural programs "3 Sat" and "1 Plus" which have a very low coverage. These programs are not attractive enough for large audiences. Furthermore, ARD and ZDF prefer to transmit their programs in the old PAL norm, because of the high costs of switching to MAC-compatible studio equipment. As a result, there is at present no convincing incitement to receive the programs transmitted over the TV-Sat system. This may gradually become changed after both ARD and ZDF have announced their willingness to also transmit some programs in the new norm (based on a memorandum of understanding in early 1991). Whether this will really influence adoption levels for the new transmission standard remains to be seen.

objectives led to a consideration of expected customer needs, and to the selection and design of appropriate institutional structures. Decisions on specific technologies were made only after reliable signals from customers and from providers of complementary assets had been taken into consideration.

The entrepreneur and project promoter had originally managed a private cable TV network in Switzerland. He thereby gained detailed insight into customer needs and requirements and into the economics of TV transmission systems. According to his experience, the number of subscribers was proportional to the number of channels transmitted. It was concluded that a new satellite TV transmission system could only get a large enough coverage if the number of channels could be considerably increased beyond five, which was the existing regulatory restraint imposed by the international standardization authority. The choice would then be to either cope with this regulatory requirement and to operate a commercially unviable system, or to find a niche in which a viable system could be operated that would not be restricted by arbitrary standards or political requirements. One country that had not signed the international agreement was Luxembourg; hence it was decided to start a satellite operating organization in this country and to launch a system with pan-European coverage.

The Société Européene des Satellites (SES) became established as a private commercial venture with some supplementary government support. Major shareholders were the Luxembourg-based broadcasting corporation (CLT) as well as some banks, media companies across Europe and private individuals. The corporate objectives were to operate a broadcasting satellite system with as great a coverage as possible, and to transmit a sufficiently large number of TV channels. These objectives could only be met with medium-power satellites, and by relying on technology which was compatible to the investment decisions of program providers, equipment manufacturers, as well as consumers, and which was in compliance with regulating authorities.

Regulating authorities were, however, seen as controlling "replaceable assets", whereas the investment decisions of program providers and equipment manufacturers were considered as being more decisive. In some countries to which programs had to be transmitted, such as West Germany, approval for a broadcasting satellite was made more difficult than approval for a telephone or data transmission satellite[23]. Astra thus got its approval as a telephone and data transmission satellite, with the intent of setting facts through operating it as a broadcasting satellite. Fast approval was thus achieved without compromising performance standards, which were regarded as crucial for compliance with customers as well as with providers of complementary assets.

---

23 Broadcasting satellites were considered as being high-power satellites, whereas medium-power satellites were classed as telephone or data transmission satellites.

Knowledge of customer requirements also showed that it is not only low price for video channel transmission, but also systems availability and reliability that are crucial to economic success. New technology can "create value" and improve comparative advantage, as long as it contributes to low channel prices without sacrifices in systems availability and reliability. Overstretched technology requirements, and over-emphasis on future generations of immature technologies, by contrast, will lead to excessive costs, uncertainties about the availability of systems, and to considerable delays. As a purely commercial venture, specialized on systems operation, with no obligation to buy from a particular supplier group or to comply with technology policy considerations, the Astra organization was free to choose a satellite best suited to its commercial requirements. It was able to "shop around" and to rely on open bidding, and was thus able to exploit economic advantages which other European satellite operating organizations were not able to[24]. Not surprisingly, Astra awarded the contract to a large U.S. satellite manufacturer who was able to offer a relatively low price and to assure delivery in less than three years[25].

During this period, Astra was still able to coordinate with TV program providers and with manufacturers of complementary equipment in order to agree on the most appropriate transmission norm. In comparison to the early and rigid specification through the TV-Sat project to which program providers were "forced to comply", Astra commissioned a market survey very late in the process; close communication with customers showed that the widely accepted PAL norm would be a "much safer bet" than any MAC standard. The final choice was completed only shortly before the satellite was launched. Through this flexible, interactive process, Astra did not just gain information about the preferred norm, but was also able to sign agreements with those program providers ready to lease channel capacity.

In addition, Astra closely coordinated with equipment manufacturers who were able to provide appropriate TV receiving equipment, satellite antennas, etc. Exchange of information and market networking with mutual benefit for both sides was sufficient to induce providers of complementary equipment. The expectation of a large European coverage induced firms to make specific investments. As an example, Amstrad developed a low-cost antenna and receiver system, and was able to gain a considerable market share across Europe. The availability of low-

---

24 The Green Paper on satellite communication published by the EEC (1990) estimates that European operating organizations have to encounter cost disadvantages of the factor two to three due to their limited opportunity to "shop around".

25 Delivery time would have been four to six years for some European manufacturers who, in addition, would have added expenditures and delays for R&D, whereas U.S. manufacturers were able to offer "off-the-shelf" products.

cost receiving equipment at just the right time, on the other hand, was an additional argument for the rapid enlargement of Astra's European customer base, and to attract additional TV program providers to transmit their program via the Astra satellite.

The Astra satellite project certainly was not without risks; the satellite was launched without enough agreements being signed by program providers, and trade journals conjectured in 1988 that the project might turn out to be a failure. Close interaction between customers, and coordination with other firms, on which Astra crucially depended, helped reduce that risk to a containable level, and allowed to exploit insider information. Favorable circumstances certainly have improved the commercial feasibility of the project in a way that was even unforeseeable to the agents directly involved. The technical breakdown of the TV-Sat 1, as well as delays with the TV-Sat 2, have further contributed to the comparative advantage of Astra. Coordination problems in connection with the MAC norm have legitimized ex-post Astra's pragmatic standardization decision. By historical coincidence, the opening of Eastern Europe in 1989 has provided further momentum to the Astra project which has become the largest European broadcasting satellite operator by the end of 1990, and which has set the de-facto-standard for satellite broadcasting.

6.3.4   The German DFS-Kopernikus Project

In 1983, the Deutsche Bundespost, the German telecommunication authority, commissioned the development and production of an integrated telecommunication satellite system which:

- was focused on *voice and data transmission*, primarily with national coverage;
- would provide *additional capabilities for broadcasting* based on new technologies developed during the TV-Sat project;
- and which should *demonstrate the capabilities of German institutions* to provide all the parts of an integrated communication system.

Contracts for the development and manufacturing of three satellites and for related earth stations were awarded to the same firms which had already participated in the TV-Sat project; purchasing continuity allowed these firms to exploit knowledge and capital equipment accumulated during former projects, and to keep R&D capacities utilized. Major tasks were divided between ANT (for the electronic payload), MBB (for the bus system) and SEL (for data transmission). At the time the contract was awarded, not one of these three firms was considered as being the appropriate partner to take on full systems responsibility. As a result, Siemens was asked to act as the general contractor, due to its perceived financial strength, but in spite of the fact that this company had announced earlier that participation in the international satellite business was not considered a strategic objective[26].

Contracts were not awarded through bidding competition. Instead, contract awards were based on worksharing agreements already established during the TV-Sat project. Similar to the process outlined in section 6.3.2, several successive stages of technical adaptation and re-specification occurred, during which price increases and project delays had to be encountered. By the time the project was completed, the cost of the overall systems came to 850 million DM. It is estimated that this was approximately 25—35% in excess of the price that would have had to be paid if the system had been procured through competitive bidding on the world market, even though it is difficult to estimate world market prices for such a custom-made system.

Disadvantages due to national and European preferences also had to be encountered for complementary services. Launching the satellite into orbit was awarded to Arianespace, the European consortium. This "lock-in" to one particular service provider resulted in high launching costs and some additional delays. The system operator, the Deutsche Bundespost, had to wait until 1989, when the first DFS Kopernikus satellite became operational; the second satellite was put into orbit in 1990. The economics underlying the project and the timing pattern were both not very favorable for commercial success, even though the project can be regarded as path-breaking in terms of technical advances. In both market segments at which it was directed, it had to run counter to some competitors who were much more favorably positioned. In *voice and data transmission*, the Deutsche Bundespost's own investments in earth-bound cable transmission and digital exchanges totally outpaced satellite investments that were pursued parallel to it[27].

In the area of *satellite broadcasting*, the few channels reserved on the DFS Kopernikus 1 satellite had to compete against Astra, which was on the market earlier and which provided many more channels with much wider coverage. TV program providers can hardly be induced to pay high annual costs for a channel, which can reach only relatively few households. Suppliers of complementary equipment (antennas, receivers), on the other hand, were not convinced that the DFS-Kopernikus satellite system, which provides TV transmission only "as a sideline" would attract enough households to amortize their specific investments.

---

26 Siemens had decided towards the end of the 1970s not to become actively engaged in the satellite communication and aerospace business, due to the perceived intensity of international competition. The company accepted the award for general contractorship for the DFS-Kopernikus satellite, without placing much emphasis on this project.

27 In 1983, the Deutsche Bundespost started an ambitious, large national investment program aimed at modernizing the earthbound telephone and data network. Since then, the role of satellites has been increasingly reduced to fulfilling a supplementary and minor function.

The comparative advantage of the system was even less visible for the consumer, the decisive though often neglected agent in the decision-making nexus. Larger, less user-friendly and more expensive antennas were required, fewer channels with less popular TV programs were transmitted, and customers were not supported by a functioning service and dealer network. The Deutsche Bundespost had not promoted the satellite system enough through information campaigns and marketing services. As a result of relatively poor customer support, the DFS-Kopernikus had hardly become known to consumers, and was not been able to reach a high-enough acceptance level. By the end of 1990, only 175 thousand households were able to receive TV signals from the DFS-Kopernikus satellite, while 730 thousand German households were equipped with receiving antennas for the Astra satellite.

Greater commercial use of DFS-Kopernikus services had also been made difficult by the pricing policies of the Deutsche Telekom, the deregulated telecommunication branch of the Deutsche Bundespost. The operation and commercial use of the DFS-Kopernikus project was organized as a small profit center, which had to bear the fixed cost of the integrated satellite system. Given the initial high price of the overall satellite system, and the dominant position of the competing terrestrial system, a large part of which has already been depreciated, it was almost impossible to ever reach amortization for the separated satellite sub-system. Customers were charged the full costs, and the acceptance level was therefore accordingly low.

The opening-up of Eastern Germany, with its urgent need for the rapid availability of voice, data and TV transmission, had provided some additional stimulus to the DFS-Kopernikus system, especially after the second satellite had become operational. The pricing of the satellite, and limited flexibility on the part of Deutsche Telekom, however, have set limits to the effective use of this system.

6.3.5   Comparison and Conclusions

These case descriptions show that the process of political decision-making reverses the sequence needed for effective governance and organization of a complex investment project. Project organization and management is not structured according to an endogenous process of "organizational design" as outlined in chapters 2 and 5, which would allow for cost minimization and program efficiency. Institutional structures are determined according to political preferences and prerogatives, and not as a result of "matching" organizational choices to the best available processes and techniques. As the TV-Sat and the DFS-Kopernikus projects demonstrate, public authorities and purchasing agents have selected a group of firms and a specific teaming arrangement. The specific form of cooperation and the organizational structure chosen turned out not to be appropriate for solving the underlying tasks. At least one of the following sacrifices had to be made:

- original objectives were only partly fulfilled or diluted;
- program costs were higher than attainable through other solutions;
- and considerable time delays had to be encountered.

As a result of the politically determined management and organizational structure, the potential customer, in both cases the West German, resp. European users of telecommunication services, have to pay higher prices, or they get inferior or delayed service for a given price level. The potential consumer surplus is reduced, and is sacrificed in order to support an inefficient structure; or else it is used for maintaining producer surpluses for a certain group of suppliers.

Increasing producer surplus by "taxing" consumers may be justified for dynamic efficiency considerations: producers may use their surplus for investments in R&D and for greater product efficiency. This would enable them to become more competitive on the world market, to reduce development and production costs and prices, and to raise consumer surplus in the future. Such arguments are often stressed in connection with support programs for a national and European supplier groups. The key question remains, whether temporary producer surpluses are used for investive purposes, or whether they are just used for compensating organizational and managerial deficiencies. So far, European satellite manufacturers have tended to use the surpluses gained from political programs as a sort of cushion: it has prevented most of them from becoming effectively involved in open, competitive, international satellite programs[28]. Repetitive national and European programs have kept a "balkanized" supplier structure alive. Most national and European satellite programs were too small, and were not launched frequently enough to allow for effective investment and restructuring; at the same time, public projects were seen as attractive enough to prevent the firms from looking out for more competitive, international programs[29].

6.4   Governance Modes for Competitive International Satellite Programs

The international telecommunication satellite industry has undergone a major restructuring phase, which will continue throughout the 1990s, during which an open, networking type of collaboration will successively be replaced by a more

---

28 During the 1980s, no single German supplier was able to gain a leadership position as systems integrator for any competitive, international satellite project.
29 There are, however, positive examples in which firms have successfully participated as suppliers to international programs. These firms, however, were often the ones neglected by national support programs. See section 6.5.

formalized, vertically-integrated industrial structure. These changes in the mode of governance and organization are interrelated with the growing share of private investment activity. Over the last ten years, the provision and utilization of telecommunication satellite services has become an increasingly commercial activity. Direct broadcasting satellites (DBS) were first operated in the United States on a private basis, and have expanded their nation-wide coverage considerably[30]. Similar services were started for the intercontinental transmission of data and information[31]. Even in strongly-regulated Western Europe, private operators of telecommunication satellites have become established[32]. Further private operators will become active all over the world, and telecommunication satellite services will expand into many new application areas[33].

These new activities must be calculated as investment projects with a clear and measurable private return. Since entry times and costs[34], as well as project risks are considerable, expenditures must be closely watched and controlled. As a result, private operators' purchasing decisions will increasingly be based on cost and delivery criteria such as

- the *purchase price* for the satellite systems;
- *operating costs*;
- reliable delivery *in time*;
- plus other characterisitics which reduce operator's costs and risks[35].

More and more private operating companies set the standard for purchasing behavior and typical customer requirements. Large international organizations such as Intelsat, Inmarsat and others are forced by their shareholders to tightly control expenditures, and are thus emphasizing similar purchasing criteria. In addition, even public operating organizations will come under increasing pressure to apply similar purchasing standards instead of subsidizing certain groups of national suppliers.

---

30 The evolution of direct broadcasting satellite services was induced by the deregulation of the telecommunication sector in the U.S. during the first half of the 1980s. Deregulation activities in other countries will lead to further inducements for the telecommunication satellite industry.

31 AT&T and PanAm-Sat operate world-wide direct broadcasting satellite services.

32 Examples are the Luxembourg-based Astra consortium, and British Satellite Broadcasting (BSB) together with Sky Television, the Logstar consortium, and others.

33 Examples are mobile telecommunication satellite services for traffic monitoring, and for cellular mobile telephony.

34 For example, just the political and regulatory process of licensing private activity for the British Satellite Broadcasting project took about five years.

35 This includes additional characterisitics such as "modular, flexible specifications" or "satellite functioning in orbit".

Market forces increasingly penetrate the whole telecommunication satellite business. The allocation of funds and resources will become separated from political decision-making. Participating agents and suppliers receive their incentives from a more "orderly distribution through imputation". This means that the value of goods of lower order (application of satellite operating services) determines the value of goods of higher order (satellite systems, sub-systems and components)[36]. The valuation of purchasing firms determines the funds allocated to the satellite supply system, and the rules for competitive differentiation between supplying firms. Efficiently organized firms will receive above-average returns, while inefficient firms will be forced to adapt, or to leave the industry. The resulting restructuring process will be analyzed in the following sections 6.4.1 to 6.4.3.

6.4.1   Integration Within Large Satellite Systems Firms

Changing customer requirements lead to a considerable restructuring within the satellite production system. The most important selection criterion is the *price of the satellite system*. Satellite systems manufacturers must be able to benefit both from economies-of-scale in production and from transaction cost advantages, which inevitably requires a large minimum efficient size. *Economies-of-scale in production* can only be exploited if a firm is able to build a certain number of satellites per year[37]. Customer demands for a more reliable track record are further enhanced by experience curve effects, through which the cost of a satellite system is a resultant of the cumulated number of satellites which a firm has produced in the past.

Indivisibilities for large assembly and test facilities lead to additional cost savings for large satellite systems suppliers. Large clean-room assembly, test and simulation facilities are highly-specific, and often have a reconstruction value of one billion dollars or more[38]. Indivisibilities in R&D require that a group of

---

36 This principle of "distribution through imputation", which was originally developed by Menger (1871), was described in chapter 2 of this study. Investment decisions for goods of higher order (upstream processes) must be based on the assessment of their contribution to the benefits of final customers. Accordingly, the choice of specific techniques of satellite communication must be based on tangible improvements in information exchange, which results in "added values" to final customers.

37 The obvious competitive disadvantage of European suppliers vis- -vis U.S. firms can be seen from the fact that the largest European manufactuers only build one satellite per year, while large U.S. firms build one per month.

38 As an example, a few large firms operate test facilities which simulate the conditions in geostationary orbit (vacuum chambers, daily changes in temperature of several hundred degrees centigrade); these facilities have been constructed for the purpose of testing satellites in the past, and represent sunk investment which would be extremely expensive to reconstruct. In-house control over such highly-specific assets offer firms sustainable first-mover advantages in bidding competition.

several hundred highly-trained specialists is regularly kept on the pay-roll, and shielded off from temporary demand fluctuations.

While some tasks of a large satellite systems, such as R&D, assembly and testing require considerable size, other specialized tasks related to the development and manufacturing of components and sub-systems can be much better performed by independent suppliers. Even though systems integrators may be interested in integrating backwards into some strategically important component segments, full integration to cover the full spectrum of activities will either not be feasible, or will offer only limited economic advantages (see section 6.4.2). Any large systems integrator will thus have to rely on a large network of specialized satellite component or sub-systems firms. This requires a tremendously complex coordination system, with transaction-specific investments of considerable size[39]. Again, large firm-size offers transaction cost savings for a large integrator of satellite systems.

In addition, new customer requirements increasingly call for a "full package" of service, and demand greater service-orientation and flexibility of satellite suppliers. Requirements such as "satellite functioning in space" force suppliers to become involved with risk assessment and insurance. Contracts which allow for changing payload specifications until shortly before the launch process, can only be offered, if a supplier can control modular, exchangable designs[40]. Only few large suppliers are ready to deal with such sophisticated customer requirements.

As a result, the group of satellite systems integrators must necessarily be highly concentrated, and the number of independent firms will be further reduced in the years to come. It is expected that only five or six suppliers worldwide will be able to effectively participate in the satellite systems business during the 1990s (see Table 6.1). Today, three large U.S. based companies (Ford Aerospace/Loral, GE/RCA, Hughes) dominate the worldwide satellite business. European systems suppliers are still too fragmented, due to their "nurturing as national champions". A major restructuring process, during which two large European systems integrators evolved[41], has been underway during the last years.

---

39 These transaction-specific investments (Williamson, 1985) cover accumulated expenditures for establishing reliable customer-supplier-relationships, related logistics and quality control procedures.

40 As an example, the Astra consortium demanded payload adaptations shortly before launching, because it wanted to remain open to customer needs "until the last minute". Given these requirements, the satellite supplier was chosen according to his ability to cope with such a contract.

41 GEC-Marconi and Matra have joined forces as "Matra Marconi Space". A second group has become established involving Alcatel, Alenia and DASA.

Table 6.1: Expected Restructuring of the Satellite Supply Sector

Systems integration level	Average annual turnover in the telecommunication satellite business (Mill.$)	Estimated number of suppliers worldwide
o Systems integrator	400	5 - 6
o Sub-system-company	100	15 - 20
o Specialized component supplier	20	40 - 60

Source: Arthur D. Little (1989, 55)

6.4.2   Upstream Networking with Specialized Suppliers

The *satellite production chain*, which is illustrated in *Fig. 6.2*, can be differen-
ciated into upstream activities (components and sub-systems manufacturing)
and downstream activities (systems integration). Upstream and downstream
activities will require different modes of governance and organization. There are
a number of reasons for the evolution towards a *dual structure* of suppliers
within the satellite supply industry, comprising both the integrated and the market mode of coordination. Customer requirements for the provision of reliable,
fully-integrated "turnkey" satellite systems can only be fulfilled by very large
suppliers, as has been explained in the preceding part. Specialized suppliers of
components and sub-systems have an incentive to interlock with large systems
integrators, because this is the only possible way to deal with demanding customers.

The *system integrator*, on the other hand, might be inclined to integrate
backwards, and to produce all components and sub-systems himself. This raises
Coase's (1937, 386f) classic question of "why can't a large firm do anything
a group of small firms can, and more". The answer must be sought in the
flexibility and specialization advantages of dedicated, small satellite supply
firms. These firms produce highly-specific components based on their cumulated production experience, and on their participation in numerous satellite

programs in the past. This knowledge is very difficult to transfer across organizational boundaries, and is characterized by long gestation periods of 20 years and more. A large satellite systems integrator would have to invest in time-consuming R&D programs, before he could successfully integrate backwards. He might be tempted to acquire a specialized satellite component supplier, even though in most cases production volume and the expected size of the business for the components fraction will be too small for him to justify corporate investment strategies.

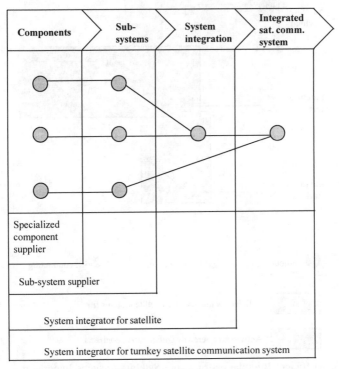

Fig. 6.2:   Production Chain for Satellite Systems

Another reason will often set limits to effective vertical backward integration: a specialized component supplier can serve the whole world-market, and can justify specific R&D investments because he can sell to *all* major satellite systems integrators. Integration within a large firm would mean to cut off part of its customer base, since large systems firms will *not* purchase from a supplier owned by that competitor. As a result, many specialized component and sub-system suppliers remain independent from satellite systems integrators[42], and follow a "global niche" strategy[43].

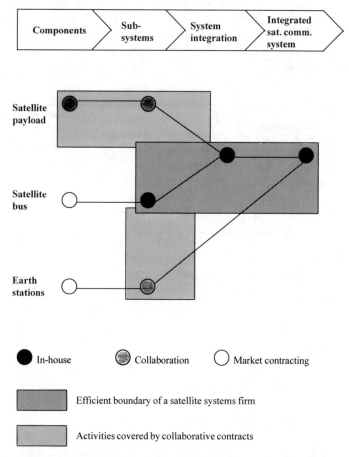

Fig. 6.3:   Efficient Boundaries for Large Satellite Systems Integrators

---

42 Some of these smaller firms may "seek shelter" within other large corporations or industrial holdings other than satellite systems integrators. In this case, the described limits to vertical integration *within* the satellite systems business are still valid, since the acquired satellite components units operate as specialized entities within more diversified industrial groups.

43 A global niche strategy involves specialization on a particular component or sub-system, for which a relatively high world-market share can be secured. Specialist suppliers following such a global niche strategy do not interfere with dominant large systems integrators, with which they often form a symbiotic relationship.

Since technology and industrial structure change continuously, and since there is imperfect information about integration advantages and disadvantages, satellite firms are changing their efficient boundaries over time. Satellite systems integration firms often do *integrate backwards*, because their production volume is large enough to fully exploit economies-of-scale and specialization for specific components in-house. Or they regard specific components and know-how areas as strategic, which they want to fully control in-house. In the last years, some electronics and data transmission technologies (primarily part of the payload sub-system) were regarded as strategically important by large satellite systems integrators. The *efficient boundaries* of a systems integrator can thus be illustrated by the shaded area in Fig. 6.3[44]. The large satellite firm will concentrate on systems integration and on the provision of the full "turnkey satellite package". It may keep some strategic parts of the pay-load subsystems in-house, and will arrange for tight sourcing-in contracts for other subsystems. Most specialized components will, however, still be produced by independent smaller suppliers, which are often interlocked into various forms of "intermediate" networking relationships.

The dual structure exposed is somewhat different to the "open network approach" favored by researchers who have analyzed the organization of the production and supply chain of textiles, machine-tools or optical instruments[45]. Since customers of satellites formulate very stringent requirements with respect to performance, quality and delivery time, a satellite systems integrator must control a rigid coordination network. He must play the role of a *hub within a tightly organized supply network*. Control is maintained through careful selection and monitoring of suppliers, through sophisticated contracts, through repetitive and binding supply relationship, and through bilateral cooperative relationships for specific, sensible parts. Alltogether, this closely controlled network resembles a complex "machinery" of tightly organized and monitored contracts.

The contractual arrangement through which a general contractor specifies all inputs, and coordinates the flow of resources as a "hub firm", most often corresponds to the fully-integrated solution. Even though ownership of specific resources required for the production of inputs is in the hands of "independent" suppliers, the general contractor often has the control rights over resources, without necessarily owning them. As long as the supplier has a real chance of switching to another general contractor, the customer-supplier relationship does not display the predominent features of a hierarchical, integrated governance mode.

---

44 The term "efficient boundaries of the firm" is explained in Williamson (1985, 96ff) and Teece (1991). See also our description in section 5.5.
45 See the network studies by Hkanson (1987), Thorelli (1986), Lorenzoni (1982) and others, which have been discussed in section 4.4.

As soon as the general contractor acts as a monopsonist, by contrast, the relationship is characterized by factual dependence, and can be described as *quasi-integration* (full control rights without ownership rights). Many international teaming arrangements in the telecommunication satellite industry can thus be characterized by quasi-integration: even though suppliers remain organizationally independent, they are nevertheless closely locked into teaming arrangements with general contractors, who can exercise control, at least for some strategically important segments of the market (as is the case for bidding for large contract awards in North America), or for a predetermined time period.

6.4.3   Downstream Diversification into Satellite Operation and Services

Since customers increasingly demand full systems and support capabilities from satellite manufacturers, large firms have developed comprehensive information systems and problem-solving capabilities. They often know at least as much as the customers, if not more, about the appropriate systems architecture and the specification of systems, sub-systems and components. Because of their comprehensive know-how, large manufacturers have often considered forward integration into the operation and service of satellite information services[46].

This trend towards forward integration is spurred on by economic incentives. The size of the business in terms of turnover is considerably higher in services than in hardware manufacturing. Of an annual worldwide turnover for satellite systems of 6 billion dollars (during the late 1980s), only about one third of expenditures are related to hardware, while two thirds correspond to satellite service revenues (Arthur D. Little 1989). The hardware part of the business is extremely price-sensitive while the service part is much less responsive to price. Hardware prices are falling continuously, while service prices remain stable. As a result, profitability and growth expectations are much more favorable for the operation of satellite based information services than for the pure manufacturing of satellite hardware systems.

Most large satellite systems manufacturers such as GE-Astro, Ford Aerospace, or Matra Marconi Space are thus actively pursuing diversification activities. The formation of the new Daimler-Benz group in West Germany was also motivated to a large extent by the potential exploitation of synergies between transportation, aerospace, and new advanced information systems[47]. The key question to be

---

46 Manufacturers argue: "Since we know more about the details of the business than service operators, we might as well start satellite-based information services on our own."

47 It remains to be seen whether the company is really able to exploit this synergy potential anticipated before merger, or whether post-merger coordination costs turn out much higher than expected.

posed in this respect is whether a satellite hardware *manufacturer* really has the appropriate competences and skills to become a satellite *service operator*, and whether economic incentives can be suitably arranged in order to exploit advantages from both hardware and services.

There are, of course, many synergies between the hardware and the service part of the business: technologies, knowledge requirements and systems capabilities are quite similar. Marketing and managerial requirements, by contrast, are *different* for both activities: while a systems hardware manufacturer has to sell to a few, very well informed agencies worldwide, the service provider becomes increasingly active in the end-user market, and has to maintain a large network of relationships with many, less informed customers. For this second reason, it is not neccesarily convincing for a large satellite systems manufacturer to actively become involved in the operation of large information service networks.

A more important *argument against forward integration* into operation and services is based on the "limits of integrated control" considerations outlined in chapters 4 and 5. A service operator must be able to source-in the best technologies and the most appropriate hardware configuration. If the service operator is owned by a hardware firm, it is no more free to choose among different suppliers. As a result, it is locked into one supplier and is running the risk of installing a less suitable, less advanced, and more expensive system which may not even be available in time. Different interests of hardware manufacturers and service providers get intertwined, and both sides may end up acting in a non-efficient way[48].

To seperate interests between hardware manufacturers and service providers, and to secure open bidding arrangements, it appears to be economically advantageous to maintain a clear separation within the *satellite communication value chain* into:

– the satellite *production chain*;
– and the satellite *service and utilization chain*.

This separation is illustrated by the vertical line in *Fig. 6.4*. Future expansion in satellite services will lead to the establishment of new, large information service firms, which operate and control both orbital and terrestrial systems. These new operating organizations will have to closely interact with hardware systems suppliers, but will most probably remain organizationally independent from them[49].

---

48 For exactly these reasons, it has proven advantageous to seperate network providers and systems suppliers in telecommunication and transportation. A major problem in energy production and distribution is caused by the inappropriate blending of both interests within large electric utilities.

49 This expectation is based on normative economic considerations. Infrastructural policy and anti-trust regulation in some countries may lead to empirical diversions, and to the sub-optimal integration of both activity areas.

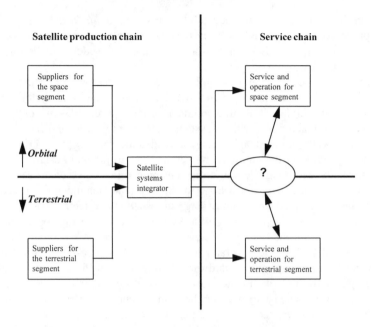

Fig. 6.4:   Organization of the Satellite Production Chain and of
            Satellite Services

Even if full integration of satellite manufacturing and satellite-based information service operation does not seem to be a suitable solution, other
equity-related modes of coordination may evolve at least for a temporary
period. Satellite producers may be well advised not to maintain majority ownership of service operators, but they might still participate through minority
ownership or other forms of collaborative arangements. Such "softer" arrangements are presently sought by many satellite systems manufacturers. However,
it is not yet clear, how stable these arangements will really be. Furthermore,
satellite systems manufacturers compete with other industrial firms which also
seek active interest in information service systems, and which will be better
prepared for lasting diversification. Large telecommunication firms diversifying into satellite-based services, as well as large network management firms
(within or from outside the telecommunication business) may have stronger
financial and managerial capabilities for establishing themselves in the worldwide information service business. As an example, the project Iridium, aiming
at worldwide coverage of mobile telecommunication services, is carried forward
by Motorola and AT&T, with active participation of three existing service pro-

viders[50]. This project is an example for the increasing importance of large systems integrators within the service and utilization chain, which tend to become organizationally separated from the satellite production chain.

6.5   An Industry in Transition: The Case of the German Telecommunication Satellite Industry

The evolution of the West German telecommunication satellite industry dates back to the first half of the 1960s. Companies like AEG, Siemens, Dornier and Siemens have closely watched ongoing developments in satellite communication, and have supported in-house R&D projects. Active involvement in this business, which appeared only slowly to become commercially attractive, was not sought at this early stage, and projects never went beyond the study phase[51]. German firms were first induced into playing a more active role for projects supported by the European Space Agency (ESA). West German financial contributions to this organization allowed national decision-makers to gain some influence in project specification and contracting decisions. Based on ESA's principles of financial back-flow, German suppliers were able to attract major workshares for components and subsystems, which allowed for the gradual build-up of technological capabilities, of specific manufacturing and test facilities, and of sophisticated systems engineering skills.

Cumulative learning and the build-up of specific investments allowed for more active influence on the evolution of technology by participants in industry, in public institutions and in research facilities. This gave rise to an understanding that stronger participation in the international business could be achieved through technological competence. Since the market for large international satellite projects was effectively controlled by other large firms, primarily from the U.S., a greater stimulus was expected from innovative home markets, which would allow for the "cushioned" development of leading-edge satellite projects with national capabilities for systems integration. The national satellite projects TV-Sat (in cooperation with the French TDF project) and DFS-Kopernikus already described in section 6.3, were expected to play a strong role in the period 1975 to 1990.

---

50 The Iridium project has been promoted by Motorola and AT&T, with a memorandum of understanding signed between Inmarsat, the American Mobile Satellite Corp. (AMSC), and the Canadian Telesat Mobile Inc. (TMI).
51 Companies did not get more actively involved because of various restrictions, some of which were truely effective at the time, while others were anticipated in the event that a West German supplier should try to penetrate into the domain of some U.S.-based firms.

Parallel to this, firms were persistently trying to participate in European and international satellite projects.

In order to support these activities, BMFT provided complementary R&D finance. Between 1975 and 1988, a total of 350 million DM of public funds was invested for satellite communication related R&D projects. Additional procurement contracts of considerable size were awarded by the Deutsche Bundespost. The experience from this federal support program was somewhat mixed: while some firms were able to gain a strong international position in specialized components and subsystems, systems integration capabilities were not effectively strengthened, at least in regard to the participation of larger German suppliers in competitive international satellite projects[52]. Systems integration capabilities remained dependent on procurement contracts for large national programs. The whole satellite production system was seriously effected as soon as large procurement contracts from the Deutsche Bundespost were reduced during the late 1980s.

During the last years, the German satellite industry has undergone a major restructuring process. Whereas about 20 German firms participated in national and international projects in the 1970s and early 1980s, the whole sector has since experienced a major consolidation process. Smaller firms were increasingly integrated into large telecommunication and aerospace firms, and the whole German aerospace sector was restructured. As a result, only two large national firms resumed responsibility for ongoing satellite communication activities: Daimler Benz acquired MBB, Dornier and AEG and consolidated their diverse activities within Deutsche Aerospace AG (DASA). Bosch Telecom merged the activities of ANT and Teldix into its space business unit. SEL was integrated into the Alcatel group, which is trying to pursue telecommunication and space-related activities across Europe on a larger scale[53]. Siemens has virtually dropped out as a producer of space and satellite-related components or systems.

This consolidation and reconfiguration of activities has clear implications on the *mapping of agents and objectives*, which is illustrated in *Fig. 6.5*. Objectives must be distinguished according to whether an organization wants to play a strong role in *satellite* communications (illustrated by the upper segment in Fig. 6.5), or in *terrestial* communication (cables and terrestial microwave transmission/represented by the lower part in Fig. 6.5). Both objectives are in conflict with each other, and they are very difficult to harmonize within one single integrated organization. On the other hand, objectives must be distinguished according to whether an organization wants to be a *producer* or an *operator* of a telecommunication system. Production-oriented firms are grouped on the left-

---

52 For an evaluation of the federal satellite telecommunication R&D support program, see Arthur D. Little (1989, chapter 2).
53 Alcatel N.V. as a holding organization is located in the Netherlands, while the core activities of this company are centered in France.

hand side in Fig. 6.5, while service-oriented firms can be found on the right hand side. Even though some firm may try to blend the activities of both sides, production and systems operation are characterized by distinct requirements and business processes, and there are good eonomic reasons not to extend the integrated mode of governance and organization too far.

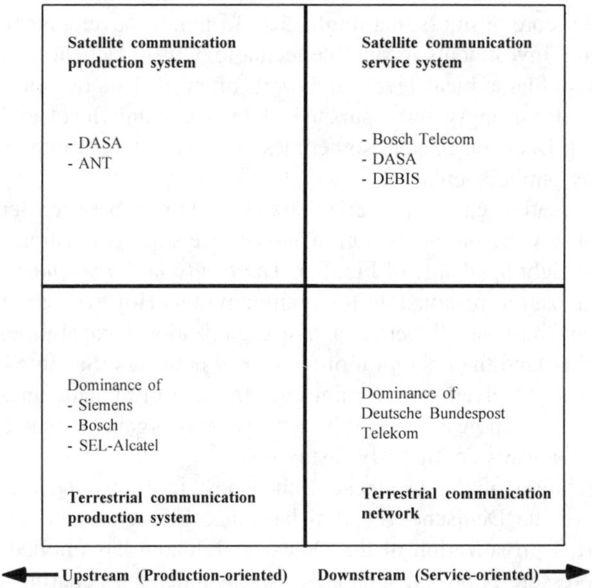

Satellite communication production system	Satellite communication service system
- DASA - ANT	- Bosch Telecom - DASA - DEBIS
Dominance of - Siemens - Bosch - SEL-Alcatel Terrestrial communication production system	Dominance of Deutsche Bundespost Telekom Terrestrial communication network

◄──── Upstream (Production-oriented)   Downstream (Service-oriented)────►

Fig. 6.5:   Strategic Groups for Telecommunication Systems in Germany

The principal reason why German firms have not been able to play a stronger role in the telecommunication satellite business is *neither* late entry to the market, *nor* limited technological competence. German firms have been involved in projects from the very beginning and have gained a high level of sophistication in many key technologies. The question must be raised why early innovation projects did not go ahead as they could have done, and why technological competence was not transformed into a comparable market presence. The most important explanation must be sought in strategic investment decisions pursued at corporate level. Firms like AEG, Siemens, Bosch and SEL did not consider *satellite* telecommunications as a target for strategic investment decisions. They regarded themselves as principal suppliers of telecommunication equipment for *terrestial* transmission, as is illustrated in the lower left square in Fig. 6.5. As principal contractors to the Deutsche Bundespost, firms within this group were able to receive a large and stable income stream, and to capture a high profit margin at relatively low risk.

Any strategic move into the development and manufacturing of large satellite systems, illustrated by the upper left square in Fig. 6.5, was either not very attractive, or was considered as being too risky by established telecommunication suppliers of terrestrial systems. The size of expected revenues was much smaller, new fields of expertise had to be explored at great expenses, and considerable risks had to be undergone. As a result, telecommunication firms participated in satellite projects only to keep track of the state-of-the-art, and to prevent any damage to their core business that might arise from new developments in satellite communication. Investments in satellite technology were tactical, often only supported at a low hierarchical level, and were often of a more defensive nature. Projects were accordingly only pursued at business unit level and not at the corporate level. Decision-makers sometimes had to be "talked into" participating in a project by public agents[54].

A similar situation can characterize strategic choices between terrestrial and satellite based services on the operation and service side, as illustrated by the two squares on the right hand side of Fig. 6.5. The *Deutsche Bundespost* has been the principal organization responsible for both activities. However, the bulk of past investments and almost all personal and organizational capabilities and skills were centered around the operation of *terrestrial* networks. Satellite communication, by contrast, received only a miniscule fraction of annual funds, only very few people were responsible for this activity, and organizational routines and allocation mechanisms continously disfavored it[55].

The deregulation of the Deutsche Bundespost in 1989, and the succeeding restructuring of the Deutsche Telekom have had no significant impact on this situation. Partial privatization of the Deutsche Telekom has implied that greater commercial pressure is put on separate business units and departments. Because of its fragile position within the organization, the department in charge of satellites was under greater pressure to earn its income than the other departments, which were able rely on large and often amortized investments of the past decades. The whole organization did not show much interest in expanding into satellite telecommunication services in a very significant way. On the other hand, the Deutsche Telekom precluded access to other organizations which were willing to invest in satellite-based telecommunication services[56].

---

54 As an example, this was the case for the TV-Sat project as well as for the DFS-Kopernikus project, both of which have already been described in section 6.3.

55 Even though some investments were made for prestige projects during the early 1980s, the limited success of these satellite projects has led to malicious glee on the part of those decision-makers favoring terrestrial transmission systems.

56 The Deutsche Bundespost Telekom still keeps a monopoly position on voice communication within Germany. Without access to this most profitable service segment, private investors are less willing to pursue major investment projects.

This kind of stalemate situation had some inherent logic as long as information transmission in the Federal Republic of Germany, as it was before 1990, was analyzed. The exisiting terrestrial telecommunication infrastructure was sufficiently well developed and geographical characteristics did not work much in favor of satellite communication. This situation has changed considerably: the restructuring process in mid-Eastern Europe has improved the comparative economic advantage of satellite transmission. This technology can most appropriately be applied for greater distances, particularly for regions with an underdeveloped status of terrestrial networks, and it allows for much greater flexibility. Information transmission to Eastern Europe and to other, more distant geographical areas can effectively be improved through satellite-based systems. Growing internationalization and increased trans-national data traffic will lead to strong growth for medium to long range communication. Satellite telecommunication systems offer the most economical and a very flexible solution, and are key for effective differentation in this high-growth market.

The exploitation of business opportunities by German firms is restricted by the present organization, and by myopic interests within the existing system of producers and service operators. The inappropriate structure, however, will not be "petrified" forever. Greater deregulation in telecommunication in Europe, access for foreign suppliers, and the formation of new firms will undermine existing "fortresses". If German firms are not willing or able to effectively grasp these new opportunities, other investment groups and international firms will be able to capture the greater part of revenues, and will become dominant in the business of communication services.

7 Structuring Financial Arrangements for Start-up Projects

In chapters 5 and 6, we have analyzed complex investment decisions and conditions under which large investment projects can be economically pursued through cooperative modes of governance and organization. We have so far neglected financial considerations, because we did not want the financial side to interfere too early into our "project structuring logic". Financial decisions will be regarded as an endogenous *result* of project structuring, as is illustrated in Fig. 7.1. Project-related *objectives* are defined first and lead to a particular configuration and sequence of project *tasks* and activities. For those activities which require highly-specific assets with low transferability, the ownership of which is distributed over two or more independent agents, cooperative modes of *governance and organization* will be chosen as the most suitable solution. The coalition of agents will then determine the most responsive form of *finance* for the joint project.

The multilateral character of *investment* will often find its correspondence in mutilateral *financial* arrangements, which are described as *project finance* in the theoretical and empirical literature[1]. The particular mode of project finance chosen in period t may in later periods influence and restrain project objectives, as well as the selection of tasks and activities (as is illustrated by the feedback loop in Fig. 7.1). We will concentrate, however, on the more influential logical sequence (illustrated by downward moving arrows in Fig. 7.1), through which the financial arrangement is endogenously determined on the basis of project objectives and task requirements.

In the following *section 7.1*, we will first describe conditions under which collaborative financial arrangements such as *project finance* can be regarded as superior and sustainable. We will then describe a particular form of project finance, the provision of financial funds for young start-up firms. Finance can be raised by two independent partners as described in *section 7.2*, or will be provided through more complex co-venturing networks (see *section 7.3*).

---

1 For theoretical analyses of project finance decisions see Grossman and Hart (1986), Hart (1988), Rudolph (1989), Shah and Thakor (1987), and Williamson (1988). Empirical descriptions can be found in Backhaus et al. (1990), Keck (1986), Nevitt (1983), and Schill (1988).

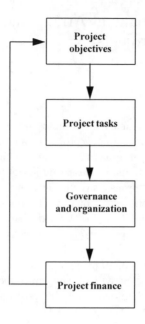

Fig. 7.1:   Multilateral Project Finance as Endogenous Result of Project
             Structuring

Our financial structuring approach is rather flexible with regard to the question whether finance is provided by private or public agents. For some particular types of projects, or during early phases of the evolution of capital markets, public agents may play a suitable and important role in supporting socially useful projects. For other types of projects and for later phases of capital market evolution, private sources of finance will be more important. Public policy for the support of start-up firms should be seen from this "infant capital market" perspective[2]. In section 7.4, we will thus analyze the experiences gained during the implementation of two public support programs in Germany, which were directed at technology-oriented young start-up firms.

---

2   The argumentation is similar to the "infant-industry" argument in development economics. The evolution of capital markets for the finance of certain types of projects will often last several decades, during which market participants have to establish reliable trading relationships. Public finance can be important for overcoming capital and product market imperfections during early phases, but will later gradually be substituted by an influx of finance from private sources.

7.1   Theoretical Reasons for Multilateral Finance

The term *multilateral finance* will be used for investment projects for which at least
two independent agents provide financial resources. Financial resources can be
provided in the form of debt, equity, or through a third, hybrid financial arrangement. These three types of finance are not merely defined as "financial instruments", but are interpreted as distinctive contract and governance modes. In terms
of *contract modes*, we will distinguish between (1) sales or rental agreements
("quid pro quo"), (2) cooperative contract modes ("quoad usum" or "quoad sortem")[3], and (3) ownership contracts ("quoad dominium"). In terms of *governance
modes*, we will distinguish between (1) the exchange of resources through markets,
(2) the temporary pooling of resources within a project, and (3) hierarchical control
within a vertically-integrated firm. These three generic types of contract modes
resp. governance modes are described by the columns in *Table 7.1.*

Table 7.1: Generic Financial Contracts and Governance Modes

	Market mode	*Cooperative mode*	*Integrated mode*
Type of *financial contract*	*Debt finance*	*Collaborative* finance	*Equity* finance
Corresponding *governance mode*	Exchange and coordination through *markets*	Temporary pooling of resources within a *project* organization	Hierarchical control within a vertically *integrated firm*
Generic *contract mode*	"Quid pro quo"	"Quoad usum" or "quoad sortem"	"Quoad dominium"
Recourse to real assets	Non-recourse-financing	Limited-recourse-financing	Full-recourse-financing
Contract duration	Fixed duration (typically less than 10 years)	Limited duration (linked to project lifetime)	Often unlimited duration ("lifetime of the firm")
Type of multi-lateral finance	Multilateral debt finance	Multilateral project finance	Multilateral equity finance

In the following we shall deal with project-type organizations, which are specifically set up for a particular investment project. The project organization will
often be characterized by limited duration in accordance with the lifetime of the
project. Institutional structures and financial contracts are "custom-tailored" according to the particular combination of assets to be involved. In most cases,

---

3   The notions "quoad usum" and "quoad sortem" have been explained in the introduction and
     in chapter 2. Both notions refer to contract modes through which agents contribute resources
     to a project, which are not owned or rented by the project organization.

finance is arranged as a "package", which can be described as a complex nexus of all three types of generic contract modes: the project organization will be established with a certain amount of equity, it will often raise additional debt finance and, what is most important, it will mobilize a considerable share of resources through cooperative contract modes ("quoad usum" and "quoad sortem" type contracts)[4]. The characteristics of the three distinct contract and governance modes are summarized in the rows in Table 7.1.

The characteristics of *pure debt finance*, which corresponds most closely to a market solution, are described in the *left column* in Table 7.1. Finance is provided by specialized agents who typically do not act as participants on the real side of the investment project. These "financial agents" provide finance on a "quid pro quo" basis, i.e. money is provided today and is repaid, together with interest, in later periods. No ownership rights get transferred[5]; financial partners do not bear the market value, nor are they considered as bearing the risk of the project, i.e. we deal with *non-recourse finance*[6]. Debt finance is typically characterized by a fixed duration, rarely exceeding more than ten years. Loans can be provided by one single agent (unilateral debt finance), or by a group of creditors (multilateral debt finance). To prevent the loss of their financial resources, loan providers may sometimes require certain management and monitoring rights, or may demand access to other resources owned by shareholders of the project. These additional contractual arrangements, however, must be seen as a diversion from the pure form of debt finance.

The other extreme form, illustrated by the *right-hand column* in Table 7.1, involves *pure equity finance* by one or more partners. Financial contracts are an inherent element of an *integrated mode* of governance and organization. Equity finance for a project can be provided by single agents (unilateral equity finance), or by a group of agents (multilateral equity finance). Multilateral equity finance, as illustrated by the lower box on the right-hand side in Table 7.1, will involve two or more partners who acquire property rights for a firm or a project in exchange for financial resources. The property rights thus acquired grant the right (1) to determine the use of resources specific to the firm or project, (2) to bear

---

4   Williamson (1988) proposes to use the word "dequity" as a hybrid form of both debt and equity, but he does not define "dequity" precisely enough. We would prefer to interpret project finance as a complex nexus of contracts, which uses pure debt and equity, as well as collaborative contract modes simultaneously.

5   Only if owners of the project are not able to repay the loan plus interest, will they be forced to hand over some of their ownership rights. To prevent expropriation, the providers of loans require a preferential treatment for repayment of their outstanding debts, often through recourse to some easily redeployable real assets such as land. Through such additional contract clauses, the pure "debt" character of financial contracts gets somewhat diluted.

6   For a distinction into non-recourse-, limited recourse- and full-recourse finance see Rudolph (1989, 292).

the market value, and (3) they allow for the exchangeability of rights to (1) and (2) (Alchian 1984, 34). Since the ownership right implies the bearing of the market value (*full-recourse financing*), financial partners want to secure themselves from expropriation of quasi-rents. Consequently, ownership rights are often combined with management contracts which grant the right to monitor the use of resources, the financial performance, and to select managers. In addition, ownership and management contracts are often supplemented by complementary service contracts through which financial partners provide additional resources such as data gathering, consulting, networking relationships, etc.[7] Equity finance contracts are most often of unlimited duration, and they are linked to the expected lifetime of an integrated firm.

Neither of these two extreme types of financial contracts, the pure market mode nor the fully integrated mode, are applicable for "complicated projects", for which asset values are difficult to determine (see section 3.3). To comply with such requirements of "complicated projects", a "complex package of finance" must often be "custom-tailored"[8], and a relatively large share of assets must be financed through *collaborative finance*. The characteristics of collaborative finance are summarized in the *center column* in Table 7.1. Collaborative finance is principally different from multilateral debt and equity finance, due to the highly critical nature of project-specific resources, the strong role of co-specific assets, the serious evaluation problems involved, and due to the limited possibilities for separating the real from the financial side of projects. The success of a project, as well as its risk and return profile are crucially dependent on the effective coordination of highly-specific, non-transferable assets which are closely held by several independent agents. Each participating investor will typically:

– be able to better assess the performance of critical assets and the related risks involved by owning key parts of the resource spectrum;
– gain a strong negotiating position vis-à-vis the owners of other, complementary assets (based on asset ownership and insider knowledge).

In order to cope with such "complicated projects", owners of critical assets will often only *grant the right* to use their resource within a project (through "qoad usum" or "quoad sortem" type contracts). They do *not* transfer ownership titles, nor do they provide their resources on a rental basis (corresponding to "quid pro quo"), because this would require determination of asset values ex-ante. The pure

---

7 The last factor, i.e. the intermediary role of financial institutions is often underestimated. This intermediary function can often be much more important than the pure provision of financial funds. It is of particular importance for the venture capital business, the reasons for which will be analyzed in sections 7.2 to 7.4.

8 In the financial sector, the terms "financial engineering", "financial design" or "finance technique" have become utilized to describe this activity.

provision of financial resources by individual agents, who do *not* own or control critical real assets would not be appropriate, because the providers of finance would have only limited knowledge of "what they get in return". Financial investors *without* ownership and control over specific assets would be easily replaceable, their negotiating position would be undermined, and they would not be capable of assessing the true performance of critical resources. In such situations of strong co-specificity, ownership titles, control rights and finance cannot be appropriately separated; the provision of finance and contributions of real assets are strongly intertwined. Collaborative modes of finance will thus involve a *complex bundle of both real and financial resources.*

In contrast to collaborative modes of finance, pure debt or equity contracts are feasible only for "non-critical" combinations of assets, for which projects can be easily evaluated, and for which the investment and finance spheres can become separated. Some agents can specialize on the pure provision of debt or equity finance, while others resume responsibility for the real side of the investment process. Only for such "non-critical" combinations of assets can the provision of finance be spread among several independent partners, who are merely interested in *financial risk diversification.* In the case of *multilateral debt finance,* a consortium of banks will provide financial funds without being involved in ownership and control of project-specific assets. Different financial partners can join the sharing of financial risks, and can set up multi-stage re-insurance arrangements. In the case of *multilateral equity finance,* asset ownership and finance will be intertwined, but will often be separated from control. A typical example is multi-agent stockholding in publicly quoted corporations: the influence of equity-owners on projects performed within the corporation will become negligible. Multilateral debt and equity finance may provide strong mechanisms for diversification and financial risk-reduction, but are not very useful for assessing or reducing risks related to highly-critical investment projects, with which we are concerned in this chapter.

Economic explanations of collaborative finance must emphasize the role of highly-specific, closely-held capital goods and knowledge bases, for which collaborative contracts "beyond debt and equity" are inevitable (see our theoretical explanations in chapters 3 to 5). As long as economic explanations are restricted to the analysis of debt or equity contracts, and of mere financial risk diversification, the phenomenon of multilateral project finance cannot appropriately be understood. Similar to the "traditional" economic explanations for cooperative investment in general, which were already discussed in section 1.3, most economic *explanations of multilateral project finance* still focus too much on:

- the argument of *financial indivisibilities*;
- on *risk-reduction* arguments; and on
- attempted *synergy* effects.

Financial indivisibilities may explain why a particular investor may be seeking additional financial funds exceeding his own budget, but cannot be used as a sufficient argument for spreading finance between different institutions. The typical size of investment for a young industrial start-up firm, for example, is not in a range which could not be "shouldered" by a single, large financier. Capital requirements for start-up firms typically range from several hundred thousand to a few million dollars for the first five years, after which part of the additional funds required can already be generated from internal cash-flow. Multilateral finance for large engineering projects may be more convincingly explained on the basis of indivisibility considerations: infrastructure projects are often financed by several independent partners whose participation is justified by fund requirements which may amount to several billion dollars. A pre-eminent example is the Eurotunnel project; even for such gigantic projects size as such is not the main argument, but is often just used as a superficial explanation for multilateral finance. Problems involved in coordinating all the parties contributing critical assets for one large "financial engineering project" are often more important than the amount of financial funds actually involved.

The *risk-reduction* argument appears to be plausible at first sight, but cannot really explain why large and risky investment projects should necessarily be financed in a collaborative, multilateral arrangement. Large and complex investment projects which require the coordination of a vast array of highly-specific resources are intrinsically uncertain, and there is no way of reducing the likelihood of failure through mere financial diversification. Only the participating agents which can effectively influence the provision of critical resources, and the "insiders" of the respective business segments are able to reduce risks by focusing on specific areas of activity. Pure "financial engineering" arrangements, by contrast, are not the appropriate mechanisms to reduce the probability of failure. All they can do is to distribute potential losses between several partners in such a way that each one of them does not have to suffer too much.

While the indivisibility and risk-reduction arguments cannot be convincingly put forth to explain multilateral project finance, *synergy* appears to be a more valid argument. Financial investors can complement each other in terms of time preference as well as risk-preference. The capital market for start-up projects, as an example, can thus be regarded primarily as a device for the transformation and equilibration of risk classes, as well as of different "duration classes" of projects. Inasmuch as financial contracts are combined with management contracts and with service contracts for the provision of information, different financial investors may be able to bring co-specific resources "to the party". As soon as as the provision of financial funds is seen in connection with these "add-on" capabilities, resource complementarity and synergy will become valid arguments for multilateral project finance.

Differential knowledge aquired through ownership and control over highly-specific assets represents a core element in the economic explanation of multilateral project finance. If different financial partners control highly-specific, but complementary knowledge-pools, and if the costs of transfering information across institutional boundaries are considerable, a project finance arrangement may offer sustainable comparative advantages. The value of the joint project being owned and controlled within a single, integrated firm would be lower than if resources remained distributed among independent agents, each being responsible for the evaluation and performance of his own assets. The attempt to pool information about asset values within one firm, and to derive an integrated, generally agreed-upon assessment of project risks and values would lead to considerable costs and delays (Rudolph 1989, Shah and Thakor 1987).

Synergy arguments based on differential knowledge and high costs of information transmission are a valid argument for the superiority and sustainability of collaborative modes of finance. Comparative advantages derive from a unique combination of distributed knowledge and financial resources. A project finance arrangement is significantly more than just a multi-party transfer of monetary wealth. The business of project finance requires detailed technology- and industry-specific knowledge. This knowledge is very difficult to acquire and is characterized by long gestation lags. Technology and industry specialists, who are able to assess and monitor a particular project, must have gained several years of "on-the-spot" experience. There is an indivisibility problem relating to the number of experts a financial investor can effectively integrate into his knowledge-pool. As a result, even very large funds and project finance organizations must rely on information which only another financial firm can provide.

In a world of uncertainty and opportunism, complementary information provided by a firm A will only be considered reliable by firm B, if A invests own money into a project, and vice versa. The provision of complementary financial funds is considered a by-product, as a *signal of reciprocal commitment* to support the validity of complementary knowledge. Distributed knowledge bases with long entry and exit lags are the *primary* argument for multilateral investment activity, while collaborative finance is used as a "secondary back-up" required to validate these knowledge-related synergies. These theoretical considerations can only reasonably be understood through an exploration of empirical projects, which are frequently financed through multilateral project finance arrangements. To illustrate our arguments, we will analyze empirical patterns of multilateral finance which have evolved in the venture capital business.

7.2   Project Finance for Start-up Companies

Venture capital and related types of financial support for start-up firms will be described as a special form of project finance: the project to be financed is a *new company* during the early phases of its existence. The evolution of the venture capital business can be described as the gradual introduction, testing and selection of contracts and governance modes, which have proven to be "robust" to this type of investment. The nexus of contracts typical for the finance of start-up projects is a combination of collaborative contracts, equity as well as debt, with a strong emphasis on collaborative contract modes (both "quoad usum" and "quoad sortem" contracts). During the lifetime of a start-up firm, the relative importance of these three elements will typically change according to the illustration in *Fig. 7.2*: collaborative contract modes will be most important during the very early phases, and will become successively substituted by equity and debt.

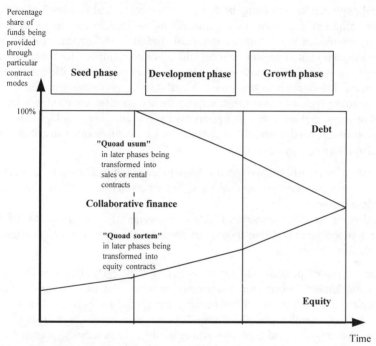

Fig. 7.2:   Relative Importance of Financial Contract and Governance Modes During the Lifetime of a Start-up Project

Particularly during the *early phases* of a start-up project, an intertwined package of collaborative contract modes as well as equity will be required. Given the high degree of uncertainty and the typical fluctuations notorious for young start-up companies, equity finance must receive much greater attention than debt finance. What is even more important is an inextricable "package" of financial as well as real assets, which must be governed and coordinated through both collaborative contract modes and equity. Highly-specific real resources, knowledge and finance is provided by several independent agents, be they venture capital firms, equity finance institutions, industrial corporations, wealthy individuals or public institutions[9]. These agents who often pursue diverse objectives, and who own a wide array of relevant resources, must be "tied together" within a multilateral project finance arrangement.

While the empirical significance and the growing importance of venture-related multilateral project finance remains undoubted, existing theoretical studies must still be considered as unsatisfactory. Based on our own empirical studies of the venture start-up process and the venture capital sector, and after reviewing most existing theoretical "explanations", we became convinced that a new theoretical explanation combining both capital theoretical and neo-institutional concepts is required. Our theoretical explanations outlined in chapters 3 to 5 were strongly motivated through these empirical studies[10]. Theoretical explanation of venture capital related project finance, which are compatible with these empirical findings, must explicitly consider the strong role of highly-specific assets and of sustainable information asymmetries. Most start-up projects, particularly those with a strong technology content, require highly-specific knowledge with long gestation lags, and are often characterized by considerable exit lags. The accumulation of knowledge and the accumulation of wealth is often distributed over *two distinct groups of agents*:

- agents who control highly-specific knowledge about technologies and markets (*entrepreneurs*/often young engineers) but who often do not own the required financial resources;
- holders of financial resources (*"financial agents"*), by contrast, do not have the appropriate knowledge about markets and technologies, which is often very difficult to access.

For new types of projects and for firms during their early life-cycle this results in a considerable information asymmetry between the two groups of agents. Incomplete contracting conditions prevail, and capital markets are "out of alignment" for considerable periods of time[11]. Given excessively high costs of information transmission, and time-consuming adjustment processes, potential trans-

---

9 See Gerybadze and Müller (1990, chap. 3) for a survey of financial institutions active in this segment of the capital market.

10 Between 1989 and 1992, we have participated in a large evaluation program supported by the Federal Ministry of Research and Technology, during which the evolution of 350 German start-up firms and of approximately 30 financial institutions was analyzed. As part of this evaluation program, existing theoretical studies from different countries were screened and new, refined concepts were developed, which have influenced our work. See also Bräunling, Gerybadze and Mayer (1989), Gerybadze (1990b, 1991b), Gerybadze and Müller (1990), Kulicke (1990), Kulicke et al. (1993), and our case descriptions in section 7.4.

11 For an analysis of incomplete contracting, and the gradual alignment of capital markets see Williamson (1988), Grossman and Hart (1982, 1988).

actions between entrepreneurs and specialized "financial agents" will often be disrupted, and the respective projects cannot be financed appropriately.

Provided there is a large enough potential of promising new projects, capital market institutions will be gradually adapted: "parties to a contract will be cognizant of prospective distortions and of the needs to (1) realign incentives and (2) craft governance structures that fill gaps, correct errors, and adapt more effectively to unanticipated disturbances. Prospective incentive and governance needs will thus be anticipated and thereafter 'folded in'" (Williamson 1988, 570). This adaptation and alignment process, however, is dependent on entry lags required to access relevant knowledge pools. A large number of potentially profitable projects will induce holders of financial resources to invest in knowledge accumulation in order to overcome information asymmetries.

Since knowledge is very specific and takes a long time to build up, "knowledge intensive" financial investors will often *not* be able to combine task-specific assets as well as financial skills in an economical way. The economics of specialization and the time to build capabilities lead to inducements for collaboration between specialized financial investors and other groups of agents. To reliably assess and monitor a particular project, the knowledge pool of one financial investor will often not be sufficient. "Bridging" or combining knowledge pools of two or more independent investors on a project-by-project basis will offer advantages to all participating agents. Efficient capital markets for the finance of start-up firms will evolve in parallel with a proven track record of completed multilateral finance projects.

7.2.1 Institutional Arrangements in the Venture Capital Business

Institutional arrangements that have evolved in the venture finance business can be classified according to the types of assets required for a project, the *types of financial contracts* used, and according to the *types of institutions* participating in collaborative finance. We will analyze the types of assets and the related types of contracts first, and will then describe three alternative groups of institutions. The most simple contractual arrangement is illustrated in *Fig. 7.3*: a single venture capital institution provides resources for a start-up firm. The *types of resources* required will involve the provision of finance, but often also management services, know-how, and in some cases even the provision of specific capital goods. Depending on the type of resources and their critical dimension, different *types of contracts* must be arranged. For *non-critical* types of resources, loan or rental agreements will be sufficient. Equity ownership rights will be transferred for those types of *critical* assets, for which the value can be more or less reliably assessed. In addition, collaborative agreements "between debt and equity" will be required for those critical assets, for which the "true" value cannot reliably be determined ex-ante.

The highly critical nature of resources to be used, the extent of information asymmetries, and the typical time and risk profile of young start-up projects will often lead to a strong emphasis on collaborative agreements during very early phases, while equity contracts will gradually become more important during the development and growth phase[12]. The composition of finance and of corresponding contract modes is illustrated in Fig. 7.3: a considerable share of resources has to be "embedded" in a start-up project in the form of cooperative agreements ("quoad usum" and "quoad sortem"/ illustrated by the light shaded area). Additional resources must be provided by the venture finance institution on an equity basis (dark shaded area), while only a relatively small fraction of financial resources can be provided on a rental or debt basis (illustrated by the white area in Fig. 7.3).

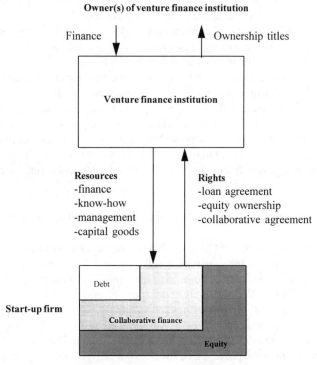

Fig. 7.3:   Finance Provided by One Single Venture Finance Institutuion

---

12 The relative importance of equity finance during the development phase of start-up firms is explained in Gerybadze and Müller (1990c, chapter 2). In the preceding chapters 2 and 3, we have explained, why equity contracts must be supplemented by collaborative agreements for the very early phase of a start-up project, during which the "true" value of critical resources cannot easily be estimated.

To gain sufficient control over the use of critical assets, which are represented by the two shaded zones in Fig. 7.3, and to monitor the use and performance of these resources, the financial investor typically asks for certain management and control rights, which are an essential element of equity contracts and collaboration agreements[13]. In addition, certain service contracts (for the provision of information, accounting, and for the establishment of useful contacts) complement the financial arrangement. The venture institution itself is owned by one or more persons or institutions. Multiple ownership is quite frequent for venture finance firms, as will be described later.

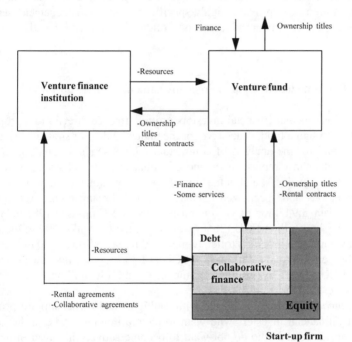

Fig. 7.4:   Venture Finance Provided through a Fund

In many cases, the venture finance institution establishes a *fund*, through which equity finance is channelled. The establishment of a fund, which is illustrated in *Fig. 7.4*, offers the advantage that more financial sources can be "tapped" without

---

13 Venture capital firms will often provide part-time management and regular controlling and monitoring through board participation. Some of these services are remunerated directly, while others are seen as an element of equity and collaboration agreements.

affecting control over the venture capital institution itself. Furthermore, the venture finance firm has greater flexibility in "packaging" several independent funds, each being targeted at particular technologies, industries, maturity and risk classes, and at different groups of shareholders. Each fund can be managed and monitored separately. Typically, the venture finance institution will own a certain percentage of the fund; in addition, it will provide fund management, and will arrange for certain service or rental agreements (as illustrated by the arrows between the venture finance institution and the fund in Fig. 7.4). Ownership contracts as well as rental agreements for certain management services will be established between the fund and the start-up firm. In addition, the venture finance institution will provide highly-specific resources (management services, know-how, establishment of contacts), often through collaborative contract modes.

7.2.2   Fund-mediated versus Direct Investment in Start-up Firms

The question whether financial investors provide finance directly to a project, or indirectly through a fund, is decisive for the understanding of strategic investment behavior, and for the analysis of contractual relations. The *indirect, fund-mediated* form of finance represents the most familiar institutional arrangement in the venture capital business, and is fairly well documented due to the work of industry associations and specialized database research organizations. According to published data, 3.9 billion ECU were raised for new VC funds in 1987 in Western Europe. About 1 billion ECU (26%) were provided by banks, 590 million ECU (15%) by corporate investors (often represented by large firms), 520 million ECU (13%) by pension funds, 480 million ECU (12%) by government agencies, 390 million ECU (10%) by insurance companies, and 140 million ECU (4%) by private investors[14].

Fund-mediated forms of finance with multiple fund ownership are primarily sought by financial investors who want to have a minority stake in the venture finance business, and who do not want to become actively involved in management and service for venture start-up firms, or for the related fund. Investment objectives are primarily of a financial nature[15], resources provided are non-criti-

---

14 See EVCA Yearbook (1988, 10f). The other, direct and *non-fund-mediated form* of venture finance is probably even more important in size, but it is not documented by statistical databases. Individual investors or groups of investors want to keep projects "hidden", while fund-managers have an incentive to make their work visible in order to attract new investors. Thus it is very difficult to get comparable information on non-fund-mediated investments.

15 The interest of a financial investor is primarily directed at portfolio diversification. He often wants to set aside a small fraction (rarely more than 5%) of his portfolio for long-term and risky assets with a high growth potential (which corresponds to a "hedging" strategy).

cal, and the financial investor cannot and does not contribute to the real side of the investment project.

Many investment projects, on the other hand, will demand an influx of highly-specialized resources in addition to finance (knowledge of a particular industry, technological capabilities, customer relations, managerial skills, etc.). Investors who, in addition to their financial contributions, are able to provide these highly-specific resources, will often be characterized by an active and more strategic interest in a particular start-up firm, or in a particular line of business. In order to pursue their strategic objectives, and in order to prevent the expropriation of quasi-rents for their resources, these investors will aquire ownership titles for a particular project, and will be less inclined to merely invest in a general fund.

We now turn to *non-fund-mediated* forms of venture finance, i.e. to direct investment in start-up firms, which may be even more important than fund-mediated investments, but for which empirical data are not published. There are no institutionalized capital markets for these types of investment, and investment decisions and financial solutions are developed on a "project by project" basis. A relatively high percentage of investments for "complicated projects" during their early lifecycle will have to be mobilized through non-formalized, collaborative arrangements "beyond capital and product markets". Investment projects typically require the use of a wide array of highly-specific resources; in such cases it will be very likely that the ownership of relevant resources is distributed across two or more independent agents. If information about the "true" value of critical resources is unevenly distributed, and if knowledge is costly to transfer across institutional boundaries, a bilateral or even multilateral project finance arrangement will be economically advantageous (Rudolph 1989, and Shah and Thakor 1987).

In the case of non-fund-mediated co-venturing, two independent financial investors A and B will provide finance plus additional resources to a project. For some of these resources, particularly those for which the value can more or less reliably be assessed, they will transfer ownership titles for the asset in exchange for ownership titles to the new project organization. For other, complementary resources, for which it is difficult to find an agreement on the "true" value, agents A and B will keep ownership titles individually, while the project organization will be enabled to make use of these critical resources. The share of assets, for which ownership rights are transferred to the project organization, is illustrated by the dark shaded area in *Fig. 7.5*; assets which are contributed to the project in a collaborative mode (through "quoad usum" and "quoad sortem" contracts), and which are owned by A and B seperately, are represented by the light shaded areas. Both types of contractual arrangements, which are often pursued in parallel, are equivalent to the alternatives "equity joint-venture" and "contractual joint-venture", which are common for cooperative investment projects (see our description in section 4.3).

Typical *institutions* which often participate in such bilateral venture finance arrangements are:

– specialized venture capital (VC) firms;
– other investment finance firms with an active interest in the venture business;
– and industrial corporations[16].

In the following, we will describe three specific institutional arrangements involving each of these groups in combination with a specialized VC-firm.

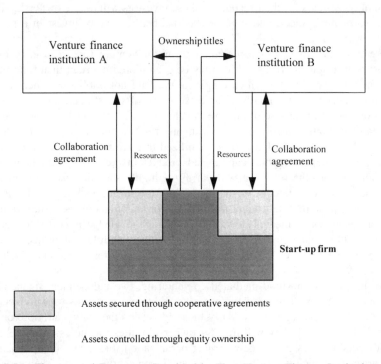

Fig. 7.5:   Finance and Resources Provided by Two Venture Finance Institutions

---

16 In addition, *private investors* represent an important group. However, they will often act as *direct*, private shareholder of the venture start-up firm, and will not be considered as an "institution", or as a separate "pole" of a bilateral project finance arrangement.

7.2.3 Two Venture Capital (VC) Firms

Venture capital firms have specialized much more than any other group of financial investors on a particular combination of knowledge pools together with the
provision of financial assets. The knowledge pool that has been built up over the
years allows these firms to more reliably assess the business potential of a particular, highly-specialized start-up project. Transaction costs for evaluating the
project ex-ante, i.e. before the investment decision is made, and for monitoring
the project after this decision has been made will be considerably lower than for
financial investors who do not possess this knowledge base. Alternatively, for a
similar expenditure on evaluation and monitoring, risks of mis-judgement can be
reduced much more effectively than if a non-experienced financial investor needs
to build up the required knowledge base during the evaluation process.

Because the knowledge pools of venture capital firms have to be so specialized, it will often be required to rely on knowledge that is provided by two
or more independent VC firms. Such firms tend to specialize according to:

- the preferred *phase* of investment and the life-cycle of firms;
- the type of *technology*;
- the specific *industry* segment;
- and on particular *regions*.

Most VC firms focus on particular *phases* of the start-up process. While some
firms prefer to invest during the initial seed phase or for the early development
phase, others prefer to invest in companies during market introduction and during
second-phase financing. Still others only want to invest at later stages (initial
public offering, leveraged buy-out)[17]. Each phase requires a very detailed understanding of specific types of risks, of appropriate contract modes, as well as a
mastering of behavioral characteristics ("how to deal with certain types of entrepreneurs"). Since start-up firms pass through several consecutive stages, and
because they often pursue different projects parallel to each other (with each
project belonging to a different phase), it will often be advantageous to combine
the knowledge pools provided by different VC firms. A seed-capital firm specia-
lizing on very early stages may want to interact closely with another financial
investor who is more interested in projects that require market introduction or
expansion. Similarly, a VC firm that invests during the market introduction phase,
may already at that stage want to "tap the expert pool" of a venture finance firm
that will become involved during the later phase of initial public offering.

VC firms also specialize in particular *technologies* and *industry* segments. As
an example, it takes considerable time to build up expertise in microelectronics,

---

17 A "standardized" classification of these phases can be found in Venture Economics (1989,
144f).

and it is expensive for a VC firm to maintain a group of experts in such a field. If the microelectronics start-up firm, in which the VC firm has an active stake, decides to diversify and become active in other fields (e. g. a related diversification into optoelectronics or into measurement and control), the financial investor specialized in microelectronics will have to access knowledge pools which will only be mastered by other VC firms.

Finally, many VC firms focus on investments in a particular *region*, especially if they want to concentrate on early-stage projects. As an example, some U.S. firms are primarily active in California, others in Massachussetts, and again others in Texas or North Carolina. If a start-up firm wants to expand its operations from California to any of these other regions, it will often be beneficial if two regionally specialized VC firms interact closely.

This pattern of specialization and the related bridging of boundaries through collaborative arrangements between financial investors is very common in the venture capital community. The specialization pattern is itself a result of an evolutionary process which typically takes 10—15 years to reach a stage at which the economics of specialization and sustainable modes of collaboration can eventually become fully exploited[18].

7.2.4   A VC Firm and a Second Finance Institution

Often, bilateral finance agreements are signed between a specialized VC firm and a more generally oriented financial institution such as a bank or a pension fund. Banks typically do not consider equity finance for start-up companies as being a significant part of their business, and will thus often seek other partners with greater experience and specific knowledge in venture management and finance. VC firms, on the other hand, are interested in good relationships with banks that can either provide complementary equity finance, or that will support their portfolio companies through loans.

Any start-up company needs both equity and debt finance with equity being relatively more important in the early stages while debt finance may increase in importance in later stages. The VC firm will concentrate on providing equity finance and additional managerial services, and is interested in frictionless support through loans being offered by other financial institutions. During the early phases of company development, the provider of debt finance is often at an information disadvantage and cannot reliably assess project risks. Specific insider knowledge contributed by a VC firm, particularly if this firm has invested its own

---

18 See our comparison of this evolutionary process between the U.S. and Western Europe in
   section 7.3.

money, will be relied upon by the bank who has to assess creditworthiness. Expected risks may be reduced, and the bank may thus be willing to offer more favorable financial conditions (lower interest rates, longer pay-back periods). The net present value of the project will be increased and all participating agents may gain from collaboration[19]. A bank may also provide complementary equity finance or additional financial services. It may act as a "bridge-finance institution", providing resources needed before the next phase of expansion can be approached; banks will often also provide services for the initial public offering of stocks. In both cases, a bank may provide additional expertise for which the specialized VC firm cannot offer the appropriate knowledge base. The financial institution and the VC firm will jointly provide a package of skills and services, which neither one of them could offer alone.

Savings banks and regional or state-owned equity finance institutions often pursue additional, *non-financial* objectives that are directed at regional and economic development[20]. They are often embedded into networks of experts and decision-makers who are willing to offer advice and help. These networks often represent very valuable knowledge pools. A VC firm that establishes links with such finance institutions can effectively mobilize these pools of expertise. Members of such a network can offer helpful advice, they can facilitate the accessibility of critical resources (such as expensive research and test facilities), or they can establish useful contacts with potential customers. The value of the start-up project will be increased, and part of this increase can be redistributed to the VC firm, to the second the finance institution as well as to other members of the network[21].

In all these cases in which specialized VC firms and other finance institutions join forces to support young start-up firms, the most important reason for collaboration is a *blending of complementary knowledge*. Each agent possesses only some fraction of the relevant know-how spectrum, and cannot easily access the other, complementary parts. Collaboration will create value and will be sustainable as long as each financial partner can effectively and repetitively contribute some unique part of the required knowledge pool. If this is not the case, and if bilateral finance is only justified by "simple" risk-sharing or financial indivisibilities, portfolio diversification would lead to similar results. Banks and other financial investors could invest in portfolios of different VC funds, and would

---

19 A tri-partite arrangement such as this will not always be as harmonious as just described. Providers of equity finance will sometimes try to gain at the expense of loan providers or vice versa.

20 In many industrial countries, such as in the U.S. or in Germany, each federal state supports or owns equity finance institutions whose objective it is to support young start-up firms.

21 Incentives to the network members need not necessarily be financial. Agents are often motivated by the "success stories" of growing start-up firms in their region.

not need to be concerned about any specifics of the business in which they invest. If, by contrast, the "specifics of the business matter", as is the case for investments in start-up projects, which demand the provision of highly critical, closely held resources, value-adding collaboration must be sought, to which each party has to contribute its own share of valuable expertise[22].

7.2.5   A VC Firm and an Industrial Corporation

Private corporations represent an important group of contributors for finance and for critical resources needed by young start-up firms. Large firms often set up their own corporate venture funds. Corporations also act as major shareholders of VC firms or of some of their funds. Their interest is most often strategic and much less influenced by motives of mere financial diversification: corporations want to have a "window on technology", and they want to monitor new developments of young start-up firms. They want to have either access to teams of talented people, keep an option on acquiring a start-up firm which may eventually control an interesting technology, or keep an option on attractive growth markets.

The corporation often has valuable assets to offer to start-up firms as well as to VC firms. It controls a large repository of technical and manufacturing skills and has detailed market expertise. It is embedded in a dense network of transactions with suppliers, customers, related specialists, and sometimes also with competing firms. Tapping this knowledge base can reduce learning costs for the start-up firm, and will often be the only way to achieve effective commercialization and growth. However, the corporation must see a benefit from letting other institutions have access to its knowledge base.

A large corporation may want to collaborate with a VC firm for several reasons. First, it may be aware of possessing strong technical, manufacturing and marketing skills, while being weak in "financial engineering skills" necessary for the venture business. Second, it may want to hold only a minority share in one particular start-up firm, while the involvement of a second, independent, though not directly competing shareholder will offer greater flexibility[23]. Third, a corporation may "keep an eye" on other firms in the portfolio of a VC firm, while forming a bilateral association to invest in a particular firm.

---

22 Bygrave and Timmons (1986), and Bygrave (1988) have shown in empirical investigations that this value-creating activity is crucial for venture capitalists who want to attain an above-average rate of return.
23 If, for example, a corporation holds 30% of a firm's shares, and a related VC firm holds another 30%, the corporation can easily acquire a majority position if the start-up firm develops in the right direction. If it does not, exit is easier than if the corporation had held 60% from the beginning.

In all these cases, collaboration between industrial corporations and specialized VC firms creates value for participating agents. The arrangement will allow an effective pooling of complementary knowledge and skills. For the corporation, participation in such a collateral arrangement is seen as being an optional investment for a particular new field of expansion. The full range of expertise distributed across participating agents can effectively be exploited, while institutional choices can be kept flexible until certain events manifest themselves (see section 3.5).

7.3 Syndicated Venturing as a Special Form of Multilateral Finance

7.3.1 Reasons for Syndicated Venturing and its Importance

Syndicated venturing represents a special form of multilateral project finance in which two or more institutions each provide equity as well as collaborative finance for a start-up firm. They remain separate shareholders, but coordinate their investments by way of information exchange, i.e. through reciprocal access to each other's pool of knowledge and management capabilities. Syndicated investment tends to grow in importance during the historical evolution of the venture capital business. It offers significant advantages over other, more "conventional" modes of finance (i.e. pure debt or equity), particularly if it is applied to investment projects during early phases of technological and industrial development. For projects implemented during pre-paradigmatic stages[24], for which the evaluation requires very specialized expertise, syndicated venturing is often the only feasible mode of finance. It can then be interpreted as a collaborative, decentralized search procedure, through which independent investors can jointly explore the potential of an investment project, for which there are no objective indicators and probabilities "at hand". Financial investors act as entrepreneurs, and they need to know significantly more about a certain line of activity than the "average" investor in the financial community. The relevant insider knowledge is highly-specific and not easily transferable; it is held by persons with long experience in a particular field, who are often closely tied to a particular investment firm[25]. *Entry*

---

24 See Teece (1986, 1987) and our description of paradigmatic and pre-paradigmatic stages in section 4.3.
25 Venture capitalists and fund managers often hold partial equity ownership in a fund or in certain projects, and they cannot easily leave their company, without being expropriated of a significant part of their past investment.

lags for a financial firm to gain that experience are long, related to the time it takes to build up a pool of experts; *exit lags* are considerable due to bonding arrangements between the investment firms, their managers and the portfolio companies.

Syndicated investment thus appears to be a *mechanism for "tapping" complementary expert pools*, which are not easily transferable between institutions. Coordinating distributed expert pools required to evaluate a venture project, though, is not an easy and unproblematic activity. Why should an agent A provide another financial institution B with strategic information on a particular project, if he does not participate in its future profits? This is different if the knowledge provider (agent A) invests himself in the start-up project. A's propensity to invest is used as an indicator for information reliability to agent B. This signal is even more amplified if A belongs to a financial institution with an established track record in the venture capital business[26]. The mere fact that company XYZ, which is known for its expertise in a specific field and for past success in venture capital investments, provides equity for a particular start-up firm, is used as a signal of reliability to the potential co-investor.

This *reputation effect*, together with personal ties across financial institutions, and inter-personal and inter-company trust relationships, can explain why co-venturing agreements are increasingly important within the venture capital community. These co-venturing arrangements cannot be explained by simple risk diversification, based on spreading risks over a portfolio of companies with measurable risk-return profiles. Instead, financial institutions reciprocally rely on complementary knowledge being captive to each institution. Each single institution participating in a co-venturing network is further "down the learning curve" to assess a particular component of risk. By jointly mobilizing their expertise without necessarily transfering their knowledge, they can reduce the likelihood of failure for a particular project.

Similarly, syndicated investment is *not* primarily driven by indivisibility considerations. Financial institutions do not team up primarily for lack of financial assets. Often, they would prefer to invest more in a particular start-up firm, but are ready to leave equity shares to another financial company in order to access that company's pool of expertise. The *pooling of complementary knowledge* appears to have a much greater priority than the pooling of finance.

---

26 A private investor A who provides equity finance for a particular firm, and who transmits information to another financial institution, may have an incentive to gain from the particular investment project at the cost of the second investor B. This danger is reduced if A works for a well-established institution that has invested in many projects, and that is sensitive about losing its reputation.

7.3.2 Syndicated Venturing in the United States

In the United States, the venture capital supply industry has attained the highest level of maturity worldwide. In addition, a much larger number of start-up firms is generated in high technology areas every year than in any other country in the world. For both reasons, syndicated venturing is most advanced and very frequently used in this country. Thus we will describe the results of empirical studies of syndicated venturing in the U.S. These findings will then be compared to syndicated venturing in Western Europe and in Germany in particular.

The *U.S. venture capital industry* has evolved over two decades as a model for financial innovations, which later became applied in other countries. There has been a strong surge in venture capital investment in the U.S. since 1978. Major explanatory factors were regulatory changes, suitable developments of capital markets, favorable growth prospects and a large potential of young high-tech companies. This surge coincided with a growing number of investments in early stage projects and in high-technology oriented companies. Early stages with a typically long time to pay-off typically involve greater risks and greater return fluctuations[27]. Technological intensity appears to be another risk factor[28]. According to Poindexter (1976), lack of information is the most important reason for failures in predicting the risk and return profile for those types of firms. Financial investors interested in this segment of the market are thus forced to overcome this lack of information. Since access to relevant knowledge bases is expensive and time-consuming, investors will try to participate in networks and co-venturing arrangements. Based on the advantages of knowledge-related complementaries and reciprocal trust building, increasingly dense networks between capitalists have become established since the mid 1970s[29]. Informal networks of venture investors were first established at a regional level, primarily in areas considered as "breeding grounds" for young start-up companies such as Route 128 in Massachussetts and Silicon Valley in California. Throughout the 1980s, close ties and co-venturing agreements became established at an inter-regional, and often also at a transnational level.

---

27 Cooper (1979) showed that the degree of uncertainty is positively corelated to the *expected time to pay-off*. Bygrave (1988) pointed out that the risk of failure is highest for the seed phase (66%), and comparatively low (20%) for later phases (expansion, bridge finance and leveraged buyout).

28 Empirical investigations summarized by Bygrave (1988) show that investment risks are greater for *technology companies* than for other types of start-up firms. These risks, however, may in some cases be balanced off by greater expected rates of return for the first group of high-tech start-ups.

29 One of the first empirical studies to validate the importance of *co-venturing* was provided by Wells (1974). Later, a number of authors became interested in this subject. See Shapero (1984) and Bygrave (1987, 1988).

Bygrave (1987 and 1988) has analyzed syndicated venturing in a comprehensive, nation-wide empirical study. He gathered data about 461 U.S. based venture
capital firms who were managing funds with a total value of 7.6 billion dollars
in 1982. These funds were strongly concentrated: the group of the 61 largest VC
firms managed 4.3 billion, or 57% of total funds, while the remaining 3.3 billion
dollars were widely distributed among the 400 smaller firms (Bygrave 1987,
145). The top 61 VC firms were also the ones most actively engaged in syndicated venturing. The most important predictors of syndicated venturing activity
were to be:

- the *size of the VC firm*;
- the *level of innovation* of the start-up firm (in the following to be called the
  "portfolio firm");
- the *stage of maturity* and the life-cycle of the portfolio firm;
- and the specific *characteristics of the industry* in which the portfolio firm
  operated.

The top 61 VC firms held shares in 73% of all portfolio companies, be it through
participation as single investor or as co-investor. An even greater percentage of
all co-investment arrangements involved one of the top 61 firms as a partner.
Furthermore, the top firms preferredly co-invested within their group of large
financial VC firms.

Bygrave (1987, 141f) distinguished between *low-innovation technical ventures
(LITV)* and *high-innovation technical ventures (HITV)*, with both groups being
differentiated by the degree of innovativeness and technical sophistication. He
showed that the extent of syndicated venturing activity was considerably more
important for high technology related projects than for start-up firms with low
technology content. The role of large VC funds as an investor for HITV was even
stronger than their share in equity ownership of all portfolio firms. A very large
share of that investment activity was maintained within syndicated venturing
arrangements, particularly through binary associations with other large VC firms.

Bygrave also compared the extent of co-venturing for investments in *early-
stage* and *late-stage* companies. He showed that co-venturing is a rather dominant
form of investment during early stages, while its importance is reduced during
later stages (Bygrave 1987, 149). Even though the average amount of investment
needed for early stage financing is considerably smaller than for later stages, and
though the typical project size for early stage project is often miniscule in comparison to the financial strengths of VC funds. Even the top 61 VC firms are
strongly inclined to participate in co-venturing arrangements.

Finally, Bygrave has compared the investment behavior for projects in *different
industries*. Consumer-related projects were characterized much less by co-venturing arrangements than upstream-related projects for specialized investment
goods. As an example, the ratio of pairs to single investments was almost five
times greater in computer companies than for investments in consumer good

companies, even though the amount of investment required in both cases was comparable (Bygrave 1987, 149). Both sectors, however, are considerably differ-ent with respect to product technology, the role of market uncertainties, as well as the level of experience needed to assess these uncertainties[30].

Bygrave concluded that syndicated venturing is neither a matter of financial risk diversification, nor influenced by the desire of VC firms to overcome finan-cial indivisibilities. Otherwise, large VC firms in the sample would have been less inclined to participate in co-venturing deals due to their own financial strength and their internal capabilities to spread risk. By contrast, his study re-vealed that *larger VC firms* were more actively engaged in co-venturing agree-ments than smaller VC firms.

What appears to be much more important as an economic argument for co-venturing is the reciprocal *"tapping of knowledge pools"*, motivated by the need to get access to specialized sets of expertise which even the largest firms cannot build-up in due time, or at an acceptable cost. This "tapping of expert pools" involves a time-consuming process, and syndicated venturing networks can be interpreted as distributed pools of financial as well as technology- and industry-specific knowledge. These elements of the distributed knowledge pool represent highly proprietary resources with long gestation lags, which can only be made accessible through collaboration.

The largest VC firms in the business were also the longest established ones in the VC business, and those who have had the greatest opportunity to establish, test and substantiate co-venturing ties. Their *capital accumulated in networks* consists of the knowledge of "where to tap" the experts and whom to trust in the VC business[31]. Their capital accumulated in the networks has become strongest *within the original high-tech regions*. 38 of the top VC firms were located in three states: California, Massachussetts and New York. Most syndicated venturing arrangements, particu-larly those in high-technology related projects and for early stage investments, were originally concluded in these three states. Based on these regional syndicated ven-turing pools, a second phase starting in the late 1970s was inititated, which involved more co-venturing agreements *between high-tech regions*, and which was directed at "tapping transcontinental expert pools". This is illustrated in *Fig. 7.6*.

Syndicated networks and expert pools appear to be more geographically dis-persed if investments in less innovative projects are considered. Inasmuch as certain technologies such as microelectronics and computers are diffused into more mature applications, knowledge of specific customer and demand condi-

---

30 For *consumer-related projects*, there are often reliable surveys available which can be "bought on the market". By contrast, sophisticated *capital goods* markets can often only be understood by very experienced "insiders".

31 For a comparable interpretation of *network relationships as investment* see Jarillo (1988), Johanson and Mattsson (1989) and our analysis in section 4.4.

tions in traditional sectors becomes critical. This knowledge is often held by venture capitalists in the more traditional industrial regions in the U.S. (such as Michigan, Illinois or Ohio). Syndicated co-venturing agreements for less sophisticated technological projects are thus characterized by arrangements through which expert pools within or between traditional regions are linked, or else through which expert in low-tech regions link up with experts in high-tech regions. See *Fig. 7.7* for an illustration.

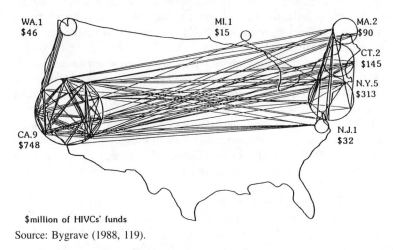

$million of HIVCs' funds

Source: Bygrave (1988, 119).

Fig. 7.6:   Syndicated Co-Venturing Agreements for High-Technology Related
            Projects

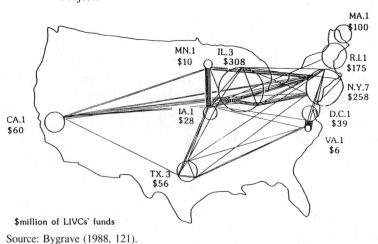

$million of LIVCs' funds

Source: Bygrave (1988, 121).

Fig. 7.7:   Syndicated Co-Venturing Agreements for Low-Technology Projects

7.3.3   Syndicated Venturing in Western Europe and in Germany

The pattern of syndicated investment is considerably different between the U.S. and Western European countries. Differences must be explained by (1) evolutionary stages of the venture capital industry, (2) by national fragmentation, and (3) by structural and regulatory characteristics specific to each country.

   While syndicated VC investment increased considerably in importance between 1977 and 1987 in Western Europe, it is still less developed than in the U.S. For a total of 15 Western European countries, 2.9 billion ECU of new VC funds were made available in 1987[32]. Of these funds, 1.2 billion or 42% were provided by single VC firms (*"no syndication"*), while 1.5 billion or 58% were invested through participation of at least two separate funds (*"syndication"*). In the U.S., a slightly higher *overall amount* is made available for venture capital than in Western Europe[33], but a much higher percentage of these funds is mobilized through syndicated venturing. See *Table 7.2* for a statistical comparison.

Table 7.2: International Comparison of Syndicated Venturing

	Percentage of funds within syndication (1)	Percentage of national syndication (2)	National as percent of total syndication (2)/(1)
United States	70*	> 65*	> 95*
Western Europe**	58.3	51.3	88
– United Kingdom	59.8	58.1	97
– West Germany	55.3	39.3	71
– France	39.4	32.5	82
– Italy	32.6	27.9	86

*   Estimates

**   Includes 15 EVCA member countries

Source: EVCA (1988)

   There are considerable national differences with respect to syndicated venturing in Western Europe; these national differences are also summarized in Table 7.2. Venture capital firms in the *United Kingdom* appear to be most actively

---

32 These countries, which are regularly monitored within the EVCA Yearbook include the EEC countries plus Austria, Sweden and Switzerland.

33 Morris (1989, 9) estimates that approximately 4 billion dollars (or approximately 3.5 billion ECU) were invested annually for VC in the U.S during the second half of the 1980s.

involved in co-venturing agreements, and they place a high emphasis on syndicated investment at the national level. At a lower level of overall funds invested in start-up projects, *West German* firms have approximately 55% of their funds committed in connection with syndicated investment projects. The role of syndicated investment at national level in Germany is, however, much less expressed than in both the U.S. and the U.K., and is also lower than for several other European countries. In *France*, 39% of VC investments are syndicated with more than 80% of all co-venturing agreements being signed at national level. In *Italy*, 33% of funds are engaged in co-venturing, 85% of which are mobilized at the national level.

National fragmentation appears to be a major impediment to the establishment of an effective European syndicated venturing network. Most network relations between financial institutions are still maintained at a national level[34]. Within each country, the suppliers' group is often "too thin", and national expert pools are not sophisticated enough to sustain an efficient syndicated venturing network. This is particularly the case for *West Germany* where most venture capital firms became established only after 1983. These firms have not had enough time to develop their own in-house expertise suited particularly to venture capital investment. Furthermore, during the first years German VC firms pursued similar lines of investment activities, and were involved in duplicated search behavior. Limited firm-specific specialization advantages, together with the build-up of competing instead of complementary expert pools reduced the opportunity for effective syndicated investment. The knowledge distribution pattern, which was introduced in section 5.3, can be described by non-exhaustiveness, and by the absence of mutual exclusiveness. Such a resource distribution pattern is certainly unfavorable for co-venturing; as a result, there is an intense competition between German VC firms, and a decreased willingness to collaborate and exchange information with each other. If co-venturing partners are sought, firms prefer to seek bilateral agreements with international and non-European partners instead of finding a suitable agreement with a national rival. Efficient national co-venturing networks have so far not gained the required momentum.

Another difference of venture capital investment in Europe as compared with the U.S. is the *strong role of government* and of *non-private* capital market participants. The federal government and the Länder states in Germany, as well as other public and semi-public institutions provide considerable funds for young start-up firms. The same is true for other European countries such as France, the U.K., Italy or for Scandinavia. Between 15 and 20% of the finance committed for VC funds are provided by government agencies (EVCA 1988, 10). Additional

---

34 Even though large banks actively pursue trans-European business strategies, informal networks between financial investors in Western Europe are still effective primarily at the national level.

public funds complement equity investments channelled through VC funds. This can be interpreted as a special form of syndicated investment, namely as the provision of complementary private and public finance, but so far it is not counted as "syndicated investment".

The question of whether finance is provided by private or public investors may be considered as less critical, as long as it does not affect the investment behavior of start-up firms. In some instances, however, the in-flow of public money will have some influence on the investment behavior of firms, and it may adversely affect the potential for the effective build-up of national syndicated venturing networks. If public funds are regarded as "easy money", while private funds are difficult to access, or considered to be combined with "uncomfortable" control rights, firms will seek public funds first, before they accept additional private shareholders. In such a situation of *venture-related crowding-out*, a viable private syndicated venturing network will have greater difficulties in becoming sustainable.

Furthermore, public institutions are often restrained with respect to the accumulation of knowledge pools, which combine financial skills with technology and industry expertise. If this is the case, the gradual build-up of financial networks and trust relationships will become retarded. There may be possibilities for effectively involving government agents in syndicated venturing. However, this requires compatible objectives between public and private agents, as well as an appropriate specialization between the two spheres. In order to study public-private syndicated venturing in more detail, we will give an account of the evolution of public support of venture capital investment in Germany in the following section.

7.4   Projects Involving Government as Financier

7.4.1   Reasons for Government Involvement in the Venturing Process

Government agencies in all industrialized countries are actively promoting industrial innovation and the diffusion of new technologies. Since young start-up firms are considered an important vehicle for the commercialization of new technologies, government involvement in the venturing process is seen as a critical element of innovation policy. Public support of R&D and of the venturing process is justified along two lines of reasoning. According to the *first argument*, government has a pre-eminent role in the *formation of markets* and in the *regulation of entry conditions* for new activities. According to the *second argument*, existing markets may require public involvement in order to *overcome market failures* and to improve the resource allocation process for ongoing activities. The differences between these two lines of reasoning are as follows: according to the *first* argument, government helps to establish new institutional structures needed to support new processes and activities; according to the *second* argument, existing institutional structures and regulatory conditions often restrain innovation activities, and these restraints can often only be offset by decisive political action.

The *formation of markets* and the facilitation of entry for new market participants is a prerequisite for a dynamic competitive system. According to the first argument, government plays an important role in the determination of legal and regulatory conditions, and must exercise some influence on entry conditions for new market participants. High entry costs and long entry times are often used as arguments for government support for specific new activities and new firms. Young start-up firms are "nurtured" by subsidies and by the preferential provision of equity finance during their early phases of development; such support of small firms is actively pursued by public and semi-public institutions at regional, state and federal level[35]. If several new firms need to become established simultaneously in order to form a viable industrial sector, public support policy refers to the *infant industry argument*. The industrialization strategy in Japan after the Second World War, as an example, was to a large extent based on this line of reasoning.

The *second argument* in support of government involvement relates to *market failures*, which are responsible for restricting certain processes and activities within existing institutional structures. For reasons of externality, indivisibility, uncertainty, or for too long a time horizon needed, private agents will invest fewer resources than would be socially optimal (Arrow 1962). Public interference in the market process is called for, to overcome the gap between privately and socially optimal activity levels. However, this argument based on market failures often *overestimates* the capabilities and the willingness of public agents to correct these failures. At the same time, this argument *underestimates* the inherent *failures of public activity*[36]. Market failures must be seen in conjunction with potential "state failures", but the interaction between both types of distortions is very difficult to evaluate and make operational for specific investment projects; this results in ambiguity: proponents of government involvement will find some arguments to support their interests, while free-market proponents will find related arguments for government *not* to interfere.

Given this arbitrary nature of "market failure" as well as "state failure" arguments, we want to suggest a *third line of reasoning* for the evaluation of public agents' involvement, which is based on our concepts of the design and organization of strategic investment projects as outlined in chapters 2 and 5. We assume

---

35 Note that the nurturing of young firms as a device to overcome institutional rigidity is not only applied by public agencies, but very often also by large corporations (in the form of spin-off and corporate venturing).

36 See Buchanan (1983), Buchanan, Tollison and Tullock (1980), Grossman (1990), and our analysis in section 8.2.

that there are *private* investors who pursue certain goals, and that there are also *public* agents who pursue other, often related objectives. If both have complementary and compatible goals, they can decide to pursue certain activities jointly. A typical example is the venture capital investment sector. Some public institutions and political decision-makers have a dedicated interest in supporting young start-up firms, or they will be interested in inititating investment activities in certain sectors for which young start-up firms play a strong role. Private agents such as young entrepreneurs and financial investors have a complementary interest: they need public institutions to support their interests and are thus willing to "join forces" with public decision-makers. Both groups will identify processes and tasks, that are particularly suited for the activities of young start-up firms. There will be some tasks to be performed preferably by private entrepreneurs; but there will also be very important related tasks which are more akin to public institutions. These tasks calling for public involvement include all activities with a strong regulatory content, for which appropriability regimes are weak, for which the time horizon is long, and for which critical resources are owned or controlled by public institutions.

This *third argument* which we propose may, at first sight, appear similar to the market failure argument outlined above, but it is in fact distinctly different. While the market failure argument often assumes that state agents display certain non-realistic characteristics (long-term orientation, willingness to accept risks, etc.), our approach is more pragmatic and directed at choice opportunities for particular investment projects. Public agents are *not* assumed to be altruistic, long-term oriented or willing to accept above-average risks. By contrast, public agents are guided by selfish motives and group-specific objectives. Objectives and processes pursued by public agents are guided and constrained by past investments in knowledge, capital goods and institutional assets. Based on these past investments, there may be certain favorable conditions, under which public agents will be more long-term oriented, more in favor of new institutional structures, and more willing to accept risk. Such favorable circumstances must be explained by resources owned and controlled by public agencies, by agency-specific knowledge bases, and by specific missions defined for public agencies.

In *Fig. 7.8*, we have illustrated the decision-making process, through which private *and* public agents can jointly implement certain investment projects, which might not be feasible through mere private acivity. Self-interested private and public agents will jointly define *strategic objectives*, and will select the *processes* required to achieve these objectives. In order to perfom the tasks required for a particular process, different agents must provide complementary resources. Some of the relevant assets will be owned by *private* agents, while others will be owned or controlled by *public* agents. Critical resources relevant for the venturing processes, as an example, which are often under the domain of public institutions, cover technological knowledge generated within public research institutions, public legislation, as well as public procurement. If complementary assets which are critical to the venturing process are owned or controlled by private *and* public agents, both will have to form coalitions. In order to secure expropriation of quasi-rents for their resources, both parties need to agree on cooperative contract and governance modes.

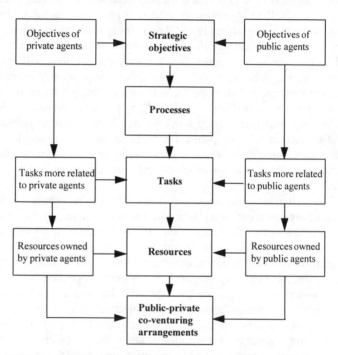

Fig. 7.8:   The Formulation of Joint Public-Private Investment Projects

Suitable *public-private co-venturing arrangements* will be derived as a specific contractual arrangement, through which private and public entities can secure their interests and ownership rights. Compatible objectives of both groups are directed at the establishment of new firms, or at the rejuvenation of the industrial structure. There may be a large variety of different public-private combinations of tasks and resources. Resources provided by public institutions can be real or of a financial nature. Sustainable modes of public-private partnership will evolve if assets and capabilities of both groups are appropriately balanced. The way in which such public-private investment projects can be implemented, will be further explored in chapter 8. In the following we will concentrate on a case description of government support of the venture capital sector in Germany; support was arranged through financial resources, which were complemented by additional services (consulting, managerial advice, networking relationships, etc.). Public financial support was first provided in the form of subsidies and loans (see our description of the TOU-program in section 7.4.2); in a later phase, public involvement was arranged through equity participation by public institutions (see our description of the BJTU-program in section 7.4.3).

7.4.2 Government as Source of Subsidies: The German TOU-program

Public institutions in West Germany had been actively involved in the venturing process for many years, though sometimes in an uncoordinated way. Original support through the European Recovery Program (ERP) helped to finance many start-up companies during the 1950s and was one of the reasons for economic prosperity in that period. Because of limited continuity and consistency within the financial system, however, many small and medium sized firms experienced a serious lack of equity after 1960. This led to the establishment of equity finance cooperations which were often owned by the Länder states[37]. In most cases, however, these new financial institutions were more actively supporting "traditional", non high-technolgy oriented firms; their institutional missions and their skill bases did not allow to effectively cope with high-technolgy start-up companies.

During the mid 1970s, decision-makers became increasingly aware of the role of high-technology oriented start-up companies for innovation and growth[38]; there was a perceived deficiency with respect to the role and position of such firms in West Germany, for which the *shortage of venture capital* in West Germany was seen as the main reason. In response to this perceived bottleneck, the West German government established a new public-private venture capital organization (the Wagnisfinanzierungsgesellschaft, WFG), in collaboration with the principal banks[39]. Experiences gained during the first years of investment activity of the WFG, together with the knowledge acquired through other public support programs, led to the conclusion that a specific program had to be designed which would be more suitably adapted to the needs of young German start-up firms. As a result, the so-called *TOU-program* for technology-based start-up firms ("*Tech-nologieorientierte Unternehmensgründungen*") was launched in 1983.

---

37 The "Mittelständische Beteiligungs-Gesellschaften" (MBG) are owned by the Länder-states, while the "Kapitalbeteiligungsgesellschaften" (KBG) were established by the banks.
38 This was initiated by (over-optimistic) studies about young high-tech firms in the U.S. See Cooper (1964), Birch (1979) and Nathusius (1979).
39 This *"Wagnisfinanzierungsgesellschaft"* provides an interesting case example for a multi-lateral public-private investment project, for which diverse, partly incompatible objectives had to be brought in line. The project in its original form did not turn out to be successful, and has undergone several stages of significant restructuring and reorganization.

The TOU-program had *two primary objectives*, the *first* of which was to enhance start-up and growth opportunities for young high-technology oriented companies, chiefly by providing financial support. The *second* objective, pursued
parallel to the first, involved the establishment of an appropriate venture capital
environment, consisting of a network of agents providing complementary services
such as management, information exchange, contract development and finance.
The particular service requirements and the financial arrangements most suitable
for the West German environment were not well known ex-ante (in 1983), even
though they had to be "custom-designed" to the specific national and regional
circumstances[40]. As a result, the TOU-program was initiated as an exploratory
program with explicitly built-in feed-back loops, and was combined with several
successive stages of evaluation.

The *support scheme* involved both financial aid and the provision of consulting services, with focus and support being differentiated into *three phases* of
project development:

– *Phase I* covered the support of *feasibility studies and preliminary project
  evaluation*. During this phase, projects were supported with a limited financial
  budget (up to 54 thousand DM), but with a high percentage of subsidies paid
  (up to 90% of costs);
– support in *Phase II* covered the more important and more expensive *product
  development phase*. Up to 1.2 million DM or 75% of project costs were paid
  for R&D;
– for the succeeding *Phase III*, which involved manufacturing of the new product and *market introduction*, the federal government provided guarantees for
  80% of loans amounting to 2 million DM, which had to be provided by
  banks[41].

Experiences gained from the differentiated support arrangements in these three
phases were quite mixed. *Phase I* support was originally sought by entrepreneurs
to validitate their projects, and to get external advice for developing the business
plan. At this stage however, there was no functioning market for start-up specific
consulting services. The transaction costs required for finding the appropriate
consultant with expertise in a specific technology or industry segment, for specifying his task and for finding an appropriate contractual arrangement were considerable. Support in the range of 10—54 thousand DM was barely sufficient for
both partners (the entrepreneur and the consultant) to work out convincing business plans. In many cases it was just used to cover transaction costs and to

---

40 The regulatory environment, the functioning of capital markets, and the behavior of entrepreneurs and financial decision-makers in Germany are *significantly different* from what can
   be observed in other countries such as the U.S. or in the U.K.
41 See the description of the scheme in Kulicke (1993, chapter2).

establish the business relationship between the two partners without, however, opening prospects for future joint work. As a result, after a very short experimentation period, Phase I support was no longer applied for. Firms interested in support during Phase I had often only considered it as an "entry ticket" into the more promising Phase II[42].

Financial support during *Phase II* provided firms with ample funds to complete their R&D work. Finance was provided as a grant and was found to be very attractive for young entrepreneurs, even though the payment procedure was sometimes criticized as being too slow and bureaucratic. Overall, more than 300 firms received support for their R&D projects between 1983 and 1989, with a total program budget of more than 300 million DM. The majority of firms completed their R&D projects successfully: by the end of 1989, more than 150 firms had completed market introduction[43].

In comparison to the funding of R&D in Phase II, the succeeding *Phase III* was accepted to a much lesser extent[44]. There were several reasons responsible for this: firms were often unwilling to switch from grants to loans. If debt finance was sought, financial investors were often willing to provide loans without government "backing". The interference of a third party (i.e. a state institution) between the entrepreneur and the financial institution was considered unnecessary and sometimes as an additional complication. Furthermore, other sources of funds from the Länder states turned out to be competing with federal money during this phase.

Appropriate financial and contractual arrangements evolved only gradually and as a result of a sequential learning process. The same was true for the evolution of complementary services and of a functioning co-venturing network. In order to explore alternative industrial arrangements, *four distinct model variants* were used in parallel for management and execution of the TOU-program:

1. for two *technology-related* program variants (for microelectronics and bio-technology), specialized project management organizations of the BMFT were selected for the execution of the program;
2. a *regional variant* was established for decentralized management and execution in six regions in West Germany;
3. 14 *technology centers* with their own management capabilities were selected to support and monitor start-up firms located within these centers;
4. finally, a *venture capital* variant was designed for those projects, for which private venture capital firms were willing to act as co-investors.

---

42 This behavior was based on a misunderstanding. Firms were allowed to apply for Phase II directly, but believed that a "good certificate" from Phase I would increase their chances for getting support in Phase II.
43 For a detailed account of program evaluation see Mayer et al. (1989) and Kulicke (1990).
44 Within the group of 170 firms that had started market introduction by the end of 1988, only 69 (41%) had applied for Phase III support.

This multi-institutional and decentralized structure turned out to be very difficult to coordinate. The capabilities, strengths and responsibilities of the various participating institutions had to be explored through a time-consuming trial-and-error process. While institutions involved in the *first model variant* were often capable of providing technological and administrative advice for the funding process, their managerial skills were often somewhat limited. The entrepreneur himself was in most cases highly technically skilled, but he demanded support for business strategies and for advice during the entrepreneurial process. Knowledge bases of start-up firms, program management organizations and external service firms were neither comprehensive nor complementary. Furthermore, objectives and responsibilities of participating agents were not appropriately "aligned". The program management institution had to play a dual role: it acted as selection and monitoring authority on the one side, and was asked for advice and cooperative support in the day-to-day entrepreneurial process on the other side. Conflicts of interests and an unclear specification of responsibilites often restricted the effective work of the program management institutions[45].

The experience was mixed for the *regional variant* and for projects supported through *technology centers* (variants two and three). Twenty different institutions involved in the two program variants displayed a dispersed spectrum of strengths and capabilities. Some were seen as very responsive to both the needs of private entrepreneurs and to the demands of public authorities; some others represented primarily the interest of one side, while there were also cases in which neither side was appropriately served. The performance of each institution can primarily be explained by its agency-specific ownership and governance structure, by accumulated skills and by the committment of dedicated, entrepreneurially-minded persons within the institution. The artificial separation of interests between a funding agency, a consulting and administration agency and the entrepreneur turned out to be detrimental. In spite of these coordination problems, a few successful projects became effectively implemented, due primarily to entrepreneurially-minded people, who acted in a project- and task-oriented way, and who were able to work against political and administrative obstacles.

The fourth, *venture capital based variant* was originally designed to overcome this separation between financial interests and institutional tasks and responsibilities. Interests of venture capitalists and funding institutions were thought to be complementary and compatible. Growth expectations and the willingness of a venture capitalist to invest in a start-up firm, according to the original idea, should be used as a signal to the funding institution that the project is viable. Unexpectedly though, it often turned out the other way round: the venture capitalist waited for funding approval and decided *then* to invest. Once an entrepre-

---

45 For a detailed account of contractual difficulties between the entrepreneurs, the program management institutions and the BMFT see Gerybadze (1991b, 24ff).

neur had received the grant for Phase II, however, he was often no longer interested in involving an additional shareholder in his project. Interests between the three parties became incompatible, and venture capitalists increasingly turned away from equity finance for TOU backed start-up firms.

Given these coordination difficulties, the intended establishment of a functioning venture finance and service network may have come at high costs. The knowledge accumulation process and the generation of comprehensive, complementary services evolved in a too decentralized, non-coordinated way, with duplicated activities and sometimes unclear responsibilities. The mobilization of private capital was made difficult through the parallel provision of grants, loan guarantees and equity finance, with the involvement of many private parties together with several independent public agencies. Experience gathered during this process, however, was very valuable.

Major lessons to be learned are that the knowledge accumulation process cannot be separated from the financial and entrepreneurial interests of the institutions involved. These interests of the participating agents, be they private or public, must be clearly specified. Market mediated forms of exchange through which "quid pro quo" relationships are established, as well as collaborative contract modes ("quo ad usum" and "quoad sortem") ought to be preferred to unidirectional transfers in the form of subsidies. Accordingly, repayable forms of finance should be preferred to non-compensated forms. Collaborative modes of interaction must become established on a reciprocal and repetitive basis, as opposed to unidirectional, non-repetitive provisions of know-how and other services. Equity-based contractual arrangements, through which the growth potential of start-up firms is assessed by risk-taking investors betting on a particular prospect are often preferable to loans or grants. These experiences have resulted in the formulation of a new scheme for the support of start-up firms in West Germany which will be described briefly in section 7.4.3.

7.4.3 Government as Co-investor: The BJTU-program

Built on the experiences gained from the TOU-program, the BMFT launched a new equity finance support program for young high-technology companies in 1988 — the so-called *BJTU-program* ("Beteiligungskapital für *junge* Technologie*u*nternehmen"). Support through subsidies was replaced by equity finance arrangements involving state-owned institutions as partners. A hidden subsidy element was still involved which can be explained by the differential risk-bearing of public and private partners[46]. Apart from this subsidy element, the BJTU-pro-

---

46 The BMFT bears a greater risk in the case of failure, and this can be evaluated as effective, though hidden, subsidy.

gram was strongly oriented towards financial arrangements which are more compatible with private capital markets:

- a supplementary and non-competitive relationship between government finance and private sources of funds was considered a key principle (the so-called *subsidiarity-principle*[47]);
- the contractual and administrative arrangement was adapted to private market requirements (*"market orientation"*);
- a flexible "quasi-price mechanism" was institutionalized, through which government agents could influence and adapt some basic parameters in accordance with market needs, and in response to private agents' behavior (*"flexible incentive mechanism"*);
- finally, exit decisions of public agents and their eventual replacement by private agents in later phases was regarded as a "dictum" (*"pre-programmed exit"*).

The BJTU-program was implemented through two distinctly different contractual arrangements, each being managed by a separate financial institution. The first arangement, which is managed by the state-owned "Deutsche Ausgleichsbank" (DAB), and which will be called the *Co-investment Model*, is illustrated in *Fig. 7.9*. The DAB will provide equity finance to start-up firms, in which another private finance institution (the "lead investor") will invest first. Both institutions will get ownership rights and will provide some services to the start-up firm. The DAB considers its equity investment as temporary, and will sell its shares at a later date. The BMFT just acts as a "back-up" needed for the case where sale values of equity will turn out to be lower than acquisition values plus management fees. To balance interests between the lead investor, the DAB and the BMFT, the following *steering parameters* can be adapted in a flexible way:

- the overall level of funds per year committed for the co-investment model;
- the type of sharing between the lead investor and the DAB;
- the type and extent of guaranties provided by the BMFT;
- and the particular distribution of capital gains primarily through agios/disagios of resale values[48].

---

47 The *principle of subsidiarity* requires that public funds are complementary to, and non-competing with private sources of funds, which corresponds to the condition of mutual exclusiveness formulated in section 5.3. This condition is necessary for public-private co-venturing agreements to become sustainable.

48 For a more detailed description of these parameters see Brunling, Gerybadze and Mayer (1989, 33).

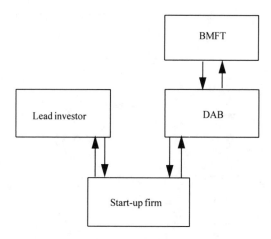

Fig. 7.9:   The Co-Investment Model within the BJTU-program

The alternative model managed by the "Kreditanstalt für Wiederaufbau" (KfW), the state-owned Bank for Reconstruction, involves re-finance arrangements for private lead investors. These private institutions will provide equity finance for start-up firms (see the *Loan-guarantee Model* as illustrated in *Fig. 7.10*), and will be responsible for ownership, management and service contracts to be negotiated with the portfolio firms. These firms can get loan finance from the KfW on more favorable terms than are available at the private capital market. The BMFT acts as "lender of last resort" for the KfW. In exchange for preferential arrangements and for public risk-bearing, the KfW will receive a certain percentage of capital gains from growing portfolio firms. The BMFT and the KfW can, to a certain extent, adapt the following *parameters*:

- the level of funds per year committed for this refinance model;
- the percentage of equity that can be re-financed by the KfW;
- the extent of risk-bearing in terms of percentage of loans guaranteed;
- and the percentage of capital gains to be distributed to the KfW.

Both models of the BJTU-program, the co-investment model and the loan-guarantee model, had to undergo some learning and adaptation. In the meantime, this has led to the establishment of bilateral and multilateral links between a large number of private finance institutions, together with the two state-owned institutions. A number of new seed-capital funds have become established, which are "embedded" into syndicated venturing networks at regional and state level. These groups will form the nucleus for a new national syndicated venturing network. While it is still too early to evaluate the BJTU-program which will be in operation until 1994, there are signs that a more efficient and self-sustainable multilateral seed capital and venture capital system will gradually evolve over the next few years.

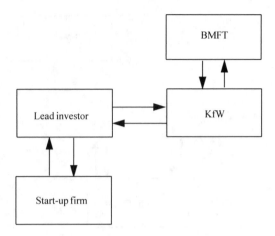

Fig. 7.10: The Loan-Guarantee Model within the BJTU Program

7.5   Conclusions for Multilateral Finance

Multilateral project finance through which two or more independent financial
partners team up to support an investment project is becoming increasingly important. Collaborative financial arrangements may be very powerful, and may
often represent the only feasible mode of governance and finance for certain
investment projects. Advantages and limits of multilateral finance, however, must
be seen from a balanced perspective and on a case-by-case basis. For some
investment projects, for which the participating agents praise the virtues of cooperation, co-venturing arrangements may *not* represent the most appropriate
mode of governance and finance. Multilateral forms of finance are only suitable
for those investment projects, for which participating agents control co-specific,
irreplaceable and durable assets[49], and for which the pattern of resource ownership distribution is balanced between partners. The type of assets required and
the resource ownership pattern should determine the most appropriate mode of
governance and finance for each particular project.

For structuring multilateral project finance and co-venturing agreements, an
extended version of our "project structuring logic" as introduced in chapters 2

---

49 See our general description of the Austrian theory of the value of complementary resources
    in section 2.4, and our analysis of specific conditions under which collaboration is superior
    over markets and integrated modes of coordination in section 5.4.

and 5 can be applied. According to the modified decision-making sequence outlined in Fig. 7.8, potential cooperation partners need to define *strategic objectives*, they have to jointly evaluate and select *processes*, and find an agreement on *tasks* and on the distribution of responsibilities. Only after a detailed analysis of *resource* requirements and of the resource distribution pattern will agents be able to design the appropriate institutional and financial arrangement. Multilateral project finance and specific co-venturing arrangements should be "custom-engineered" and endogenously derived as a result of this proposed project structuring approach.

In contrast to the most frequently heard arguments for multilateral finance, there is some doubt that the investment size and the risk level connected with a project are sufficient arguments for cooperation. Given favorable conditions for both entry to and exit from specific resources[50], any size of an investment project and any risk level could be "shouldered" by a single large firm issuing shares to a large group of anonymous agents. Or else it could be arranged from within a loose market network of specialized agents. Collaborative institutional arrangements will become only economically superior, if resources are very difficult to access, if assets are tightly held by independent agents, and if strong information asymmetries prevail.

A further, very important characteristic for multilateral project finance is the extent of *co-specificity between financial and real assets* (specific knowledge and capital goods). The need for multilateral finance can hardly be deduced from the character of financial assets alone. Money as a resource is easily accessible and replaceable. The numbers and types of owners of money required for a large project are no more relevant than sailing on an the ocean requires the knowledge of which rivers its water has flown from. For highly-specific *real* assets, the *"relevance of source"* is important, while for purely financial assets the source does not matter much. Such an "irrelevance of source" argument applicable for financial assets, is no longer valid if we are concerned with revenue streams generated over many periods, and which are based on the coordination of highly-specific real assets. Providers of finance must then have profound knowledge about specific resources and about suitable contractual arrangements which have proven to be effective in coordinating the underlying combination of real assets. Participating agents are then required to provide knowledge *and* finance, *not just* finance.

For certain complex, large and highly-specific investment projects, "knowledge how to do", "knowledge how to choose" (Nelson and Winter 1982, 60f) and "knowledge how to design and implement contracts" will become a much more

---

50 These conditions can be defined by entry cost and entry time, resp. by exit cost and exit time, as outlined in section 4.1.

critical asset than money itself. Distributed expert pools and complementary knowledge bases represent the most important asset within a multilateral contractual arrangement, and finance provided by the partners will merely be used as a secondary resource, or as a type of "glue". It has been shown in sections 7.1 and 7.2, that financial funds are often primarily used to "back-up" knowledge complementarities between independent agents. The fact that investor A has committed financial funds for a project for which he is believed to control specific knowledge, is used as a signal for investor B to commit financial resources. The selection of the most appropriate insitutional arrangement to make a project economically feasible and financially "sound", is then primarily a matter of "tapping" distributed expert-pools which are "backed up" by multilateral finance.

This interconnectedness between financial and real assets has some profound implications on the question, whether *public agents* should be involved in an investment project, or in a certain type of innovation activity. The often-heard argument that government agencies should be included because finance mobilized from private sources would not suffice, is not convincing. In this role as "dull generators of funds" for projects which cannot secure enough private finance, government agents will easily become misused, and tend to support second or third best projects. According to our "project structuring logic" outlined in the preceding , government agents should only be involved in those types of projects, for which they own and control critical resources, which are irreplaceable and which cannot easily be accessed by private agents. This would be primarily the case for projects,

– for which the government exercises a strong influence on the venturing process through the *legal and regulatory framework*;
– for which government institutions constitute a major share of demand, and for which they possess the relevant *knowledge of customer needs*;
– for which government agents themselves are members of the *relevant, distributed expert pool*;
– for which the government can provide *supply-side stimuli* for the formation of projects and for the generation of business prospects;
– and for which *tax policies* and *capital market regulation* strongly affect the outcome of projects.

All these arguments are of relevance for the national and international venture finance network, the working of which can only be understood through a detailed analysis of the *interplay between market forces and government finance and regulation*. This venture finance network can only be effective, if all participating agents bring complementary resources other than finance "to the party", if their objectives are compatible, and if the resource ownership pattern is appropriately balanced. The way in which our proposed "project structuring logic" can be further developed for a number of different public policy "issues" other than venture capital will be further explored in the subsequent chapter.

Part IV: Policy Implications

8   New Cooperative Solutions and Public-Private Partnerships

8.1   The Need for New Cooperative Solutions

Many economic, ecological and social problems and challenges during the 1990s will increasingly demand cooperative solutions, through which relatively large groups of agents have to coordinate their activities at a regional, national, and often even at a global level:

- *ecological problems* such as the increased production of CO_2, the deforestation in tropical zones, and the related greenhouse-effect can only be solved through decisive and coordinated activities at a global level;
- *global competition* and the international division of labor will undergo a major restructuring process, and will increasingly call for international cooperation and for new forms of economic coordination;
- the development and dissemination of fusion technologies increasingly involves companies from different industries, government agencies, research laboratories as well as universities;
- the political and economic transition process in *Eastern Europe* can only be envisaged as a well-coordinated economic development program involving governments and private investors in both the Eastern and the Western part of the hemisphere;
- if the *North-South conflict* is to be resolved, new collaborative solutions are inevitable. The reconsideration of new concepts and the creation of new institutions for economic policy and development aid are of particular concern.

Greater degrees of collaboration will be necessary for many of these problems due to the extent of *ecological interdependance* at regional, international and global level (as paraphrased by the term "spaceship earth"). The increased application of generic, "chain-linked" *technologies* of a systemic nature (Kline and Rosenberg 1986, and Teece 1991) requires new solutions, for which many independent agents possess only a very narrow range of the resource spectrum. High degrees of *specialization* related to capabilities and distributed knowledge bases call for novel solutions of project organization and implementation.

Despite these challenges, however, flexibility and responsiveness is restrained by the narrow framework which we often apply to the design of institutional structures. We still think in too narrow and inappropriate concepts when it comes to the formulation of organizational solutions required to solve complex tasks.

Our minds are captivated by rather rigid models of organizational design which distinguish between *simplified "polar solutions"* such as:

- the distinction between *markets* and *hierarchies*;
- the distinction between *market* coordination and *government* involvement;
- and, third, the distinction between the establishment of *new institutions* vs. the reliance on *old institutional structures*.

As we have shown in chapter 4, new developments in neo-institutional economics challenge the rigid binary distinction between *markets and hierarchies*. The solution of complex problems involves new configurations of activities, only part of which can appropriately be solved by either markets or integrated modes of governance and organization. Many activities will have to rely on hybrid forms "between markets and hierarchies" (Thorelli 1986).

Similarly, the rigid distinction between *markets and politics* (Lindblom 1977), or between market and government-mediated modes of coordination appears to be inappropriate. Pure market coordination cannot function effectively for many of the problems and challenges outlined above[1]. But this cannot imply that market coordination can be substituted or compensated for by *government* forms of coordination; nor should we rely on established routines of government involvement. Government institutions themselves have often become obsolete and bureaucratic structures, which were originally established to solve the problems of the past. Disillusion with established routines for the public goods allocation process, and shortcomings of the social welfare systems will prohibit effective government involvement for solving most of the problems outlined above. New collaborative solutions and public-private partnerships may dynamize established public resource allocation processes. The traditional antagonism between industry and government may be overcome inasmuch as new investment projects are seen as as complex arrays of activities, many of which will require new coordination mechanisms *"between market and politics"*.

In *Fig. 8.1*, the three distinct modes of governance and organization, namely markets, hybrid modes of collaboration and integration are illustrated along the *horizontal axis*. On the *vertical axis*, we distinguish between three modes of political coordination: purely private ("market coordination"), purely public ("government coordination"), and mixed forms of public-private coordination[2]. A

---

1   A typical example is the transition process in Eastern Europe, which cannot be implemented as a process of pure market coordination before the basic foundations for the effective functioning of markets have been established.

2   The political coordination mechanism can be described as a nexus of contracts, the most important elements of which are property rights and control rights. Pure *public coordination* can accordingly be characterized by public ownership and government control. *Private coordination*, on the opposite side, is defined by private ownership and autonomous private control. Numerous intermediate forms of political coordination may be envisaged.

certain investment project in an initial period to will encompass a chain of diverse activities, some of which may best be governed through integration while others will involve collaboration. Relatedly, some activities may best be coordinated through government ownership or control, while others will involve mixed modes of public-private coordination (see the dark shaded area in Fig. 8.1).

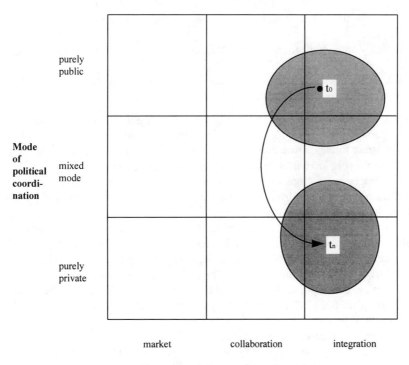

Fig. 8.1:   Public-Private Interaction and Modes of Governance and Organization

During the life-cycle of a project, the appropriate modes of governance and organization, and the related forms of political coordination will often change. While predominantly government-mediated coordination processes may be required during very early phases, mixed public/private coordination will become more important as the project evolves. Successively, a greater part of activities can be governed through markets or hybrid modes of coordination, and public agencies will become less influential. In a final stage, in period t_n, most activities will become coordinated in a private way, while more integrated modes of governance and organization may become dominant. We have assumed in Fig. 8.1, that integration within one or a few firms will be the final mode of governance and organization, but it can also be imagined that disintegration and market transactions will be more appropriate for a particular set of activities in later phases of their life-cycle.

In order to develop the most suitable institutional arrangement for a project to be implemented in a particular time period, we have to ask:

– What are the best contractual arrangements for *each single activity* within a project?
– Which contractual arrangements should be chosen for the *set of core activities*?[3]
– Which contractual arrangements must be chosen to allow for the comprehensive *coordination* of *all* activities?

In chapters 2 and 3, we have distinguished between generic contract modes such as ownership contracts, sales and service contracts, and intermediate, collaborative contract modes. Ownership contracts are the most important element for the analysis of core activities, and for assessing changes in institutional arrangements. Important notions of institutional restructuring such as privatization, deregulation, and nationalization must be interpreted as a specicic reconfiguration of ownership and control rights.

Unfortunately, many of these notions often get confused, not only in public debate, but also in the literature and even in announcements made by informed observers. We will speak of *deregulation,* if *control rights* for core activities are transferred from public institutions to private agents[4]. Deregulation is illustrated by a vertical arrow pointing downward on the right side in *Fig. 8.2.* The opposite form of institutional change, i.e. the transfer of control rights *into* the public domain, will be called *increased regulation.*

Regulation or deregulation can be attained without any change in *ownership rights,* even though the transfer of property rights will empirically be connected to a transfer in control rights. A public authority that restrains access to a particular activitiy does not need to have ownership of resources; it exercises its control through sheer legislative or regulatory power. Similarly, ownership rights can be transferred without a similar transfer of control rights. We will speak of *privatization* only, if ownership titles for resources, which are specific to core activities

---

3 For each project, some activities will typically assume a core function. Core activities will allow to control the greatest part of the revenue stream and the most critical array of knowledge. Agents who control the core activities are able to control the whole project.
4 These control rights can govern core activities, or they can be used to determine the use of critical resources needed for these activities. The second way of control will be the essential one. As an example, the Deutsche Bundespost controls the *activity* of voice telecommunication primarily through its exclusive control of the earthbound transmission and switching network, which are the *critical resources.*

are transferred from public institutions to private agents. This is illustrated by a downward moving graph on the left side in Fig. 8.2. The opposite case of transfer of ownership titles from private agents to public institutions will be called *nationalization* (marked by an upward moving graph on the left side in Fig. 8.2).

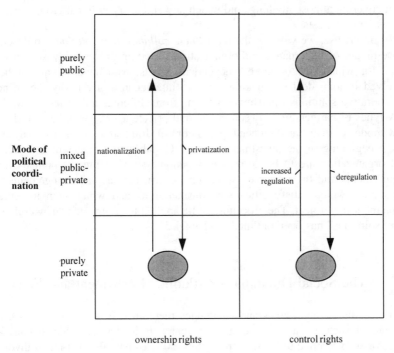

Fig. 8.2:   Privatization and Deregulation of Activities

It is very important to specify in detail, which type of institutional change is arranged for which type of activity. Otherwise, institutional changes get misdirected and will not lead to the desired results. It is very often not clearly specified whether in fact the core activities are affected by deregulation or privatization. The main reason for this confusion in terms can be explained by the fact that competing political groups will often only agree on compromised and diluted forms of institutional change. Confusion over the type of institutional change is often the only way to attain support in a diverse constituency. Institutional reforms that have been decided upon can then be transmitted by each party in a way most attractive to its electorate.

A typical example is the attempted privatization and deregulation of telecommunication services in Western European countries. In effect, only a very limited form of partial deregulation of a few activities has occurred, and deregulated activities often do not represent the core activities[5]. In order to prevent such ineffective compromising and the related notational confusion, we suggest that the underlying contractual arrangements for the major activities related to a particular investment project should be clearly specified. If this is *not* done, the words "new collaborative solution" may easily become mis-used as a very broad term covering almost anything, and which any and every political group may use for its own interests.

To be precise, we will use the term *"new collaborative solution"* to describe those modes of governance and organization for complex, large investment projects, for which two or more independent agents, who have so far not been involved in joint decision-making, have to interact in a novel way. These new collaborative solutions often involve firms from different industries, as well as new types of partnership between public and private agents, who have to devise new modes of distributed ownership and control. Joint strategies must be defined at the beginning of the investment process. Collaborative modes of governance and organization are to be derived endogenously, taking into account the task requirements and the resource ownership pattern. contractual arrangements are negotiated, which satisfy efficiency considerations and which help to rapidly implement the project. The procedure to be applied to attain such "new collaborative solutions" has been outlined in chapter 5.

8.2   The Social Dilemma for "Public" Investment and Finance

Many of the problem areas and challenges mentioned in the preceding section 8.1 are of such a scale and complexity that it is hard to imagine that private investors can respond to them appropriately. At least partial government involvement in regulation, finance or ownership would appear to be useful. For some very large and complex issues such as the CO_2 problem, for economic restructuring in Eastern Europe, or for large telecommunication and space projects, international collaboration between several nations seems to be the only way to overcome national restraints related to capital assets and knowledge bases. This rationale for public involvement and for collaboration between nation states, however, is built on the fiction that a few single agents ("nation states") can rationally decide and purposefully interact with each other.

The opposing view of public choice theorists that nation states are totally heterogenous collections of individuals and diverse interest groups, which must

---

5   As an example, the deregulation of the telecommunication sector in Germany has kept the core activities (voice communication), and the most critical resources (the network) within the domain of a still publicly-owned monopoly (the Deutsche Bundespost Telekom).

be organized on an "issue by issue" basis, will set limits to the rational design of large and complex investment projects. Any single, large project will become very difficult to legitimize, to finance and to implement. This problem is only inappropriately solved through the fiscal policy regime that has become established in almost every industrialized, democratic country. This fiscal policy regime involves *forced transfers* between taxpayers and recipients of public expenditure. The extent of these transfers typically ranges between one quarter and one half of national income[6]. The "public transfer machinery" is often legitimized on the basis of historical processes, and through the alleged public good character of certain activities and programs.

Both arguments built on traditions and on public good considerations must be challenged, since any non-compensated transfer will generate its own distortions and inefficiencies[7]. Non-compensated transfers represent rents to recipients who will invest in rent seeking; this rent seeking must be considered as socially inefficient because the process in itself creates no value while utilizing scarce resources (Buchanan, Tollison and Tullock 1980, and Buchanan 1983). Depending on the transfer process and the related decision-making mechanism, a considerable share of national resources will be wasted for rent seeking investments as well as for maintaining the fiscal policy machinery[8].

Proponents of public finance for certain activities and investment projects counter-argue, that positive or negative externalities will set limits to the allocation of resources through compensated, purely private transfer mechanisms. Spillovers will undermine the functioning of individualized compensation mechanisms due to the limited appropriability of benefits, and due to non-attributable costs[9]. *Public goods* can be considered as a special form of externality, or as a limiting case for which benefits are totally inappropriable, and for which costs are totally non-attributable. Complete inappropriability and non-exclusiveness serves as an argument for taxing the general public and for making the public good available to everybody (Buchanan 1969).

More recent research on the social dilemma for the provision of public goods has increasingly attacked this view of pure public goods as being a limiting case. This research suggests that there are very few discernible areas which display the features of pure public goods described above (Marwell and Ames 1981, Isaac, Walker and Thomas 1984, and Weimann 1990). On the contrary, most investment

---

6 Public expenditures as a percentage of gross domestic product for the year 1986 range from 26% in Japan, 33% in West Germany, 35% in the U.S., 43% in the U.K., and have reached 49% in Italy and 54% in Sweden.

7 See also our description and critique of non-compensated transfers for the support of young start-up firms in sections 7.4 and 7.5.

8 Costs for collection, administration, monitoring, etc. must be considered as non-trivial.

9 The original arguments of externality by Pigou (1932), Coase (1960), Arrow (1962) and Buchanan (1969) are summarized in Laffont (1988, 112ff) and Wolf (1988, 21).

projects or programs for which public involvement and finance is sought are characterized only by *partial* inappropriability and by partial non-exclusiveness. Hence it is not justifiable to involve the public in general, but only those potential beneficiaries and those agents which are directly or indirectly affected. Accordingly, the social dilemma for the provision of public goods is then reduced to a much more narrowly defined collective choice problem for a particular group of agents.

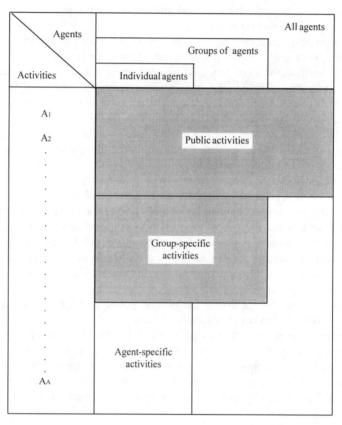

Fig. 8.3:   Decomposition of Tasks and Activities Related to Public Goods

We would even go as far as to say that there are *no pure public goods at all.* Any public good is a bundle of activities, some of which display public features, whereas some other, related activities must be considered as private or group-specific. Any "public good" or any large investment project can in this way be unbundled into activities which are appropriable and exclusive to specific groups of agents. In *Fig. 8.3*, we have mapped the activities related to the provision of a "public good" along the vertical axis. Only a few activities represent purely public activities. All other activities can either be attributed to individual agents, or to particular groups of agents. In addition to this partitioning of public goods into activities on the *production* side, the *consumption* of public goods or of discernible components thereof can be attributed to particular groups.

As a result, the social dilemma of the provision of public goods can be reduced to a mere configuration problem. It can be solved by an appropriate partitioning of projects or programs, and by the responsive break-down into activities and sub-groups of potential beneficiaries. Activities attributed to individual agents can be allocated and coordinated through the *market*. Activities attributable to specific groups must be organized through *contractual arrangements* (involving both hybrid modes of collaboration and integration within firms). Only the remaining, and often rather small, percentage of activities which are totally inappropriable and totally non-exclusive should then be reserved for some form of *public involvement*, being financed through mechanisms of fiscal policy, if necessary through non-compensated transfers.

The complexity of the process of provision of public goods can be compared to architecture and to city planning: the design problem related to a new city or a major urban renewal process is typically so complex that it would be insoluble if it could not be decomposed into smaller tasks and sub-problems. In 1964, an American architect, Christopher Alexander, proposed that the design of communities should be modularized and decomposed into sub-systems. Each sub-system could be planned, built, and implemented fairly independently. In addition, the whole urban renewal project could be carried forth in a more flexible and persistant way, since changes in the design of some modules (houses or modular parts of houses) could be easily integrated as the project unfolds[10].

Quite similarly, the "social architecture" of public goods requires the decomposition of public choice problems into modules of activities, only some of which will necessarily display features of a pure public good (complete inappropriability as well as complete non-exclusiveness). Most other activity modules will be specific to particular groups or even to particular agents. For these group-specific, and empirically much more important lines of activity, the social choice problem is reduced to a matter of organizing beneficiaries of positive externalities, and of maintaining transfers between benefactors and beneficiaries; in the case of negative externalities, it will be a matter of organizing transfers netween perpetrators and victims.

The original proposition of Coase (1960), who argued that most externalities might be solved by making external costs tangible to their sources, and by ar-

---

10 See Alexander (1964) and Alexander and Manheim (1963), cited by v. Hippel (1990).

ranging for appropriate compensation mechanisms, can thus be validated *after* the externality problem has been decomposed. This decomposition and reduction of complexity is a necessary first step.

Unfortunately, Coase's powerful theoretical argument runs into a serious problem of implementation. The problem lies in the difficulty of bringing about the kind of bargain or contract he envisages between the sources and the victims of negative externalities. In practice, the difficulty (which implies costs) of accomplishing such transactions between perpetrators and victims, or between benefactors and beneficiaries, is likely to be so formidable as to preclude the bargain being struck at all. However, to the extent these formidable transaction costs can be avoided or surmounted, markets can overcome externalities and continue to function efficiently (Wolf, 1988, 23).

The costs related to accomplishing transactions are a function of the number of agents involved, of the complexity of tasks and activities, and of the ease with which benefits and activitiy costs can be made tangible to particular agents or groups. If the social choice problem can be decomposed and simplified in the way described above, transaction costs and contractual arrangements will become feasible, which then allows for a cheaper and more efficient provision of the so-called public good within the existing network of institutions, or within new networks that may evolve as the appropriate institutional setting.

8.3   How to Design Complex, Collaborative Projects

Complex problems which appear to be insoluble at first sight, can become solvable through an appropriate reconfiguration of tasks, resources and agents. This will be called the *design* or the problem-solving architecture for a complex project[11]. Extremely large and complex problems can be made tangible through (1) decomposition and task-partitioning, (2) modularization, (3) through changes in agents' participation and (4) through novel solutions for organizational structure and finance.

We do not assert, though, that *any* complex problems can be solved that way. Many of the pertinent social, ecological and political problems described in the first part of this chapter are so immensely complex and interwoven into the fabric of global conflicts, that is is very hard to imagine sensible solutions. However, even some overly complex and global problems can be decomposed into sub-problems and can thus become solvable at a lower level of the "problem archi-

---

11 The methods used for project design are equivalent to systems engineering applied for large construction projects, for planning space programs or for software programming. In chapter 5, we have introduced a general framework for planning such large and complex projects.

tecture". As an example, part of the CO_2 problem is caused by deforestation in tropical zones. The two countries where this is carried out on a major scale are Brazil and Indonesia. In these countries, land zoning and the transformation of forests into arable land are a major cause. A considerable part of these activities is itself influenced by state legislation and tax policies, part of which can be changed by decisive action[12].

Most of the very large and global problems will only be solvable inasmuch as they are decomposed into national or even regional sub-problems. International coordination will never be achieved if one country has to incur a major share of costs for a problem solution, for which the benefits will accrue to all other nations. This is primarily the explanation why many international environmental programs are not very successful. More appropriate solutions can be expected if a considerable share of benefits can be appropriated within the country which bears the costs of environmental improvement[13]. Only if one nation has successfully demonstrated an appropriate solution will decision-makers in some other countries become convinced of the advantages of applying similar solutions. The same logic applies for regional decomposition of problem solutions, and the diffusion of these solutions between different regions within one country[14]. Regional task partitioning leads to early and containable problem solutions; successfully demonstrated solutions can then spread to other areas, and may become applied at a more aggregate level, as is illustrated in *Fig. 8.4.*

To achieve a solution at a regional or national level, it may often be required to decompose activities even further. This is achieved by forming sub-groups of agents who agree on particular tasks. As an example, even environmental policies in North Rhine-Westphalia, which presently is the most environmentally conscious state in the Federal Republic of Germany, were first promoted by small groups of agents with a primary interest in developing solutions to specific prob-

---

12 We do not want to underestimate the political difficulties of changing legislation or tax regulation in developing countries. In such cases, however, even some apparently minor changes can result in major improvements. Some changes in tax depreciation schemes in Brasil over the last years have, for example, resulted in a considerable reduction of deforestation programs.

13 This is the case for the purification of rivers which flow *within* one country; costs incurred for pollution control upstream are more than compensated by costs reductions for water purification at downstream locations within the same country. Tangible benefits and cost reductions will lead to a more dedicated pollution control policy, than if the benefits of purified water would be appropriated by citizens of another state located downstream.

14 As an example, environmental protection policies which were first implemented in North Rhine-Westphalia, due to a relatively high benefit/cost ratio of environmental control measures in a heavily-polluted region, were afterwards applied in Baden-Württemberg, and will later spread to other German Länder states.

lems. Solutions developed and implemented at *low* levels were then applied at a more aggregate level and spread on to related applications.

The basic principle is to "keep things clear and simple" in the first instance. This means that the perception of a problem has to be very precise, and that goals should be specified coherently and in an operational way. This is only feasible if the (decomposed) problem is not too large and complex. A clear perception of a problem and the formulation of coherent and compatible goals is only feasible if the group of agents concerned is small enough. Small groups of agents form close conversation circles and will agree more easily on a particular problem solution[15]. The effectiveness of the small group's activity is enhanced since each member receives a large share of group benefits and is thus willing to bear its own burden related to costs and risks[16]. The effectiveness of the group is stipulated if there are too many agents with diverse interests or with non-compatible resource capabilities, if objectives and tasks are too general and non-operational, and if problem solutions involve too many activities for which members of the group cannot control the required resources.

To prevent such a *dilusion* of objectives and task responsibilities, it is important to decompose projects to the lowest operational level, to formulate sub-tasks and to reduce group sizes as well as the scope of the problem. However, it is indispensible that a "grand design" is kept in mind; this "grand design" provides the overall direction, and contains "dense" information about the integrated problem solution that must be repetitively transmitted to participants of subgroups. Problem analysis and problem synthesis must be intertwined. This can be achieved by greater *modularity* between sub-tasks and elementary "building blocks". Modularity implies that solutions developed for one particular sub-task can be more easily coordinated with and applied to related tasks. Modularity is also very important for the transfer of solutions from low aggregation levels (particular groups or regions) to higher aggregation levels (national or even international).

---

15 Diffusion studies have emphasized the strong role of small conversation circles and communication networks for innovations to gain a critical mass of supporters. Members of such sub-groups prefer to interact among themselves and will realize greater benefits and lower costs related to an innovation, than if a much larger population would be involved. The innovation will attain a greater degree of acceptance within the sub-group, and once all members have been converted, they can go on evangelizing other sub-groups. See also Gerybadze (1992, section 4).

16 Costs and benefits tangible for each member as well as reciprocal risk-bearing are the prime arguments of Olson's (1968) theory of the effectiveness of small groups.

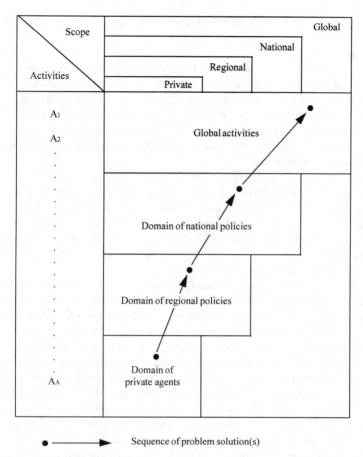

Fig. 8.4: Regional Task Partitioning and Aggregated Project Design

8.4 Effective Management of Public-Private Partnerships

Public-private partnerships are often troubled by very high coordination costs and by inappropriate management and contral mechanisms[17]. Several independent agents participate in the projects and they are often not willing to disclose their

---

17 The costs of coordination and management costs related to large collaborative projects have been outlined by Stopford and Wells (1972), Gullander (1976) and Porter and Fuller (1986). These authors have concentrated on privately maintained projects. For public-private partnerships, coordination and management is even more difficult due to different incentive structures and liabilities.

true objectives. The contributions and rewards of each member in a coalition can often not be specified clearly enough (Alchian and Demsetz 1972). The rewards for positive contributions, the responsibilities, and the consequences for negative behavior can often not be attributed directly enough to individual members. Incentives will become misaligned and individual agents will be inclined to demand too high a share for their (positive) contributions, whereas they tend to "dump" the burden of inappropriate behavior on all members of the group (Olson 1968). There is often no appropriate command and control mechanism, which would allow effective execution and monitoring of the required tasks and of each individual agent's contribution.

The complicated managerial problems to be encountered during a collaborative project are often not anticipated well enough during the early implementation phases. Each project is "new" and "unique", and new groups of agents are formed, whose behavior cannot easily be predicted. It is possible, however, to define some generic characteristics for the management of complex, collaborative projects that can help to structure the projects, to specify tasks and responsibilities, and to monitor and improve project execution.

The most critical parameter certainly is *group size*. The larger the number of independent agents, the more complex and more expensive will be the coordination requirements. Effective management will become unfeasible beyond a certain group size. This is one of the reasons why many projects with public participation fail, and why projects pursued by industry associations are often not very effective[18]. This does not imply that projects such as these cannot, in principle, be managed effectively. Nor does the requirement of small group size imply that certain large and complex projects, for which many independent resource-owners have to be included, cannot effectively be pursued. Important characteristics required for effective management can be fulfilled even for extremely large and complex projects, and even if public agents' involvement is considered necessary. Partitioning of such large projects into manageable subprojects will often be feasible; tasks and responsibilities can be decomposed in such a way that the group size for each separate task can be kept sufficiently small.

For a group of agents that is sufficiently small, it is then necessary to specify clearly all the objectives and activities to be pursued, and the resources that will be required. The agents who will be involved must agree on joint objectives that must be as precisely defined as possible. Furthermore, they must agree on a particular process and a sequence of activities. Critical resources must be controlled by these agents in a comprehensive, complementary and

---

18 The reason for this is, that *efficiency objectives* are impaired by *equal opportunity objectives*. Fairness principles work against small group size and concentrated control, and are thus serious impediments against effective management.

balanced way[19]. If critical resources cannot be controlled in a *comprehensive* way, the group will become dependent on outside suppliers; failure to secure the in-flow of resources from external suppliers will often be used by group members as an excuse for not performing their sub-tasks in the expected way. If the resources and capabilities of the group members are not *complementary*, duplicated activites and rivalrous relationships will reduce the effectiveness of the coalition. If contributions from individual members are not *balanced* enough, cooperative relationships will be undermined and dominance by some members may be a result. In all three cases, the effectiveness of the group's outcome will be reduced and the collaborative project will not become sustainable.

Even if the group size can be kept sufficiently small, if all members agree harmoniously on objectives, processes and tasks to be performed, and if the resource ownership pattern is appropriately balanced, effectiveness of the group's outcome will be reduced if *coordination and control mechanisms* are not suitably adapted and implemented. Each partner's *risks and liabilities* must be sufficiently specified. The contributions of each individual member must be precisely determined. Failure and low performance during some sub-tasks must be attributed to individual members and not just to the group as a whole. Individual members must be able to bear an above average share of risk, and be able to earn an above average share of return. If such an incentive structure cannot be established due to monitoring problems and uncertainty (Alchian and Demsetz 1972), collaborative projects can only be effective if participating members can build on a long sequence of successful joint projects in the past[20].

Coordination and monitoring tasks that are already considerable in a small group but which increase considerably with group size, with task complexity and with the degree of uncertainty, cannot appropriately be performed by a "group of equals". Collaboration between agents of comparable strengths implicitly leads to the understanding of "equal opportunities" and a sharing of management responsibilities. For many cooperative projects, however, centralized management and control is crucial for performance, at least for securing the most critical process steps. *Quasi-hierarchies* must be established, through which the members

---

19 The methodology for planning such large, collaborative projects has been outlined in chapter 5. Critical assets were defined as those resources that are difficult to access and replace, and which are highly-specific to the particular activity pursued by the group of agents. For large, public-private investment projects, it is required that each agent brings critical resources other than finance "to the party".

20 As has already been pointed out in the cooperation literature (Buckley and Casson 1988, and Axelrod 1984), past collaboration success "breeds new success". Project members cannot effectively evaluate other members' actual performance contributions, but know from past experience that they have always "acted in a reliable way".

of the cooperation must agree on one central manager responsible for the coordination and monitoring of decomposable tasks.

This *central task manager* or *coordinator* can be selected on a temporary basis, and can be replaced by another coalition member as the task proceeds. Selection of the central coordinator must be based on criteria which contribute to project performance. Instead of applying arbitrary or political selection mechanisms[21], the following criteria should be applied:

- the person selected should be *in control of the most critical resources* required for the particular process step;
- the person must be able to *influence or assess customer needs*, and to specify the requirements to be met for the next process stage;
- the central manager should be able to *bear a relatively high portion of consequences* of his decisions.

Some agents in every coalition will control a slightly bigger share of critical resources than others and will often possess unique capabilities. These agents must have a greater influence in nominating the central coordinator. Better knowledge and closer access to customer needs and to specifications being defined for the process steps to follow will help to direct activities more effectively towards a final and desired outcome[22]. Finally, the selection of a central coordinator who has to bear a relatively high proportion of the consequences, will lead to greater incentives to promote a positive outcome, while only those individuals who are willing to bear risk will be attracted. The willingness to bear risk must be a distinctive characteristic for a potential central manager and it can be used as a yardstick to exclude a number of other candidates.

Central coordinators with the characteristics outlined above are important for effective management and execution of each single process step. Larger, more complex projects will require an additional layer of *integrated centralized coordination*. A person displaying the same characteristics as outlined above is to be given preference for this assignment as the overall project coordinator. In addition, this person must have the resources and capabilities to effectively direct and control all other managers of sub-projects. The performance and success of large and complex collaboration projects is crucially dependent on the vision, strength, and decisiveness of such a centralized project coordinator[23].

---

21 Central managers are often selected for a cooperation project because someone is "available for the job", or because of proportional political representation. Selection mechanisms such as these will hardly contribute to the sucess of a collaboration project.

22 This principle of "retrograde evaluation" known from the project management literature is closely related to Menger's (1871) principle of "distribution through imputation" which has already been outlined in section 2.4.

23 The role of a central *project coordinator* has been shown to be decisive for large investment projects. An illustrative explanation can be found in Crecine (1986). See also Herten (1988) and Mowery (1987) for a description of this role in international aerospace projects.

The managerial failure of many large collaborative projects, be they pursued by private corporations or with government involvement, can be explained by the inability to allocate resources to this core function of the central project coordinator. Private corporations that set resources aside for joint-ventures or other collaborative projects, often tend to delegate this activity to "second class managers" who have no direct access to top management decisions. Publicly supported collaboration activities, on the other hand, often lack sufficient support at the political level; or else, they suffer from an inappropriate and inflexible allocation of funds, and they are insufficiently shielded from day-to-day political decisions. Such problems of resource allocation and managerial decision-making, which are often notorious for projects with public involvement, can seriously restrain the work and the motivation of the central project coordinator.

In order to overcome this dilemma, a *dual leadership structure* can be implemented; a strong central project manager is responsible for the performance of the collaborative venture. He gets support from, and direct access to leaders in the parent organization(s) who may be called *"champions"*. These have a very high and exposed position and can mobilize financial resources and other support from the parent organization(s). If the project is supported by private companies, an "industry champion" will typically be a highly exposed member of the board of the parent organization. If government involvement is required, a high-ranking person acting within public administration will have to play the role of a "political champion". "Champions" will often act as influential members of the advisory board of a collaborative venture, and will thereby have the position of a much-needed bridgehead for the central project coordinator[24].

The formation of the most effective management structure will be the result of a process of *phased introduction*. Collaborative projects are typically characterized by a process of "sequential hardening": during the initial study phase, a loose, network-type structure with informal communication flows, and loosely structured contractual agreements will often suffice. Typical examples are some basic research agreements or early feasibility studies for large engineering projects. In an intermediate phase, more formal collaborative contracts must be signed, depending on the task to to be performed, and on the characteristics of resources to be used. In later phases, when an R&D project is transferred to large-scale manufacturing, or if a large engineering plant is actually built and operated, a more structured, often integrated organization will be formed. The type of management structure, the selection of the most appropriate central manager(s) and the contractual arrangement through which support from parent organizations will be secured, must be designed endogenously, and in respondence to task requirements and to the resource ownership pattern characteristic for each relevant project stage.

---

24 For a description of the dual leadership structure, the role of "champions" and the central coordinator see Gerybadze (1992, sections 4 and 5).

8.5   New Forms of Financing Public-Private Partnerships

New types of collaborative projects demand new ways of financing them. We have proposed a method through which complex projects can be decomposed into separable activities, each of which may best be performed through a distinctive mode of governance and organization. Each activity will be characterized by a different time profile of the related revenue stream, and financial arrangements must take different time preferences and risk-preferences of participating agents into consideration. New modes of collaborative finance involving public as well as private agents must be developed for each separate activity, and must be "fine-tuned" to specific task and resource requirements.

Depending on the revenue stream related to a particular project activity, its time horizon and its expected risk profile, finance can be provided by:

- cash-flow;
- loans;
- equity;
- or grants and donations.

Finance from *cash-flow* will only be feasible if a positive revenue stream can be expected for all periods, if no large up-front investment has to be borne, and if the respective activities are characterized by a very low level of risk[25]. If the activity is characterized by some up-front investments for which the time horizon and the level of risk can be kept within a relatively narrow range, finance from *loans* will be feasible. Larger degrees of uncertainty, and a very long time horizon (measured by the time it takes to amortize the investment), will no longer allow a particular activity to be financed by debt. *Equity finance* has to be provided, and financial investors will demand ownership and control rights to prevent expropriation. This is illustrated in *Fig. 8.5* in which the time horizon of investment is measured along the vertical axis, while the level of risk is measured along the horizontal axis. Finance from cash-flow and through debt will only be feasible for combinations of low risk and a short time horizon, as illustrated by the bottom left-hand corner in Fig. 8.5. The more we move in the northeastern direction, the more activities of a particular project will have to be financed by equity.

The time horizon and the level of risk for an investment activity may become so large that a sensible investment calculus will no longer be feasible. Investors will no longer be willing to provide any substantial amounts of equity for the project in question. The project can then only be pursued if some of the agents

---

25 We are concentrating here on cash-flow from a particular project activity, and we do not consider cases in which one activity is financed by revenues from another project activity, or even by cash-flow generated by a different project.

are willing to provide *grants* or donations. These represent unidirectional transfers, through which no (future) ownership rights are acquired[26].

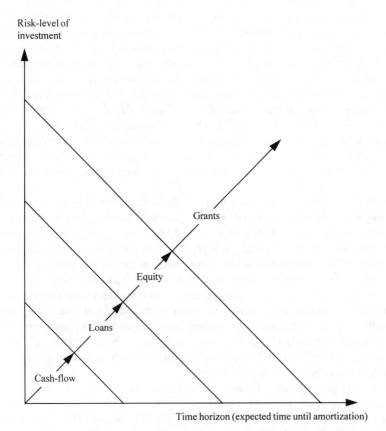

Fig. 8.5:   Types of Finance Dependent on the Time Horizon and on Risk-Levels

The kind of agent who will provide the appropriate financial resources will be
made dependent on the type of finance required, on objectives and capabilities of
investors, and on the particular process phase. The question whether a particular
project or a particular activity is financed privately or through public funds is

---

26 The financing of long-term oriented, basic R&D in a government-owned laboratory or
   university is not considered as a grant but as equity investment, as long as the government-
   owned institution will own and control future outcomes.

then decided accordingly, and *not* on the basis of ad-hoc decisions or predetermined institutional or political prerogatives.

As is illustrated in *Fig. 8.6, private investors* will be more important for investment activities which are primarily financed by customer revenues (cash-flow), loans and equity finance. *Public institutions* will rarely be involved in financing activities that can be supported by customer revenues, except in cases in which public institutions themselves represent a major share of the market[27]. *Loan finance* is a domain of specialized private institutions, even though in many countries a certain fraction of loans will be provided by public finance institutions, sometimes at preferential conditions. *Equity finance* will typically be provided by specialized private agents, who have built up specific skills and capabilities allowing them to better assess and monitor a certain project. Equity finance will most often be offered by private companies, who expect to exploit potential synergies between this new project, and their existing portfolio of activities.

Public agents, by contrast, will typically only become involved in a few equity-financed projects, and will be more active in providing *grants* than private investors (as illustrated in the bottom part of Fig. 8.6). Equity finance from public investors will be advantageous in fields in which public institutions have accumulated skills and capabilities enabling them to assess and control a project activity better. In addition, political priorities may lead to the support of some investment activities (for example education and basic R&D), and public institutions may accumulate appropriate knowledge bases for related, succeeding investment projects. If these conditions (specific knowledge bases of public institutions, generally-supported political priorities to further enhance certain knowledge bases) are not fulfilled, public agents should refrain from financing certain investment projects through equity finance.

A greater part of public finance will often be provided in the form of *grants or donations*. This form of finance is appropriate for those activities, for which no investment calculus can sensibly be applied, and for which benefits *cannot* be easily attributed to particular groups. It may be questioned, as in section 8.2, to which extent certain activities are typically considered to be "public", truely intangible and "social". The group-specific fraction of such activities can often more appropriately be financed through grants and donations by wealthy private individuals, foundations, and by industry associations or interest groups.

---

27 This is the case for all activities normally considered as being "public", such as defense, transportation, telecommunication and energy. Consequent deregulation and privatization of these areas may, in many cases, lead to the continuous retreat of public institutions as customers.

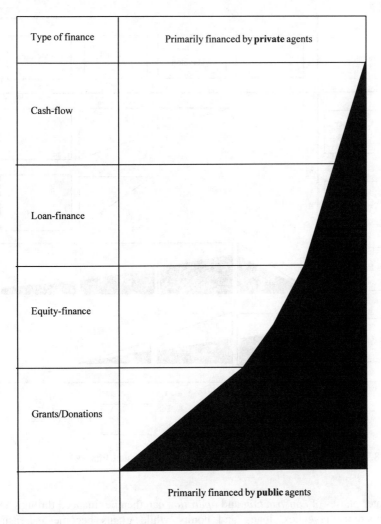

Type of finance	Primarily financed by **private** agents
Cash-flow	
Loan-finance	
Equity-finance	
Grants/Donations	
	Primarily financed by **public** agents

Fig. 8.6:   Private and Public Finance of Investment Activities

The type of finance needed to support a large and complex investment project can thus be suitably adapted to task requirements, and may be differentiated for each squential project phase. This is illustrated in *Fig. 8.7*. The whole investment project is decomposed into (1) the exploration or study phase, (2) design and development, (3) the phase of construction, and (4) the period of operation. During the early phase of *exploration*, finance can only be secured from grants or equity. The *development* phase will be financed by equity, by grants being reduced with the stage of development, and from customer revenues being set aside for project-specific R&D.

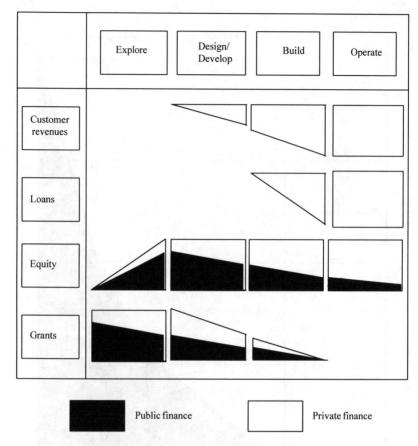

Fig. 8.7:   Types of Finance Differential by Major Project Phases

Later phases of *construction* and *operation* can then be financed through a mix of customer revenues, loans and equity while grants become increasingly abolished[28]. Public finance, be it in the form of grants or equity, will thus — under normal circumstances — only be required during the early exploration and development phases. In Fig. 8.7, the shaded area in each box represents the share of finance being provided by public institutions. After projects have been "triggered-off" by some support from public institutions, the additional, often larger

---

28 This will only be different for inappropriately designed projects, which will depend on a continous influx of subsidies.

part of funds required may be mobilized from private sources. After the project has successfully passed the construction period, it can more or less be operated and financed as a private venture. Except for very few truly "public" activities and for some early trial phases, the majority of investment projects can be removed from the public arena, and can be supported and maintained primarily as private business activities[29].

8.6   Some Concluding Principles

In this final section, we will outline some basic guidelines, which should be applied for strategic investment planning and for a new design of public policy. The *first* and most important guideline is the *principle of structural openness*. Investment processes should not be constrained too much by existing institutional and political structures. Decision-makers in established institutional settings often try to pursue (1) what is good for themselves within their institution, (2) what is good for the institution, and only with third priority: (3) what is needed for a particular investment project. Executives of large firms will opt for governance and organization of an investment project within the hierarchical structure of their corporation. Representatives of small, independent firms will praise the virtues of the market mode of governance and organization. Representatives of government institutions will try to extend the scope and control of public agencies.

As opposed to this biased perspective, we would propose as a *second principle: let the project determine what is the best solution.* There are always projects which can best be maintained through market transactions, while others should be governed and organized within integrated firms; still other projects will demand hybrid modes of collaboration. Relatedly, there are some projects which can most efficiently be maintained in the *private* arena, while others should be governed and controlled by *public* agencies; still other projects will demand mixed modes of public-private partnerships for their implementation.

The basic criterion for the selection of the most appropriate mode of governance and organization should be, *third*, an *economic principle: select those contractual arrangements for each project, for which the costs of operating institutions can be minimized.* For some projects, the costs of operating markets will

---

29 There may be some convincing reasons for keeping activities financed in the public domain, such as the desire to maintain a level of social responsiveness and equal opportunity for different social groups (i.e. serving distant locations with a mail network), or if the private business community is not developed enough to "shoulder a high enough level of investment". An appropriate regulatory environment and the formulation of adequate incentives will often help to overcome such early impediments to the working of private markets.

be comparatively low, while for other investment projects, large integrated firms may help to save transaction costs[30]. For a number of other investment projects with broad constituencies and pretentious resource requirements, comparatively low costs of operating institutions can only be achieved through some involvement of public agencies[31].

Costs of operating alternative institutional settings are, to a large extent, affected by fixed investment in capital goods and knowledge bases. Certain institutions or coalitions offer cost advantages, because participating agents can mobilize their capital good portfolio and their knowledge base more efficiently and in a more flexible way. As a *fourth principle*, decisions about agent participation and the appropriate mode of governance and organization should primarily be based on a detailled *evaluation of resource capabilities and comprehensive, complementary asset bases*. As long as government agencies control critical assets, they should be involved in strategic investment processes. As soon as private agents control all relevant assets, investment projects can be pursued as purely private activities.

Because many large investment projects are characterized by a very high degree of asset complementarity, since highly-specific assets are distributed over many independent agents, and because the costs of solving the dominant design problem are often considerable, *new collaborative solutions* must often be sought. These new collaborative solutions help to solve some of the problems involved, but they often also create new, in many cases unexpected and underestimated problems and complications. A *fifth principle* thus implies to *balance the cost savings from new collaborative solutions with the potential cost increases* incurred by an inappropriate design of multi-agent collaborative arrangements.

This discrepancy between multi-agent participation and efficiency can often only be solved, if a project is *decomposed* into sub-projects and activities, which demand similar strategies, and for which similar asset bases are required. As a *sixth principle, complex large projects should always be partitioned and decomposed into "strategic project units"*. Strategies to be pursued, the relevant resource-spectrum, as well as the appropriate modes of governance and organization must be determined for each task and sub-unit selectively. Activities should be managed and performed by those agents and institutions, which control the

---

30 This criterion of the costs of operating institutions to be minimized has been introduced by Coase (1937). See also our descriptions in section 3.3 and 4.2 to 4.4.

31 It may sound implausible at first sight to argue for government involvement leading to *reductions* in the overall costs of operating institutions. One has become familiarized with a pattern of government involvement typically leading to *greater* costs of administration; this last effect must be explained by established public agencies creating unnecessary overhead costs. We propose instead, that government involvement should only be constrained for those projects, for which it can really help to reduce the overall costs of contracting and of operating institutions.

most relevant critical assets and knowledge bases "on the spot". Decentralized control by the owners of the most critical assets, and "bottom-up-processes" of decision-making are very important.

Project decomposition and task partitioning must be complemented by *project synthesis* and *integration*. For many large and complex investment projects, spontaneous market organization will *not* lead to the desired results. A decisive *entrepreneurial function* for collecting information, coordinating resource-flows, and "packaging" the whole project is required. For purely private investment projects, this role can be performed by a *private entrepreneur* or systems integrator. For private and semi-private investment projects, a *political coordinator* must play a strong role[32]. As a *seventh principle*, new collaborative projects require a *strong central function of governance and control being distinctively different from both hierarchical control and spontaneous market organization*. "Top-down processes" of decision-making must complement the underlying "bottom-up-processes" and must be designed in a way which best corresponds with the decentralized structure of asset ownership and task control.

We thus propose a new framework for public policy and for public-private investment projects. This framework is imbedded into an evolutionary perspective, in which the role and participation of institutions is made dependent on the historical path of investment and knowledge accumulation. Public involvement and the role of political coordinators is endogenized. The overall project coordinator acts as political entrepreneur who discovers new ways of solving a problem jointly with all agents involved. He does not operate within a framework of constructivist rationalism, presuming full knowledge about the best possible solution; nor does he attempt to impose an authoritarian policy upon a group of firms. Instead, he tries to grasp the movements and undercurrents for a specific empirical change situation. His principal aim is to discover an improved, and practicable solution, for which he can convince the key decision-makers. A typical sequence of such a discovery procedure or joint problem-solving process may involve the following five steps:

- collect information in order to be able to reduce the complexity of the project, and to decompose it into manageable sub-tasks;
- gather information about processes, tasks, distributed assets and knowledge bases of all major decision-makers to become involved;
- develop strategies and find out if there is a core of joint strategies together with a need for collaborative activities;
- design an appropriate set of coordination mechanisms and incentives, and review it with the parties involved;

---

32 For a detailed description of the role of private entrepreneurs and political coordinators see Picot, Laub and Schneider (1989, 28ff) and Gerybadze (1992, sections 4 and 5).

– implement, manage and evaluate the process over a consistently long enough time-span.

The proposed framework can provide an appropriate model and a strong tool for solving large and complex investment projects. It can be used for project reengineering in many application areas such as industrial R&D and innovation, infrastructure planning, industry restructuring, privatization resp. deregulation, as well as for regional policy and for environmental protection.

References

Abernathy, W.J., Utterback, J.M. (1978), Patterns of Industrial Innovation, *Technology Review*, 80, pp. 40—47.

Albach, H. (1988), Kosten, Transaktionen und externe Effekte im betrieblichen Rechnungswesen, *Zeitschrift für Betriebswirtschaft*, 58, 11, pp. 1143—1170.

Alchian, A.A. (1977), *Economic Forces at Work*, Indianapolis.

Alchian, A.A. (1984), Specificity, Specialization and Coalitions, *Journal of Institutional and Theoretical Economics*, 140/1, 1984, pp. 34—49.

Alchian, A.A., Demsetz, H. (1972), Production, Information Costs, and Economic Organization, *American Economic Review* 62, pp. 775—795.

Alexander, C. (1964), *Notes on the Synthesis of Form*, Cambridge, Mass.

Alexander, C., Manheim, M.L. (1963), Four Computer Programs for the Hierarchical Decomposition of Sytems which have an Associated Linear Graph, Research Report R63—27, MIT, Cambridge, Mass.

Ansoff, H.I. (1968), *Corporate Strategy*, Harmondsworth.

Aoki, M., Gustafsson, B., Williamson, O.E. (Eds. 1989), *The Firm as a Nexus of Treaties*, London.

Arrow, K. J. (1962), Economic Welfare and the Allocation of Resources for Invention, in: Nelson (1962).

Arrow, K.J. (1971), Agency and the Market, in: Arrow, K.J., Intrilligator, M.D. (Eds.), *Handbook of Mathematical Economics*, Volume III, Amsterdam.

Arthur, W.B. (1988), Competing Technologies: An Overview, in: Dosi et al. (1988), *Technical Change and Economic Theory*, London.

Arthur, W.B. (1989), Competing Technologies, Increasing Returns and Lock-in by Historical Events, *Economic Journal* 99, pp. 116—131.

Axelrod, R. (1984), *The Evolution of Cooperation*, New York.

Backhaus, K., Sandrock, O., Schill, J., Uekerman, H. (Eds. 1990), *Projektfinanzierung*, Stuttgart.

Backhaus, K., Uekerman, H. (1990), Projektfinanzierung. Eine Methode zur Finanzierung von Großprojekten, *WiSt* 19, 3, pp. 106—112.

Bain, J. (1956), *Barriers to New Competition*, Cambridge, Mass.

Ballwieser, W., Schmidt, R.H. (1981), Unternehmensziele und Finanztheorie, in: Bohr, K., (Hrsg. 1981), *Unternehmensverfassung als Problem der Betriebswirtschaftslehre*, Berlin.

Bamberg, G., Spremann, K. (1988), *Capital Market Equilibria*, Berlin, Heidelberg, New York.

Bamberg, G., Spremann, K. (1989), *Agency Theory, Information, and Incentives*, Berlin, Heidelberg, New York.

Bartlett, C.A., Ghoshal, S.(1989), *Managing Across Borders. The Transnational Solution*, Boston.

Bartlett, F.C. (1932), *Remembering*, Cambridge, Mass.

Baumol, W.J. (1992), Horizontal Collusion and Innovation, *The Economic Journal* 102, January, pp. 129—137.

Baumol, W.J., Panzar, J., Willig, R.D. (1982), *Contestable Markets*, New York.

Baumol, W.J., Willig R.D. (1981), Fixed Costs, Sunk Costs, Entry Barriers, and Sustainability of Monopoly, *Quarterly Journal of Economics*, pp. 405—431.

Baur, C. (1990), *Make-or-Buy-Entscheidungen in einem Unternehmen der Automobilindustrie — empirische Analyse und Gestaltung der Fertigungstiefe aus transaktionskostentheoretischer Sicht*, Munich.

Berg, C.C. (1981), *Organisationsgestaltung*, Stuttgart.

Berg, S.V., Duncan, J., Friedman, P. (1982), *Joint Venture Strategies and Corporate Innovation*, Cambridge, Mass.

Bernholz, P. (1971), Superiority of Roundabout Processes and Positive Rate of Interest: Simple Model of Capital and Growth, *Kyklos* 24, pp. 687—721.

Bernholz, P., Faber, F. (1976), Time Consuming Innovation and Positive Rate of Interest, *Zeitschrift für Nationalökonomie* 36, pp. 247—367.

Bernholz, P., Faber, M. (1973), Technical Productivity of Roundabout Processes and Positive Rate of Interest: A Capital Model with Depreciation and n-Period Horizon, *Zeitschrift für die gesamte Staatswissenschaft*, 129, pp. 46—61.

Bidlingmaier, J. (1967), Begriff und Formen der Kooperation im Handel, in: Bidlingmaier, J., Jacobi, H., Uherek, E.W., *Absatzpolitik und Distribution*, Wiesbaden.

Birch, D.L. (1979), *The Job Generation Process*, Cambridge, Mass.

Black, F., Scholes, M. (1973), The Pricing of Options and Corporate Liabilities, *Journal of Political Economy* 81, pp. 637—654.

Bleicher, K. (1987), Strategien der Unternehmensakquisition und -kooperation, Unpublished paper, St. Gallen University, St. Gallen.

Bleicher, K. (1991), *Integratives Management*, Frankfurt/Main, New York.

Blois, K.J. (1972), Vertical Quasi-Integration, *The Journal of Law and Economics* 20, 2, pp. 253—273.

Böhm-Bawerk, E. v. (1921), *Positive Theorie des Kapitals*, 4. Edition, Jena.

Bräunling, G., Gerybadze, A., Mayer, M. (1989), Ziele, Instrumente und Entwicklungsmöglichkeiten des Modellversuchs "Beteiligungskapital für junge Technologieunternehmen", Fraunhofer-Institut für Systemtechnik und Innovationsforschung, Karlsruhe.

Brealey, R., Myers, S. (1988), *Principles of Corporate Finance*, 3. Edition, New York.

Buchanan, J.M. (1969), *Cost and Choice. An Inquiry in Economic Theory*, Chicago.

Buchanan, J.M. (1983), Rent Seeking, Noncompensated Transfers, and Laws of Succession, *Journal of Law and Economics* 26, April, pp. 71—85.

Buchanan, J.M., Tollison, R.D., Tullock, G. (Eds. 1980), *Toward a Theory of the Rentseeking Society*, College Station.

Buckley, P.J., Casson, M.C. (1985), *Economic Theory of the Multinaltional Enterprise. Selected Papers*, London.

Buckley, P.J., Casson, M.C. (1988), A Theory of Cooperation in International Business, in: Contractor and Lorange (1988).

Burmeister, E. (1980), *Capital Theory and Dynamics*, Cambridge.

Burns, T., Stalker, O.M. (1961), *The Management of Innovation*, London, New York.

Business International Corporation (1987), *Competitive Alliances. How to Succeed at Cross-Regional Collaboration*, New York.

Bygrave, W.D. (1987), Syndicated Venturing in the U.S.: An Empirical Study, Centre for Entrepreneurial Studies, Babson College.

Bygrave, W.D. (1988), Venture Capital Investing: A Resource Exchange Perspective, Ph.D. Dissertation, Boston University, Boston.

Bygrave, W.D., Timmons, J.A. (1986), Venture Capital's Role in Financing Innovation for Economic Growth, *Journal of Business Venturing* 1, pp. 161—176.

Cantillon, R. (1905), *Essay on the Nature of Trade in General*, London.

Cantwell, J.A., Dunning, J.H., (1991), MNE's, Technology and the Competitiveness of European Industries, *Aussenwirtschaft* 46, pp. 45—65.

Chakravarthy, B.S., Doz, Y. (1992), Strategy Process Research: Focusing on Corporate Self-Renuval, *Strategic Management Journal* 13, pp. 5—14.

Chakravarthy, B.S., Lorange, P. (1991), *Managing the Strategy Process*, Englewood Cliffs.

Chandler, A.D. (1962), *Strategy and Structure*, Cambridge, Mass.

Chandler, A.D. (1977), *The Visible Hand*, Cambridge, Mass.

Chandler, A.D. (1990), *Strategy and Scope*, Cambridge, Mass.

Chesnais, F. (1988), Technical Cooperation Agreements between Firms, *STI Review* [OECD Directorate for Science, Technology and Industry], 4, pp. 51—115.

Cheung, S.N.S. (1983), The Contractual Nature of the Firm, *Journal of Law and Economics* 26, pp. 1—21.

Clark, J.B. (1893), Genesis of Capital, *Yale Review*, November.

Clark, K.B. (1985), The Interaction of Design Hierarchies and Market Concepts in Technological Evolution, *Research Policy*, 14, pp. 235—251.

Clark, R. (1981), The Four Stages of Capitalism: Reflections on Investment Management Treatises, *Harvard Law Review* 94, pp. 561—583.

Coase, R.H. (1937), The Nature of the Firm, *Economica*, 4, pp. 386—405.

Coase, R.H. (1960), The Problem of Social Cost, *Journal of Law and Economics* 3, pp. 1—44.

Coase, R.H, (1972), Durability and Monopoly, *Journal of Law and Economics* 15, pp. 143—153.

Coase, R.H. (1974), The Market for Goods and the Market for Ideas, *American Economic Review, Papers and Proceedings* 64, pp. 384—392.

Commons, J.R. (1934), *Institutional Economics*, Madison, Wisconsin.

Commons, J.R. (1970), *The Economics of Collective Action*, Madison, Wisconsin.

Contractor, F.J., Lorange, P. (Eds. 1987), *Cooperative Strategies in International Business*, Lexington, Mass.

Contractor, F.J., Lorange, P. (Eds. 1988), Cooperative Strategies in International Business, *Management International Review*, Special Issue.

Cooper, A.C. (1964), R&D is More Efficient in Small Companies — in the Sense of Getting More Results per Dollar of Expenditure, *Harvard Business Review* 42, pp. 75—83.

Cooper, A.C. (1979), Strategic Management: New Ventures and Small Business, In: Schendel, D.E., Hofer, C.W. (Eds.), *Strategic Management*, Boston, Mass.

Coopers & Lybrand (1986), Corporate Odd Couples, in: *Business Week*, July 21, p. 99.

Cowan, R.A. (1989), Backing the Wrong Horse: Sequential Choice Among Technologies of Unknown Merit, Mimeo, New York University, May.

Crecine, J.P. (1986), Defense Resource Allocation: Garbage Can Analysis of C3 Procurement, In: March, J.G., Weissinger-Boylan, R. (Eds.), *Ambiguity and Command*, Marshfield.

Cyert, R.M., March, J.G. (1963), *A Behavioral Theory of the Firm*, New Jersey.

Davenport, T.H. (1993), *Process Innovation. Reengineering Work through Information Technology*, Cambridge, Mass.

Davenport, T.H., Short, J.E. (1990), The New Industrial Engineering: Information Technology and Process Redesign, *Sloan Management Review*, Summer, pp. 11—27.

Davidow, W.H., Malone, M.S. (1992), *The Virtual Corporation. Structuring and Revitalizing the Corporation of the 21st Century*, New York.

Demsetz, H. (1988), *Ownership, Control and the Firm. The Origination of Economic Activity*, Oxford.

Dosi, G., Dosi, C., Nelson, R.R., Silverberg, G., Soete, L. (Eds. 1988), *Technical Change and Economic Theory*, London.

Dosi, C., Perez, C. (1988), Structural Crises of Adjustment: Business Cycles and Investment Behaviour, in: Dosi et al. (1988).

Dunning, J.H. (1988), *Explaining International Production*, London.

Eschenburg, R. (1971), *Ökonomische Theorie der genossenschaftlichen Zusammenarbeit, Schriften zur Kooperationsforschung*, Volume 1, Tübingen.

EVCA (1988), *European Venture Capital Association* [EVCA Yearbook], London.

Faber, M. (1979), *Introduction to Modern Austrian Capital Theory. Lecture Notes in Economics and Mathematical Systems*, Volume 167, Berlin, Heidelberg, New York.

Faber, M. (Ed. 1986), *Studies in Austrian Capital Theory, Investment and Time, Lecture Notes in Economics and Mathematical Systems*, Volume 277, Berlin, Heidelberg, New York.

Faber, M., Proops, J. (1990), *Evolution, Time, Production and the Environment*, Berlin, Heidelberg, New York.

Fama, E.F. (1970), Multiperiod Consumption-Investment Decisions, in: *American Economic Review* 60, pp. 163—174.

Fama, E.F. (1980), Agency Problems and the Theory of the Firm, *Journal of Political Economy* 88, 2, pp. 134—145.

Farmer, D.H., Macmillan, K. (1976), Voluntary Collaboration vs. 'Disloyalty' to Suppliers, *Journal of Purchasing in Materials Management* 12, 4, pp. 3—8.

Farmer, D.H., Macmillan, K. (1979), Redefining the Boundaries of the Firm, *The Journal of Industrial Economics* 27, pp. 277—285.

Fisher, I. (1965), *The Theory of Interest*, New York.

Frank, H. (1986), *Project Finance*, Vienna.

Frese, E. (1988), *Grundlagen der Organisation. Die Organisationsstruktur der Unternehmung*, 4. Edition, Wiesbaden.

Fusfeld, D.R. (1958), Joint Subsidiaries in the Iron and Steel Industry, *American Economic Review* 48, pp. 578—587.

Gaitanides, M. (1983), *Prozeßorganisation*, Munich.

Galbraith, J.R. (1977), *Organization Design*, Reading, Mass.

Galbraith, J.R. (1983), Strategy and Organization Planning, *Human Resource Management* 22, 1/2, pp. 64—77.

Gerlach, M. (1988), Alliances and the Social Organization of Japanese Business, Ph.D. Dissertation, University of California, Berkeley.

Geroski, P.A. (1992), Vertical Relations between Firms and Industrial Policy, *The Economic Journal* 102, January, pp. 138—147.

Gerth, E. (1971), *Zwischenbetriebliche Kooperation*, Stuttgart.

Gerybadze, A. (1982), *Innovation, Wettbewerb und Evolution. Eine mikro- und meso-ökonomische Untersuchung des Anpassungsprozesses von Herstellern und Anwendern neuer Produzentengüter*, Tübingen.

Gerybadze, A. (1987), Maßgebliche Einflußfaktoren für die Entwicklung der technologischen Leistungsfhigkeit der deutschen Avionikindustrie im Vergleich zu Frankreich und Großbritannien, Report to the Federal Ministry of Research and Technology, Arthur D. Little International, Wiesbaden.

Gerybadze, A. (1988), *Raumfahrt und Verteidigung als Industriepolitik? Auswirkungen auf die amerikanische Wirtschaft und den internationalen Handel*, Frankfurt/Main, New York.

Gerybadze, A. (1990a), Technological Forecasting, in: Tschirky, H., Hess, W., Lang, P. (Eds.), *Technologie-Management*, Zurich.

Gerybadze, A. (1990b), Erfolgs- und Mißerfolgsfaktoren von jungen Technologieunternehmen in der Bundesrepublik Deutschland, Fraunhofer-Institut für Systemtechnik und Innovationsforschung, Karlsruhe.

Gerybadze, A. (1991a), Innovation und Unternehmertum im Rahmen internationaler Joint-Ventures — eine kritische Analyse, in: Schneider, D., Laub, U. (Eds.), *Innovation und Unternehmertum*, Wiesbaden.

Gerybadze, A. (1991b), Marktwirtschaft und innovative Unternehmensgründungen. Erfahrungen aus dem Modellversuch "Förderung technologieorientierter Unternehmensgründungen (TOU)", in: Oberender, P., Streit, M. (Eds.), *Marktwirtschaft und Innovation*, Baden-Baden.

Gerybadze, A. (1992), The Implementation of Industrial Policy in an Evolutionary Perspective, in: Witt, U. (Ed.), *Explaining Process and Change: Approaches to to Evolutionary Economics*, Ann Arbor.

Gerybadze, A., Müller, R. (1990), Finanzierung von jungen Technologieunternehmen. Zur Hypothese der Kapitalmarktdiskrepanz in der Bundesrepublik Deutschland, Fraunhofer-Institut für Systemtechnik und Innovationsforschung, Karlsruhe.

Ghemawat, P., Porter, M.E., Rawlinson, R.A. (1986), Patterns of International Coalition Activity, in: Porter (1986).

Grochla, E. (1959), *Betriebsverband und Verbandbetrieb. Wesen, Formen und Organisationen der Verbände aus betriebswirtschaftlicher Sicht*, Berlin.

Grochla, E. (1982), *Grundlagen der organisatorischen Gestaltung*, Stuttgart.

Grossman, G.M. (1990), Promoting New Industrial Activities: A Survey of Recent Arguments and Evidence, *OECD Economic Surveys*, 14, pp. 87—127.

Grossman, S., Hart, O. (1982), Corporate Financial Structure and Managerial Incentives, in: McCall, J. (Ed.), *The Economics of Information and Uncertainty*, Chicago.

Grossman, S., Hart, O. (1986), The Costs and Benefits of Ownership: A Theory of Vertical and Lateral Integration, *Journal of Political Economy*, 94, pp. 691—719.

Gullander, S. (1976), Joint Ventures in Europe: Determinants of Entry, *International Studies of Management and Organizations*, 6, pp. 85—111.

Gutenberg, E. (1983), *Zur Theorie der Unternehmung*, Berlin, Heidelberg, New York.

Hagedoorn, J., Schakenraad, J. (1989a), Strategic Partnering and Technological Co-operation, in: Dankbaar, B., Groenewegen, J., Schenk, H., Perspectives in Industrial Economics, Dordrecht.

Hagedoorn, J., Schakenraad, J. (1989b), Partnerships and Networks in Core Technologies, Paper for the Conference on "The Economics of Technical Change", Maastricht, November.

Hahn, F.A. (1966), Equilibrium Dynamics with Heterogeneous Capital Goods, *Quarterly Journal of Economics* 80, pp. 633—646.

Hahn, F.A. (1970), "Some Adjustment Processes", *Econometrica* 38, pp. 1—17.

Håkansson, H. (Ed. 1987), *Industrial Technological Development: A Network Approach*, London.

Håkansson, H. (1989), *Corporate Technological Behaviour. Cooperation and Networks*, London.

Haley, C.W., Schall, L.D. (1979), *The Theory of Financial Decisions*, 2. Edition, New York.

Hammer, M., Champy, J. (1993), *Reengineering the Corporation. A Manifesto for Business Revolution*, New York.

Harrigan, K.R. (1985), *Strategies for Joint Ventures*, Lexington, Mass.

Harrigan, K.R. (1986), *Managing for Joint Venture Success*, Lexington, Mass.

Harrigan, K.R. (1988), Strategic Alliances and Partner Assymmetries, in: Contractor and Lorange (1988).

Hart, O. (1988), Incomplete Contracts and the Theory of the Firm, *Journal of Law, Economics and Organization*, 4, 1988.

Hax, A.C., Majluf, N.S. (1984), *Strategic Management. An Integrative Perspective*, Englewood Cliffs.

Hayek, F.A. v. (1945), The Use of Knowledge in Society, *American Economic Review* 35, pp. 519—530.

Hayek, F.A. v. (1978), The Errors of Constructivism, in: *New Studies in Philosophy, Politics, and the History of Economic Ideas*, 3. Edition, London.

Heidorn, W. (1985), *Fixkostenleverage und Risiko der Unternehmung*, Göttingen.

Herten, H.-J. (1988), *Internationales Projekt-Management. Gestaltung der grenzüberschreitenden Projektkooperation im Großanlagenbau sowie in der Luft- und Raumfahrtindustrie*, Cologne.

Hicks, J.R. (1965), *Capital and Growth*, Oxford.

Hicks, J.R. (1973), *Capital and Time: A Neo-Austrian Theory*, Oxford.

Hinsch, C., Horn, N. (1985), *Das Vertragsrecht der internationalen Konsortialkredite und Projektfinanzierungen*, Berlin.

Hippel, E. v. (1987), Cooperation between Rivals: Informal Know-how Trading, *Research Policy* 16.

Hippel, E. v. (1988), *The Sources of Innovation*, Oxford.

Hippel, E. v. (1990), Task Partitioning: An Innovation Process Variable, *Research Policy* 19, pp. 407—418.

Hirschman, A.O. (1970), *Exit, Voice, and Loyalty. Responses to Decline in Firms, Organizations, and States*, Cambridge, Mass.

Hirshleifer, J. (1970), *Investment, Interest and Capital*, Englewood Cliffs.

Horwitch, M. (1989), *Post Modern Management*, New York.

Hutter, M. (1989), On Economic Theory as a Theory of a Self-Referential System, Discussion paper 3—89, University Witten-Herdecke.

Imai, K.I., Baba, Y. (1991), Systemic Innovation and Cross-Border Networks. Transcending Markets and Hierarchies to Create a New Techno-Economic Paradigm, in: OECD (1991).

Imai, K.I., Itami, H. (1984), Mutual Infiltration of Organisation and Market — Japan's Firm and Market in Comparison with the U.S., *International Journal of Industrial Organization* 1.

Imai, K.I., Nonaka, I., Takeuchi, H. (1985), Managing New Product Development: How Japanese Companies Learn and Unlearn, in: Clarke, K.B., Hayes, R.H., Lorenz, C. (Eds.), *The Uneasy Alliance*, Boston, Mass.

Isaac, R.M., Walker, J.M., Thomas, S.H. (1984), Divergent Evidence on Free Riding: An Experimental Examination of Possible Explanations, *Public Choice* 43, pp. 113—149.

Jaksch, H.-J. (1975), Die Mehrergiebigkeit längerer Produktionsumwege in einem linearen Vielsektorenmodell, *Zeitschrift für die gesamte Staatswissenschaft*, 131, pp. 92—105.

Jarillo, J.C. (1986), Entrepreneurship and Growth: The Strategic Use of External Resources, Ph.D. Dissertation, Harvard University, Graduate School of Business Administration, Cambridge, Mass.

Jarillo, J.C. (1988), On Strategic Networks, *Strategic Management Journal*, January-February, 9, pp. 31—41.

Jarillo, J.C., Ricart, J.E. (1987), Sustaining Networks, *Interfaces*, September-October, 17, pp. 82—91.

Jensen, M.C., Meckling, W.H. (1976), Theory of the Firm: Managerial Behaviour, Agency Costs and Ownership Structure, *Journal of Financial Economics*, 3, pp. 305—360.

Johanson, J., Mattsson, L.G. (1989), Interorganizational Relations in Industrial Systems: A Network Approach Compared with the Transaction Cost Approach, *International Journal of Management and Organization*.

Joskow, P. (1987), Contract Duration and Relationship-Specific Investments, *American Economic Review* 77, pp. 168—185.

Kanter, R.M. (1983), *The Change Masters*, New York.

Kappich, L. (1989), *Theorie der internationalen Unternehmungstätigkeit — Betrachtung der Grundformen des internationalen Engagements aus koordinationskostentheoretischer Perspektive*, Munich.

Katz, M.L., Shapiro, C. (1986), Technology Adoption in the Presence of Network Externalities, *Journal of Political Economy* 94, 4, pp. 822—841.

Keck, J. (1986), *Die Projektfinanzierung*, Constance.

Kern, H., Sabel, C., Herrigel, G. (1989), Collaborative Manufacturing, Unpublished paper, MIT, Cambridge, Mass.

Kester, W.C. (1980), Today's Options for Tomorrow's Growth, in: *Managing Projects and Programs, Harvard Business Review Book*, Cambridge, Mass.

Kester, W.C. (1987), An Options Approach to Corporate Finance, In: *Handbook of Corporate Finance*, 6. Edition, New York.

Khandwalla, P.N. (1977), *The Design of Organizations*, New York.

Khanna, T. (1990), *Foundations of Neural Networks*, Reading, Mass.

Kirzner, I. (1973), *Competition and Entrepreneurship*, Chicago.

Kirzner, I. (1989), *Discovery, Capitalism and Distributive Shares*, Oxford.

Klein, B., Crawford, R.G., Alchian, A.A. (1978), Vertical Integration, Appropriable Rents, and the Competitive Contracting Process, *Journal of Law and Economics* 21, October, pp. 297—326.

Kline, S.J., Rosenberg, N. (1986), An Overview of Innovation, in: Rosenberg, N., Landau, R. (Eds.), *The Positive Sum Strategy*, Cambridge, Mass.

Knight, F.H. (1965), *Risk, Uncertainty and Profit*, New York.

Kodama, F. (1986), Japanese Innovations in Mechatronics Technology, *Science and Technology Policy*, 17.

Kodama, F. (1992), Technology Fusion and the New R&D, *Harvard Business Review*, July-August, pp. 70—78.

Kodama, F., Oshima, K. (1988), Japanese Experiences in Collective Industrial Activity: An Analysis of Engineering Research Associations, in: Fusfeld, H.I., Nelson, R.R. (Eds.), *Technical Cooperation and Competitiveness, Center for the Study of Science and Technology Policy*, New York.

Kogut, B. (1988), A Study of the Life Cycle of Joint Ventures, in: Contractor and Lorange (1988).

Koopmans T.C. (1951), The Analysis of Production as an Efficient Combination of Activities, in: Koopmans, T.C. (Ed.), *Activity Analysis of Production and Allocation*, New York.

Kosiol, E. (1962), *Organisation der Unternehmung*, Wiesbaden.

Kulicke, M. (1990), Modellversuch "Förderung technologieorientierter Unternehmensgründungen" (TOU) — Zwischenbilanz zum 31.12.1989, Fraunhofer-Institut für Systemtechnik und Innovationsforschung (FhG-ISI), Karlsruhe.

Kulicke, M. (1993), *Chancen und Risiken junger Technologieunternehmen. Ergebnisse des Modellversuchs "Förderung technologieorientierter Unternehmensgründungen"*, Heidelberg.

Laage-Hellmann A. (1989), *Technological Development in Industrial Networks, Comprehensive Summaries of Uppsala Dissertations from the Social Sciences 16*, Uppsala.

Lachmann, L.M. (1977), *Capital, Expectations, and the Market Process. Essays on the Theory of the Market Economy*, Menlo Park.

Laffont, J.-J. (1988), *Fundamentals of Public Economics*, Cambridge, Mass.

Lawrence, P.R., Lorsch, J.W. (1967), *Organization and Environment. Managing Differentiation and Integration*, Cambridge, Mass.

Levin, R., Klevorick, A., Nelson, R.R., Winter, S.G. (1984), Survey Research on R&D Appropriability and Technological Opportunity, Unpublished paper, Yale University, Saybrook.

Lindblom, C.E. (1977), *Politics and Markets. The World's Political-Economic Systems*, New York.

Little, Arthur D. (1989), Analyse der Marktstellung und der Entwicklungschancen der deutschen Industrie im Bereich der Nachrichtensatellitentechnik, Report to the Federal Ministry of Research and Technology, Wiesbaden.

Lorange, P. (1985), Cooperative Ventures in Multinational Sellings: A Framework, Unpublished paper, Wharton School, University of Pennsylvania, Philadelphia.

Lorenzoni, G. (1982), From Vertical Integration to Vertical Disintegration. Paper presented at the Strategic Management Society Conference, Montreal.

Lorenzoni, G., Ornati, O.A. (1987), Constellations of Firms and New Ventures, Working Paper 87—1, Graduate School of Business Administration, New York University, New York.

Lundgren, A., Björklund, L. (1989), Economic Changes in Industrial Networks, Unpublished paper, Stockholm.

MacNeil, I.R. (1980), *The New Social Contract*, New Haven.

Majd, S., Pindyck, R.S. (1987), Time to Build, Option Value, and Investment Decisions, *Journal of Financial Economics*, 18, pp. 7—27.

March, J.G. (1989), *Decisions and Organizations*, New York.

March, J.G, Simon, H.A. (1958), *Organizations*, New York.

Mariti, P., Smiley, R.H. (1983), Cooperative Agreements and the Organization of Industry, *The Journal of Industrial Economics*, 31, pp. 437—451.

Martin, J. (1978), *Communication Satellite Systems*, Englewood Cliffs.

Marwell, G., Ames, R.E. (1981), Economists Free Ride, Does Anyone Else?, *Journal of Public Economics* 15, 9181, pp. 295—310.

Mayer, M. (1989), Modellversuch "Förderung technologieorientierter Unternehmensgründungen (TOU)", Zwischenbilanz zum 31.12.1988, Fraunhofer-Institut für Systemtechnik und Innovationsforschung, Karlsruhe.

McDonald, R., Siegel, D. (1986), The Value of Waiting to Invest, *Quarterly Journal of Economics*, November, pp. 707—727.

Mellerowicz, K. (1958), *Betriebswirtschaftslehre der Industrie*, 3. Edition, Freiburg.

Menger, C. (1871), *Grundsätze der Volkswirtschaftslehre*, Vienna.

Miles, R.E., Snow, C.C. (1984), Fit, Failure and the Hall of Fame, *California Management Review* 26, 3, pp0.10—28.

Milgrom, P., Roberts, J. (1992), *Economics, Organization and Management*, Englewood Cliffs.

Mintzberg, H. (1979), *The Structuring of Organizations. A Synthesis of the Research*, Englewood Cliffs.

Mintzberg, H. (1983), *Power in and Around Organizations*, Englewood Cliffs.

Mises, L. v. (1963), *Human Action*, New York.

Morgan, G. (1986), *Images of Organization*, Beverly Hills.

Morris, J.K. (1989), An Overview of the Venture Capital Industry, in: *Pratts Guide to Venture Capital Sources,* 13. Edition, *Venture Economics*, Needham, Mass.

Moss, S.J. (1981), *An Economic Theory of the Firm*, Oxford.

Mowery, D.C. (1987), *Alliance, Politics and Economics. Multinational Joint-Ventures in Commercial Aircraft*, Cambridge, Mass.

Mowery, D.C. (Ed. 1988), *International Collaborative Ventures in U.S. Manufacturing*, Cambridge, Mass.

Nathusius, K. (1979), *Venture Management. Ein Instrument zur innovativen Unternehmensentwicklung*, Berlin.

Nelson, R.R. (1959), The Economics of Invention. A Survey of the Literature, *The Journal of Business* 32, pp. 101—127.

Nelson, R.R. (Ed. 1962), The Rate and Direction of Inventive Activity: Economic and Social Factors, A Report of the National Bureau of Economic Research, Princeton.

Nelson, R.R., Winter, S.G. (1982), *An Evolutionary Theory of Economic Change*, Cambridge, Mass.

Nevitt, P. (1983), *Project Financing*, London.

Nickell, S. (1978), *The Investment Decisions of Firms*, Cambridge, U.K.

Nordsieck, F. (1934), *Grundlagen der Organisationslehre*, Stuttgart.

Ochsenbauer, C. (1989), *Organisatorische Alternativen zur Hierarchie*, Munich.

OECD (1986), *Technical Cooperation Agreements between Firms. Some Initial Data and Analysis*, Paris.

OECD (1990a), Innovation-Related Networks and Technology Policy-Making, Preliminary Document for the Technology Economy Programme (TEP) by the Council at Ministerial Level, OECD, Paris.

OECD (1990b), Technological Innovation: Some Definitions and Building Blocs, Preliminary Document for the Technology Economy Programme (TEP) by the Council at Ministerial Level, OECD, Paris.

OECD (1991), *Technology and Productivity — The Challenge for Economic Policy*, Paris.

OECD (1992), *Technology and the Economy — The Key Relationships*, Paris.

Ohmae, K. (1985), *Macht der Triade*, Wiesbaden.

Ohmae, K. (1990), *The Borderless World. Power and Strategy in the Interlinked Economy*, London.

Olson, M. (1968), *Die Logik des kollektiven Handelns*, Tübingen.

Ouchi, W.G. (1980), Markets, Bureaucracies and Clans, *Administrative Science Quarterly 25*, 2, pp. 129—142.

Ouchi, W.G., Bolton, M.K. (1987), The Logic of Joint Research and Development, *California Management Review 30*, 1, pp. 9–33.

Pellengahr, I. (1986a), Austrian versus Austrians I: A Subjectivist View of Interest, in: Faber (1986).

Pellengahr, I. (1986b), Austrian versus Austrians II: Functionalist versus Essentialist Theories of Interest, in: Faber (1986).

Penrose, M. (1959), *The Theory of the Growth of the Firm*, Oxford.

Pettigrew, A. (Ed. 1988), *The Management of Strategic Change*, Oxford.

Picot, A. (1982), Transaktionskostenansatz in der Organisationstheorie: Stand der Diskussion und Aussagewert, in: *Die Betriebswirtschaft* 42, pp. 267—284.

Picot, A (1984), Specificity, Specialization, and Coalitions: Comment, *Journal of Institutional and Theoretical Economics* 140, 1, pp. 50—53.

Picot, A. (1989), Zur Bedeutung allgemeiner Theorieansätze für die betriebswirtschaftliche Information und Kommunikation: Der Beitrag der Transaktionskosten- und Principal-Agent-Theorie, in: Kirsch, W., Picot, A. (Eds.), *Die Betriebswirtschaftslehre im Spannungsfeld zwischen Generalisierung und Spezialisierung*, Wiesbaden.

Picot, A. (1990), Division of Labour and Responsibilities, in: *Handbook of German Business Management*, Stuttgart, Heidelberg.

Picot, A., Dietl, H. (1990), Transaktionskostentheorie, *WiSt*, 4, pp. 178—183.

Picot, A., Laub, U., Schneider, D. (1989), *Innovative Unternehmensgründungen. Eine ökonomisch-empirische Analyse*, Berlin, Heidelberg, New York.

Pigou, A.C. (1932), *Economics of Welfare*, London.

Piltz, D.J. (1991), Stichwort: Gesellschafterbeiträge (Einlagen) Quoad Dominium, Quoad Usum, Quoad Sortem, *Deutsches Steuerrecht*, 8, pp. 251—252.

Pinchot, G. (1985), *Intrapreneuring*, New York.

Pindyck, R.S. (1988), Irreversible Investment, Capacity Choice, and the Value of the Firm, *American Economic Review* 78, pp. 969—985.

Pisano, G.P., Russo, M.V., Teece, D.J. (1988), Joint Ventures and Collaborative Arrangements in the Telecommunications Equipment Industry, in: Mowery, D.C. (1988).

Poindexter, J.B. (1976), The Efficiency of Financial Markets: The Venture Capital Case, Ph.D. Dissertation, University of Utah.

Porter, M.E. (1980), *Competitive Strategy. Techniques for Analyzing Industries and Competitors*, New York.

Porter, M.E. (1985), *Competitive Advantage. Creating and Sustaining Superior Performance*, New York.

Porter, M.E. (Ed. 1986), *Competition in Global Industries*, Boston, Mass.

Porter, M.E (1990), *The Competitive Advantage of Nations*, London, Basingstoke.

Porter, M.E., Fuller, M.B. (1986), Coalitions and Global Strategy, in: Porter (1986).

Prahalad, C.K., Hamel, G. (1991), Nur Kernkompetenzen sichern das Überleben, *Harvard Manager*, 2, pp. 66—78.

Pratt, J.W., Zeckhauser, R.J. (1985), *Principals and Agents: The Structure of Business*, Boston.

Reekie, W.D. (1984), *Markets, Entrepreneurs and Liberty: An Austrian View of Capitalism*, Brighton.

Reimann (1991), Formenerfordernisse beim Abschluß von Gesellschaftsverträgen, *Deutsches Steuerrecht*, pp. 154—156.

Reinhard, B. (1991), Die Einlage Quoad Sortem und ihre Darstellung in der Handelsbilanz, *Deutsches Steuerrecht*, 18, pp. 588—591.

Reiss, W. (1979), Substitution in a Neo-Austrian Model of Capital, *Zeitschrift für Nationalökonomie*, 39, pp. 33—52.

Reiss, W. (1981), *Umwegproduktion und Positivität des Zinses: eine neo-österreichische Analyse*, Berlin.

Richardson, G.B. (1972), The Organization of Industry, *Economic Journal*, 82, pp. 883—896.

Robbins, L. (1932), *An Essay on the Nature and Significance of Economic Science*, London.

Roberts, K., Weitzman, M.L. (1981), Funding Criteria for Research, Development, and Exploration Projects, *Econometrica* 49, pp. 1261—1288.

Rudolph, B. (1989), Finanzierungstheorie und Allgemeine Betriebswirtschaftslehre, in: Kirsch, W., Picot, A. (Eds.), *Die Betriebswirtschaftslehre im Spannungsfeld zwischen Generalisierung und Spezialisierung*, Wiesbaden.

Salter, W.E.G. (1960), *Productivity and Technical Change*, Cambridge, U.K.

Say, J.B. (1802), *Cours d'Économie Politique*, Paris.

Scherer, F.M. (1980), *Industrial Market Structure and Economic Performance*, 2. Edition, Chicago.

Schill, J. (1988), *Verbundgeschäfte, Projektfinanzierung und Kooperation als Finanzierungsinstrumente im Maschinen- und Anlagenbau*, Frankfurt/Main.

Schmalensee, R., Willig, R.D. (Eds. 1989), *Handbook of Industrial Organizations*, Amsterdam.

Schmidt, R.H. (1981), Ein neo-institutionalistischer Ansatz der Fianzierungstheorie, in: Rühli, E., Thommen, J.P. (Eds.), *Unternehmungsführung aus finanz- und bankwirtschaftlicher Sicht*, Stuttgart.

Schmidt, R.H. (1981), Grundformen der Finanzierung. Eine Anwendung des neo-institutionalistischen Ansatzes, in: *Kredit und Kapital* 14, pp. 186—221.

Schmidt, R.H. (1986), *Grundzüge der Investitions- und Finanzierungstheorie*, 2. Edition, Wiesbaden.

Schmitt, W. (1989), *Internationale Projektfinanzierung bei deutschen Banken*, Frankfurt/Main.

Schneider, D. (1973), *Unternehmungsziele und Unternehmungskooperation. Ein Beitrag zur Erklärung kooperativ bedingter Zielvariationen*, Wiesbaden.

Schneider, D. (1980), *Investition und Finanzierung*, 5. Edition, Wiesbaden.

Schneider, D. (1988), *Zur Entstehung innovativer Unternehmen. Eine ökonomischtheoretische Perspektive*, Munich.

Schramm, W. (1936), *Die betrieblichen Funktionen und ihre Organisation*, Berlin, Leipzig.

Schumpeter J.A. (1934), *Theorie der wirtschaftlichen Entwicklung*, 3. Edition, Berlin, Munich.

Scousen, M. (1990), *The Structure of Production*, New York.

Shackle, G.L.S. (1955), *Uncertainty in Economics and other Reflections*, Cambridge, U.K.

Shah, S., Thakor, A.V. (1987), Optimal Capital Structure and Capital Financing, *Journal of Economic Theory*, pp. 209—243.

Shand, A.H. (1984), *The Capitalist Alternative. An Introduction to Neo-Austrian Economics*, New York, London.

Shapero, A. (1984), The Entrepreneurial Event, In: Kent, C.A. (Ed.), *The Environment for Entrepreneurship*, Lexington, Mass.

Siebert, H. (1990), *Technologische Entwicklung und Vorproduktbeschaffung*, Frankfurt/Main, Bern.

Simon, H.A. (1960), *The New Science of Management Decision*, New York.

Simon, H.A. (1961), *Administrative Behavior*, 2. Edition, New York.

Simon, H.A. (1978), Rationality as Process and as Product of Thought, *American Economic Review* 68, pp. 1—16.

Smith, A. (1776), *An Inquiry into the Nature and the Causes of the Wealth of Nations*, London.

Smith, C.W. (1989), Agency Costs, in: Eatwell, J., Milgate, M., Newman, P. (Eds.), *Finance. The New Palgrave*, New York, London.

Spremann, K. (1986), *Finanzierung*, 2. Edition, Munich.

Spremann, K. (1989) Agent and Principal, in: Bamberg and Spremann (1989).

Stephan, G. (1983), Roundaboutness, Non-Tightness and Malinvaud-Prices in Multisector-Models with Infinite Horizon, *Zeitschrift für die gesamte Staatswissenschaft*, 139, pp. 660—667.

Stephan, G. (1985), Competitive Finite Value Prices: A Complete Characterization, *Zeitschrift für Nationalökonomie*, 45, pp. 35—54.

Stigler, G.J. (1948), *Production and Distribution Theories*. The Formative Period, New York.

Stigler, G.J. (1968), *The Organization of Industry*, Homewood.

Stiglitz, J. (1987), Technical Change, Sunk Costs, and Competition, *Brookings Papers on Economic Activity*, 3, pp. 883—937.

Stopford, J.M., Wells, L.T. (1972), *Managing the Multinational Enterprise*, New York.

Streit, M.E., Wegner, G. (1988), Information, Transaction and Catallaxy — Reflections on Some Key-Concepts of Evolutionary Market Theory, Discussion Paper 367—88, University Mannheim, Mannheim.

Teece, D.J. (1986), Profiting from Technological Innovation: Implications for Integration, Collaboration, Licensing, and Public Policy, *Research Policy* 15, 6, pp. 285—305.

Teece, D.J. (1987), Capturing Value from Technological Innovation: Integration, Strategic Partnering, and Licensing Decisions, in: Guile, B.R., Brooks, H. (Eds.), *Technology and Global Industry. Companies and Nations in the World Economy*, Washington, D.C.

Teece, D.J. (1988), Firm Boundaries, Technological Innovation, and Strategic Management, in: Dosi et al. (1988).

Teece, D.J. (1991), Technological Development and the Organization of Industry, in: OECD (1991).

Teubner, G. (1991), Die vielköpfige Hydra: Netzwerke als kollektive Akteure höherer Ordnung, in: Krohn, W., Küppers, G. (Eds.), *Emergenz und Selbstorganisation*, Frankfurt/Main.

Thompson, J.D. (1967), *Organizations in Action*, New York, London, Sidney.

Thorelli, H.B. (1986), Networks: Between Markets and Hierarchies, *Strategic Management Journal* 7, 1, pp. 37—51.

Tirole, J. (1989), *The Theory of Industrial Organization*, Cambridge, Mass.

Twaalfhoven, F., Hattori, T. (1982), *The Supporting Role of Small Japanese Enterprises*, Schiphol.

Ulrich, H. (1968), *Die Unternehmung als produktives soziales System. Grundlagen der allgemeinen Unternehmungslehre*, Bern, Stuttgart.

UNCTC (1988), *Transnational Corporations and Economic Development, Fourth Survey, United Nations Center on Transnational Corporations*, New York.

Van de Ven, A.H., Joyce, W.F. (Eds. 1981), *Perspectives on Organization Design and Behavior*, New York.

Venture Economics (1989), *Pratt's Guide to Venture Capital Sources*, 13. Edition, Needham, Mass.

Weder, R. (1989), *Joint Venture. Theoretische und empirische Analyse unter besonderer Berücksichtigung der chemischen Industrie der Schweiz*, Basel.

Weimann, J. (1990), Soziale Dilemmata, *WiSt* 2, February, pp. 83—85.

Weitzman, M.L., Newey, W., Rabin, M. (1981), Sequential R&D Strategy for Synfuels, *Bell Journal of Economics*, 12, pp. 574—590.

Weizsäcker, C.C. v. (1971), *Steady State Capital Theory*, Berlin, Heidelberg, New York.

Wells, W.A. (1974), Venture Capital Decision Making, Ph.D. Dissertation, Carnegie Mellon University, Pittsburg.

Wenger, E., Terberger, E. (1988), Die Beziehung zwischen Agent und Prinzipal als Baustein einer ökonomischen Theorie der Organisation, *WiSt* 17, 10, pp. 506—514.

West, M.W. (1959), The Jointly Owned Subsidiary, *Harvard Business Review* 37, 4, pp. 165—172.

Williamson, O.E. (1964), *The Economics of Discretionary Behavior. Managerial Objectives in a Theory of the Firm*, Englewood Cliffs.

Williamson, O.E. (1967), Hierarchical Control and Optimum Firm Size, *Journal of Political Economy*, pp. 123—138.

Williamson, O.E. (1975), *Markets and Hierarchies. Analysis and Antitrust Implications*, New York.

Williamson, O.E. (1985), *The Economic Institutions of Capitalism. Firms, Markets, and Relational Contracting*, New York.

Williamson, O.E. (1988), Corporate Finance and Corporate Governance, *Journal of Finance* 18, 3, pp. 567—591.

Williamson, O.E. (1990), Comparative Economic Organization: The Analysis of Discrete Structural Alternatives, Paper presented at the annual meeting of German academic teachers of business economics, Frankfurt/Main, June.

Williamson, O.E., Wachter, M.L., Harris, J.E. (1975), Understanding the Employment Relation: The Analysis of Idiosyncratie Exchange, *Bell Journal of Economics* 6, Spring, pp. 250—280.

Winter, S.G. (1982), An Essay on the Theory of Production, In: Hymans, S.H. (Ed.), *Economics and the World Around it*, Ann Arbor.

Winter, S.G. (1987), Know-how and Competence as Strategic Assets, in: Teece, D. (Ed.), *The Competitive Challenge*, Cambridge, Mass.

Wolf, C. (1988), *Markets or Governments. Choosing between Imperfect Alternatives*, Cambridge, Mass.

Index